The Economy of China

The Economy of China

Linda Yueh

Fellow in Economics, St Edmund Hall, University of Oxford, UK

Edward Elgar
Cheltenham, UK • Northampton, MA, USA

Published by
Edward Elgar Publishing Limited
The Lypiatts
15 Lansdown Road
Cheltenham
Glos GL50 2JA
UK

Edward Elgar Publishing, Inc.
William Pratt House
9 Dewey Court
Northampton
Massachusetts 01060
USA

A catalogue record for this book is available from the British Library

Library of Congress Control Number: 2009940697

Mixed Sources
Product group from well-managed
forests and other controlled sources
www.fsc.org Cert no. SA-COC-1565
© 1996 Forest Stewardship Council
FSC

ISBN 978 1 84542 194 6

Printed and bound by MPG Books Group, UK

Contents

Figures

Tables

Preface

The transformation of the Chinese economy has been impressive. In the past three decades, China has experienced a remarkable rate of economic growth that has propelled it from being one of the poorest countries in the world to becoming its third largest economy. It is also a complex economy with a mix of characteristics derived from being both a transition economy and a developing country. That is, a country that is dismantling the previously planned economy and moving toward a market one, while at the same time contending with all of the well-known challenges of economic development. Due to its rapid emergence as the world's third largest economy, China's prospects are increasingly intertwined with those of the global economy. During the 2008 global financial crisis, the ability of China to sustain its growth in the midst of the worst downturn since the 1930s has become an issue of interest to a wide set of policy-makers, academics, as well as interested observers.

This book sets out to introduce the reader to the path of China's economic development since 1979. The intention is to provide a picture of this economy to a wide range of readers interested in gaining a better understanding of the complex Chinese growth path by emphasising the ways in which institutional change – laws, policies, institutional reforms – has played a key role in developing the market mechanisms central to China's success. Although a book of this kind can have a tendency to focus on the trees and miss the forest, that will be resisted here. This book is an introduction to the economy of China. There are other works which can provide a deeper treatment of each of the topics. I hope to show the forest in this book, and what a remarkable forest it is.

Although no book will be comprehensive given the scale of the economy and the remarkable pace of transformation over three decades, this volume will highlight the key areas of this extraordinary economy. The book's analysis of the main topics will give an overview of developments within China's economy so that the reader can better assess the prospects of continuing growth. For instance, the book assesses the reforms of the labour market and asks whether China has achieved a sufficient degree of productivity to sustain its growth, which I consider important in thinking about how the economy will evolve and where it is in need of further reform. Also, given China's importance in the global economy, the final chapter analyses the various ways in which China's opening has affected not only its own development but also how it has influenced the world in the past few decades. Undoubtedly, China's future is intertwined with the rest of the world, such that its prospects will affect the path of the global economy. Despite its success thus far, China's tale is not finished and there is still a long way to go before it reaches the standard of living of the West. For the sake of one-fifth of the world's population, my hope is that it will do so.

Abbreviations

ADR	alternative dispute resolution
AMC	asset management company
BCS	Budgetary Contracting System
BIS	Bank for International Settlements
BRS	Budgetary Responsibility System
CBRC	China Banking Regulatory Commission
CDB	China Development Bank
CHIP	China Household Income Project
CIC	China Investment Corporation
CIETAC	China International Economic and Trade Arbitration Commission
CIRC	China Insurance Regulatory Commission
CPI	consumer prices index
CRS	Contract Responsibility System
CSRC	China Securities Regulatory Commission
DSU	Dispute Settlement Understanding
EEFSU	Eastern Europe and the former Soviet Union
EPS	Epidemic Prevention Service
ETDZ	Economic Trade and Development Zone
FDI	foreign direct investment
FIE	foreign-invested enterprise
GATT	General Agreement on Tariffs and Trade
GDP	gross domestic product
GNP	gross national product
HRS	Household Responsibility System
HTDZ	High-technology Development Zone
ICBC	Industrial and Commercial Bank of China
ILO	International Labour Organization
IPO	initial public (stock) offering
IPRs	intellectual property rights
JV	joint venture
LLC	limited liability company
M&As	merger and acquisitions
MCH	Maternal and Child Health Service
MFN	Most Favoured Nation

MLE	maximum likelihood estimation
MOL	Ministry of Labour
MPL	marginal product of labour
MR	marginal revenue
MRP	marginal revenue product
NBS	National Bureau of Statistics
NERI	National Economic Research Institute
NPL	non-performing loan
NSSF	National Social Security Fund
OECD	Organisation for Economic Co-operation and Development
OLS	ordinary least squares
OPC	Open Port City
PBOC	People's Bank of China
PPP	purchasing power parity
PQML	Poisson Quasi Maximum Likelihood
PRC	People's Republic of China
QFII	qualified foreign institutional investors
R&D	research and development
RCMS	Rural Cooperative Medical Scheme
RMB	*renminbi*
SAFE	State Administration of Foreign Exchange
SASAC	State-owned Asset Supervision and Administration Commission
SCB	state-owned commercial bank
SEZ	Special Economic Zone
SIP	share issue privatisation
SIPO	State Intellectual Property Office
SME	small and medium-sized enterprise
SOB	state-owned bank
SOEs	state-owned enterprises
SWF	sovereign wealth fund
TFP	total factor productivity
TRIPs	Agreement on Trade-related Aspects of Intellectual Property Rights
TVE	township and village enterprise
UNCTAD	United Nations Conference on Trade and Development
VA	value-added
VMP	value of marginal product
WOFE	wholly owned foreign-owned enterprise
WTO	World Trade Organization

1. Introduction

The extraordinary emergence of China during the past three decades has been a hallmark of the global economy, heralding a 21st century world that looks quite different from the previous one. This book serves as an introduction to the economy of China during its reform period since 1979. The aim is to explain China's remarkable transformation from a centrally planned to a more market-oriented economy through the institutional reforms utilised to support such marketisation and eventually global integration. This is a challenging process, as China is not only in transition but is also a developing economy with many of the problems associated with being a primarily rural, poor country.

The theme of the book is that China's marketisation process is one that entails a gradual introduction of market forces into areas of the economy, which also requires both dismantling the structure of the centrally planned economy and developing market-oriented incentives. The creation of various types of institutions to support this process of establishing markets will be examined closely. For instance, these include corporate laws to establish private firms, reforms to the wage structure to incentivise labour productivity, and industrial policies designed to attract foreign investment. China undertook much dismantling of institutions from the centrally planned period, but it also must now build the additional institutional foundations to support a more market-oriented economy. This book seeks to explore the interplay between growth and institutions in China, a topic which is of relevance to China and also to the economic development and growth literature.

The structure of the book covers the transformation of the major sectors in the Chinese economy and the reforms associated with the main economic growth factors, such as labour, capital, and technological innovation. The second chapter analyses China's growth model in terms of transition from central planning, economic development challenges, and eventual integration with the global economy. Institutional reforms have underpinned the gradual marketisation process, and legal reforms look to be increasingly important as China becomes a global player. The next four chapters focus on the reform of the factors that drive economic growth, namely, enterprises, labour, entrepreneurship and capital markets (banking and financial sectors). The latter chapter also touches on China's indirect role in the 2008 global financial crisis as a pointer to future reform. In each of these chapters, institutional reforms are highlighted. For enterprises, the mixture of 'institutional innovations' such as the Contract Responsibility System (CRS) and corporate laws accompany the process of reforming state and collectively owned firms as well as helping to establish privately owned ones and attract foreign investors. In terms of labour and entrepreneurship, reforming the wage structure and dismantling the lifetime employment system fed into the development of a labour market that was driven by supply and demand, and allowed entrepreneurs to operate. Governance of capital markets and the restructuring of the banking system constitute a good illustration of the importance of institutional reforms of markets. The global financial crisis of 2008 provides an unmistakable impetus for further cross-border regulation of international capital markets that involves China as a major economy.

A detailed exploration of the interplay between legal and economic reforms follows in a chapter dedicated to this central quest on as to how laws and markets evolve in China. The subsequent chapter explores the key issue for long-run growth – innovation and patents – covering the domestic and some of the international aspects of the intellectual property rights system. The penultimate chapter turns to the social foundations of growth, including education, pensions, the health system and lingering inequality, as well as poverty. It points to the ongoing institutional reforms in progress to support China's marketising economy in those areas. The final chapter concludes the book with an examination of China's external sector development, namely, policies concerning trade, investment, and exchange rates. An assessment of the impact of China's re-emergence in the global economy is also included. The legal and institutional backdrop was most apparent in the ways that China treated foreign investors early on in its reform period, and the chapter concludes with an assessment of how China will fare in an increasingly rules-based international economic system. Therefore, the book assesses China's marketisation process in terms of how major sectors of the economy have been transformed and the areas in need of continuing reform to sustain its transition and continued development. The gradual injection of market-oriented incentives coupled with institutional reform is the approach highlighted throughout the book.

China's reform path can be roughly divided into three parts: rural reforms in the late 1970s, urban reforms in the mid 1980s and opening up to the global economy, which took off in the early 1990s and culminated in accession to the World Trade Organization (WTO) in 2001. The following provides a brief overview of these pillars of China's transformation as an introduction to the volume and begins first with an analysis of the centrally planned period (1949–78) that provided the backdrop to market-oriented reforms which started at the end of 1978.

1. THE IMPETUS FOR REFORM

The impetus for introducing market-oriented reforms in China stemmed from the structural imbalances that favoured industry over consumption, deriving from the centrally planned economy from 1949 to 1978. Despite the high levels of investment and rapid growth (estimated to be 12.3% in real annual gross domestic product (GDP) growth) in 1978, the Chinese economy by the end of the 1970s had standards of living that were not much better than in the 1950s. In the indicative category of grain consumption, average per capita food grain availability in 1977 was similar to the 1955 level. Average grain consumption of the rural population for 1978–80 was actually lower than that for 1955–57, whereas it was slightly higher in urban areas (Riskin 1987).

Within the state-owned sector which encompassed nearly all of industrial output during the command or administered economy, the general freeze on wages after 1957 and the entry of new workers into the lowest rungs of the wage ladder caused the average wage in real terms to fall 17% between 1957 and 1977. Only a large increase in the labour force participation rate – from 30% of the urban population in 1957 to 55% in 1980 – enabled the average per capita income of wage and salary earners to increase by 62% in real terms within that period. Neglect of 'non-productive' investment caused the small housing space of 4.3 square metres per urban resident in 1952 to decline to 3.6 square metres in 1977 (World Bank 1983).

However, China did achieve numerous economic and technological triumphs, including industrialisation, which had eluded so many developing countries. On the innovation front, these included a large machine-building industry, satellites, nuclear weapons, large ships and giant hydraulic presses, and synthesis of insulin. However, these achievements did not translate into an improvement in the real standard of living, technological advances or improved productive efficiency (Chow 1994; Borensztein and Ostry 1996).

Most of China's industrial growth had come from increases in factors, especially fixed capital, rather than an increase in the efficiency of use of inputs. Even the growth in labour productivity was achieved mainly by increases in the amounts of physical capital per worker. For instance, estimates of the capital-labour index indicate an increase from 100 in 1952 to 373 in 1978 (Riskin 1987). This was due to the structural shifts towards more capital-intensive heavy industries following the Soviet model which were later reversed.

This was the crux of the problem of 'structural imbalance' that required reform. Another part is due to systematic reasons familiar to centrally

planned economies, stemming from the deficiencies in the system of economic organisation, planning and management. This tension became a
principal theme of the new economic strategy announced at the Third
Plenum of the 11th Central Committee in December 1978, which marked
the start of the reform period in China (Chang 1988).

Finally, there was also a problem of high urban unemployment which
reappeared in 1978. In 1979, the urban unemployed were thought to
number upwards of 10 million or about 9.5% of the estimated non-
agricultural labour force of 104 million (China's National Bureau of
Statistics (NBS) 1999). Before 1976, unemployment was largely avoided,
by such means as some 20 million urban residents being sent to the countryside after the Great Leap Forward of the late 1950s and early 1960s.
Their return likely contributed to the subsequent rise in unemployment
figures. The estimated 17 million youth who were sent out to the countryside from 1966 to 1976 were urban residents (Chang 1988). Moreover,
during this period, job placement was handled by the state labour
bureaux, which were responsible for placing school-leavers, demobilised
soldiers, returned youth from the countryside, and released convicts.
The burden on the already disorganised state apparatus resulted in many
job-seekers spending long periods of time 'waiting for work'. Enterprises
were forbidden to recruit workers and individuals could not seek jobs in
compliance with the state's goal of providing full employment. This commitment resulted in general overstaffing (a form of 'disguised unemployment') (Knight and Song 2005). This problem was perhaps exacerbated
by a continuing gap between urban and rural incomes which resulted in
an oversupply of labour at existing wages. The numbers were dependent
to some extent on administrative suppression of the movement of labour
through a prohibition on rural-urban migration. Other contributing forces
include the favoured sector in China's development strategy being heavy
industry, which is capital-intensive.

Therefore, high urban unemployment, stagnating levels of food consumption, deteriorating urban housing conditions, falling real wages,
widespread rural poverty resulting from the emphasis on industrialisation
in urban areas and sluggish productivity growth – all despite rapid economic growth conventionally measured – could be viewed in the context
of the deficiencies of central planning. A reassessment of the structural
imbalances and systematic flaws – flaws in the planning, management,
and incentive systems under the planned economy – pointed to a number
of problems in the economy. These included high levels of capital accumulation, coupled with a lack of efficiency and low levels of consumption.
There was a neglect of agriculture and light industry as well as of maintaining living standards. The struggle to overcome these structural and

systematic imbalances led to the introduction of market-oriented reforms, whilst retaining a planned portion of the economy consistent with a high degree of governmental control, since unlike other transition economies, China did not embrace marketisation alongside political reform. This became known as the 'dual track' transition path of the Chinese economy, in which a planned segment was maintained alongside the market sector.

2. RURAL REFORMS

Market-oriented reforms started with rural development and liberalisation at the end of 1978, which resulted in the unexpected success of Township and Village Enterprises (TVEs) by the early 1980s (Oi 1999). Farmers became part of a system of residual claimants who could retain returns on their work product after remitting the required portions to the state. This characterised the accompanying liberalisation of agriculture. Once this 'dual track' system, known as the 'household responsibility system' (HRS), was adopted, output grew in rural areas. Agricultural output growth soared, peaking in 1984. This spectacular success caused the subsequent claim that Chinese economic reforms began in the countryside. Reorientation of the economy through this type of institutional innovation increased the share of national income going to households by 10 to 15 percentage points (NBS 1999). National savings and investments remained robust through the 1980s on account of this structural shift. This also minimised the adjustment required by the economy because while government savings was falling, investment was maintained at relatively high levels. Thus, Chinese households helped to maintain macroeconomic stability during this period. And, as a result, China's financial system began to diverge from the standard command economy model, which has low levels of private savings, with subsequent difficulties when governmental revenues declined, and began to resemble the structure of a market economy.

The TVEs or rural enterprises had become ensconced in the collective organisational structure in the countryside. They were permitted to develop in order to provide inputs for the quite successful agricultural industry in rural areas. TVEs also became vehicles for absorbing surplus labour from agriculture. What was not anticipated were the profound changes they engendered in the economy as a whole. In 1983–84, a short time after the introduction of market-oriented reforms, most communes were abolished (Riskin 1987; Lin et al. 2003). Their functions were divided between townships that assumed responsibility for governmental operations and local economic committees that took over economic management. This permitted the TVEs to become more independent as well as being profit-oriented entities. At their peak during the post-1978 reform period, TVEs accounted for around one-third of industrial output in China.

3.   URBAN REFORMS

The next phase of reform was in urban areas. There were three main so-called 'institutional innovations' in the state sector that characterised its successful reorientation toward the market in the 1980s and 1990s. They were the Budgetary Responsibility System (BRS), the Contract Responsibility System (CRS) and permitting direct borrowing (Riskin 1987; Naughton 1996; Lin et al. 2003). Since 1980, under the BRS, the central government shares revenues (taxes and profit remittances) with local governments. For local governments which incur budget deficits, the contract sets the subsidies to be transferred to the local governments. This fundamentally reshaped fiscal relations between central and local government. Then, the CRS in 1985 permitted state-owned enterprises (SOEs) to pay a fixed amount of taxes and profits to the state and retain the remainder. In principle, so long as the SOEs deliver the tax and profit remittances specified in the contracts, they are free to operate. Also in that year, state grants for operating funds and fixed asset investments were replaced by bank loans. Local governments and SOEs are allowed to borrow directly from banks. Since 1991, local governments and SOEs were further permitted to borrow from households and other institutions. With World Trade Organization (WTO) accession in 2001, foreign banks were also gradually permitted to extend domestic credit.

The result of the urban reforms is a decentralised state sector where autonomous local governments, SOEs and local state-owned banks (SOBs) have increasingly important roles in determining resource allocation, while central government has become less important, even though ownership has not been fully reformed. Based on China's experience, it is sometimes argued that a market economy could be compatible with state ownership if managerial incentives were introduced. Decentralisation has occurred in almost all areas of decision-making in production, pricing, investment, trade, expenditure, income distribution, taxation and credit allocation (Naughton 1996). The decentralisation reforms may indeed have improved the technical efficiency of the state sector, but by the standards of allocative efficiency and intertemporal stability, the decentralised state sector is a major institutional cause of macroeconomic instability and of the divergent development of regional economies.

Therefore, decentralisation and institutional innovations within the state sector were important for China's development in the post-1978 period in urban as well as rural areas. However, the retention of the planned track engendered 'soft' or non-binding budget constraints for SOEs and non-performing loans (NPLs) held by SOBs. Even though SOE inefficiency and unemployment were not concomitant until the late 1990s, it did eventually surface as a major source of difficulty in the Chinese economy. Thus, 'soft budget' constraints, remain perhaps the most difficult issue for reform of the state sector in China.

4. EXTERNAL SECTOR DEVELOPMENT

In 1978, the reform period began when market-oriented measures, which included the 'open door' policy designed to encourage international trade and foreign direct investment (FDI), were implemented. China's approach to economic reforms, though, is and has been gradual as it tends to adopt policies slowly. China's reform programme progressed in a gradualist approach that has also been referred to as 'crossing the stream while feeling the stones'. China's approach is to wait until a particular policy has been successfully implemented in one region before the 'experiment' is extended nationally. As a result, China's 'open door' policy did not move forward until reforms were implemented in urban areas in the mid 1980s and then did not pick up until Deng Xiaoping's game-changing tour of the first-opened southern coastal provinces in 1992. Since then, China has been tremendously successful in attracting FDI and had also become the world's second largest trader some decade and a half later.

The first reforms in the area of FDI policy created what are known as Special Economic Zones (SEZs). SEZs were first introduced in 1979 in the south-eastern coastal provinces of Fujian and Guangdong and located in urban areas (Lardy 1991; Naughton 1996). The SEZs are similar to special customs areas. Foreign invested enterprises (FIEs) received preferential treatment, including up to 50% reduction in custom duties, with respect to corporate income tax and granted duty-free imports. This resulted in extremely rapid growth in these areas due to their attractiveness to foreign investment. Guangdong was the leading exporter among provinces in China by the mid 1990s on account of the successful growth of the SEZ city of Shenzhen on the Hong Kong border and that of the capital city, Guangzhou. Although the SEZs were successful, the Chinese authorities believed that they tended to attract investment in low-technology and light industrial sectors. These were indeed consistent with China's comparative advantage in abundant, low-cost labour. However, China was keen to attract more advanced technologies and the combination of these factors paved the way for future reforms and eventual membership of the WTO.

China's further trade liberalisation measures, leading up to membership of the multilateral trading body, the World Trade Organization, in 2001, set the stage for its opening. Over the period 1990–2000, Chinese manufactured exports grew by 16.9% per annum, compared with 10.3% for the rest of East Asia, and its world market share tripled from 1.7% to 4.4% (Lall and Albaladejo 2004). China's share of the global export market grew even faster after 2000, accounting for over 7% of world merchandise exports after WTO entry.

Manufactured goods comprise around 90% of its merchandise exports (Lall and Albaladejo 2004). China has emerged as the largest exporter of manufactured products in the developing world. The growth of its manufactured exports has been among the fastest achieved by developing countries, and they are not, as sometimes thought, based only on cheap labour. The exports span a broad range of technologies, so reflecting an impressive range of competitive strengths, and are diversifying and upgrading with amazing rapidity.

Moreover, despite the lack of full convertibility of its capital account, China in the 1990s had become the second largest host country for foreign direct investment after the US, the eighth largest capital supplier in the world, and the largest among developing countries (not including flows through Hong Kong, which reverted to China in 1997) (World Bank 1997). The stock of FDI is impressive, although there is some dispute over the figure on account of 'round tripping', whereby capital leaves China and returns to take advantage of foreign capital concessions. The ten biggest investors contributing to its impressive inflow of FDI are Hong Kong, the Virgin Islands, Japan, South Korea, the United States, Taiwan, Singapore, Western Samoa, the Cayman Islands and Germany. The top two sources of funds were from Hong Kong, a conduit for investors from Europe, Asia and the US, and the Virgin Islands, used as a channel for Chinese money 'round tripping' to qualify for various tax perks given to foreign investors.

However, WTO accession for China required numerous forms of trade liberalisation and reciprocal entry into the domestic market. China reduced the number of products subject to non-tariff barriers (that is, quotas and licences) from an estimated 1200 in the early 1990s to approximately 200 a decade later. The pace of tariff reform was also rapid, with rates at less than 20% across the board following a significant tariff reform in 1997. Three more tariff reforms preceded accession in 1999, 2000 and 2001, so that average rates were nearer to 15% with the lower tariffs in manufacturing. The reduction in tariffs required by accession were not as severe as a result. An important feature of China's trade regime has been the provision of exemptions or reduced rates for goods imported for production of exports and direct investment, which accounted for about 60% of imports in 2000.

As with all WTO members, China moved toward a regime based on tariffs, so quotas, licences and designated trading were to be phased out. State trade of commodities is still permitted, though, subject to WTO rules. China agreed to be bound by all industrial and agricultural tariffs, so that the average tariff on manufactured goods was reduced to 6.95% and 17% on agriculture upon accession. Notably and specifically regarding textiles, China became integrated into the General Agreement on Tariffs and Trade (GATT) Uruguay Round on textiles and clothing. By 2005, all existing quotas on China's exports of textiles and clothing ended, and by 2008, any special textile safeguards also came to an end. It coincided with the phase-out of the Multi-fibre Agreement at the start of 2005, which had previously allocated quotas for output to different countries. As such, China's antici-pated gain in market share was considerable, perhaps as much as 50% of the US market. However, subsequent safeguards against Chinese exports of textiles and clothing were imposed by the US and Europe, while smaller exporters such as Bangladesh were threatened, leaving this area still less than fully liberalised. Therefore, although there remain issues concerning agricultural products and access to China's domestic market, the general outlook is that of an economy which is quickly opening its borders and becoming all the more globally integrated. Indeed, within a few years of joining the WTO, China had become the second largest trader in the world and among the top three trading partners of the European Union and United States.

5. CONCLUSION

This brief overview of the Chinese economy highlights the gradual and piecemeal fashion of economic reforms. The major waves of reforms in the late 1970s, mid 1980s, early 1990s and early 2000s have culminated in an economy that is increasingly market-oriented. This book will delve into the major aspects of growth, transition and development to give a fuller picture of the economy of China.

As China is expected to become as important an engine of growth in the world as the United States over the coming decades, understanding the nature of its marketisation process and the fragilities in its institutional system are more important than ever before. No longer a country for specialist investigation, China has arrived on the global stage as an economy that needs to be analysed and assessed in order to gain a general view of the global economy.

2. Economic growth: 30 years of market transition, economic development and global integration*

1. PRE-1978 PERIOD

Following the turmoil of the Cultural Revolution, China embarked on an economic reform programme characterised by the Four Modernisations of agriculture, industry, national defence, and science and technology (see, for example, Riskin 1987; Chang 1988). At the Third Plenum of the Eleventh Central Committee in December 1978, the Chinese authorities resolved to make economic development a top priority. In urban areas, economic reforms were intensely implemented from 1984 after the initial reforms in rural areas proved to be successful.

The remarkable growth rate of China since 1979 was prefaced by a centrally planned economy which provided the impetus and background against which to understand the later reforms. The periods of the centrally planned economy can be roughly generalised into the following periods: (1) the beginning of the socialist economy, including the redistribution of land, from 1949 to 1952; (2) the cooperative movement from 1952 to 1956; (3) the communisation movement from 1956 to 1958; (4) the Great Leap Forward, where industrialisation initially followed the Soviet model of emphasis on heavy industry to the neglect of light industry and agriculture, from 1958 to 1961; (5) a period of economic recovery until 1966; (6) the decade of the Cultural Revolution from 1966 to 1976 when progress, including economic progress stalled; (7) a period of economic reforms geared toward a greater degree of marketisation from 1978 to 1984; and (8) the earnest implementation of market-oriented reforms from 1984 to the present.

This chapter will identify some of the main drivers of the later market-oriented reforms by exploring key sectors of the economy in the pre-reform period.

2.   CHARACTERISTICS OF A PLANNED ECONOMY

A centrally planned economy differs from a market economy in many ways. Economic resources are owned by the state instead of being in private hands. Prices are determined administratively rather than by the market forces of supply and demand. Decisions concerning consumption, production, distribution and investment are centrally determined.

Some of the macroeconomic characteristics of a command economy include households comprising a modest share of national income. In 1978, households controlled 55% of disposable national income in China (NBS 1999). In contrast, the figure is around 90% for market economies such as the US and Japan (Naughton 1996). In those economies, government services are afforded through the taxation of private incomes, whereas in command economies, government activities are financed by the profits that accrue to them from state enterprises. Accordingly, household savings are a relatively small portion of national savings, as most of national savings is carried out by state enterprises.

The state then also carries out most investment, financed by transferring the profits of state enterprises to state revenues. The state maintains the terms of trade between the state enterprise sector and the household sector on terms favourable to state enterprises to ensure the flow of state revenue. The 'mark-up' on consumer goods is large, while wages are controlled at stable levels. For instance, the terms of trade were mainly determined in the early years of the Chinese command economy by agricultural price policies, otherwise known as the 'scissors' gap', so named after similar policies in the Soviet Union in the 1920s (Knight 1995). In other words, there are price distortions which are designed to channel resources to the state sector. Again, consistent with this deliberate setting of the terms of trade, bank lending is limited to short-term finance of trade and inventories.

A final and well-known characteristic of a centrally planned economy is the persistent shortage of goods (see Kornai 1992). Control of household income is important to the government because the market for consumer goods is one in which households with independent choices and hard budget constraints determine the demand for goods. A rough balance must be struck between supply and demand. In command economies, this tends to be imperfect. Shortages arise from two sources. First, the government channels so many resources into investment and heavy industry that there is little left for households. In order to keep shortages within limits, the government maintains tight control over household income or tries to. Second, shortages result from the soft budget constraints of state enterprises. Most enterprises do not face bankruptcy as a possibility. As a result, firms seek growth without constraint, resulting in an unlimited desire for investment. Therefore, when enterprises are given modest amounts of autonomy, their demand for inputs tends to expand until total demand hits total available supply of resources; generating a built-in tendency to become 'shortage economies'.

It is worth mentioning at this point, before we delve into aspects of the development of the economy, that the Chinese economic system described during this period was subject to major political upheavals. The Great Leap Forward from 1958–62 was preceded by the rapid formation of agricultural communes from April–September 1958, which was disruptive in itself. The second Five Year Plan (1958–62) was severely interrupted. Misguided agricultural and industrial policies caused famines and curtailment of industrial output. The second disturbance was the Cultural Revolution of 1966–76. Having lost ground as a result of the Great Leap Forward, Chairman Mao sought to regain political control through a Cultural Revolution. Economic planning and agricultural production were disrupted.

2.1 Enterprises

In 1949, the central government took over industrial enterprises belonging to the previous government of the Republic of China, which fled to Taiwan. Private enterprises were tolerated for a short while before they became joint ventures, mainly in 1953 after the 'five-anti' movement. By 1956, however, private enterprises had mostly been eliminated. Before, former owners had been permitted to share the profits of jointly owned enterprises with the state partner and exercised some control over management. This ceased after 1956, heralding the era of state-owned enterprises (SOEs).

For the key industries, a Soviet-style of central planning was undertaken, beginning with the First Five Year Plan in 1953. State-owned enterprises were administered by some 20 ministries in the State Council and coordinated by a State Planning Commission. Targets were established for output, and important material inputs were centrally distributed to the enterprises through a bureau of material supplies. The output of SOEs was distributed by the state, with prices determined by a price commission. Most of the profits of SOEs were given to the state, providing a major source of government revenue. Funds for capital construction and expansion were approved by the state. However, by the 1960s, SOEs and local governments began to keep a significant portion of their depreciation funds and used them to finance investments.

As a result of enterprises obtaining inputs through a central allocation, remitting output for central distribution and exerting no control over profits, there was no responsiveness to price signals. The main concern of enterprise managers was to obtain sufficient material and labour inputs to fulfil production targets, and in turn, they tended to overstate input requirements to ensure their fulfilment. There was much inefficiency under this system, seen in the under-utilisation of productive capacity and the stockpiling of inventory.

The First Five Year Plan was indeed 'Stalinist' in the sense of establishing urban industries, setting up central management systems, embarking on long-term planning, and providing for scientific and technical education. Therefore, the First Plan created a large-scale, capital-intensive producer goods industry, accompanied by a highly centralised mode of planning, a hierarchical management system, and a distorted structure of incentives which then comprised industry in China.

These distortions from centralisation led to a series of State Council directives in late 1957 and 1958 that decentralised the planning and management system for industry, commerce and finance. Under the Soviet-type system, the government set specific target outputs for individual industries to maintain their objective of heavy industrialisation. Establishing these targets, or quotas, required making certain assumptions, such as the production capacity of industries, the supply of resources, the technical coefficients of industries (that is, required amounts of specific inputs per unit of output), and the opportunities for foreign trade. A perennial challenge was to expand the economy in the direction desired by the planners, while avoiding or minimising shortages of some products and surpluses of others in aiming for full utilisation. The objective of matching supply and demand required the maintenance of certain balances, such as a materials balance for production and distribution of goods; a labour balance to allocate labour supply; an energy balance between fuel for power production and allocation; financial balances, consisting of transfers to the population of income and expenditures, the state budget, the credit plans of the banking system, among others. The central plan also had to encompass the development of health care, educational and other cultural systems, which were largely administered through the SOEs.

Central plans were vertically organised, whereby the plan for each economic sector was supervised by the relevant central ministry, including producer goods and raw materials. Initially, 28 goods were covered in 1952; this had reached 235 by 1956. In addition, provinces and localities also made plans that were 'horizontally' organised by territory and covered all sectors within the relevant jurisdiction where the enterprises were under provincial or local control. Centralisation tended to favour a vertical structure, as heavy industry tilted the share of industries away from light industrial goods which were under provincial/local control. The state was also concerned with reducing the sharp regional inequities in the level of development and distribution of services and central control over resources was essential to achieve this end.

However, the costs of centralisation were high. As the desired structural shifts were brought about, any advantage was outweighed by the size and complexity of the economy. This was especially notable after the sudden end of the private sector in 1956 which dramatically increased the number of enterprises under the direct control of the central planning apparatus and simultaneously eliminated the role of the market in distributing many goods and services, which were then handled only by the state distribution channels.

Many problems of coordination, control and incentives were revealed as a result of this degree of centralisation. Central decisions were often based on inadequate or erroneous information, while local governments which had the information could not use it, as many activities fell within the sphere of vertical planning. Further, under the consolidated budget system, local expenditures were centrally determined and bore no relation to local revenues, which reduced the incentive for localities to increase revenues and engage in local development efforts.

The push for decentralisation also received a boost when Soviet credit dried up after 1955. The government had then to plan for small or medium-scale projects, which were faster to begin production and capable of providing more employment. Decentralisation occurred with increased enterprise authority and mostly greater local administrative power. As a result, there was greater attention to light industry, especially consumer goods, and a slight increase in the role of the market. In order to make market-oriented incentives effective, there was also a rollback of the authority of provinces and localities and consequently a reduced role for the powerful regional Party apparatus that dominated provincial administrations. By 1958, provinces and localities were granted permission to plan for all enterprises within their territory, including those operated by the central government.

However, decentralisation was effectively rescinded as sectoral imbalances grew. Both the centre and the provinces drew up targets and the plans began to diverge strongly. For this and other reasons, centralised leadership was reasserted with the Great Leap Forward in 1957–58. By 1961, the economic planning system was as centralised as before 1957.

Disastrous effects of the Great Leap Forward, 1963–65 marked a period of readjustment and recovery. Industrial policy focused investment in a small number of sectors regarded as high priority for economic or strategic reasons. Agricultural policy became a priority. Foreign trade also benefited.

However, the return to rigid centralisation in the early 1960s meant that the economy was soon facing many of the same problems as before the 1957–58 reforms. At this time, more far-reaching discussions began resulting in a second decentralisation reform in 1964, though it was not as significant as the first reforms. By 1966, this ended with the Cultural Revolution.

2.2 Agricultural Production

In the early 1950s, land was confiscated from the landlords and redistributed. In the mid 1950s, Chairman Mao reorganised the cooperatives into communes – a type of collective unit where land is owned collectively by its members. By the end of 1955, 59% of peasant households were organised into elementary cooperatives. Two years later, a very high 88% of all rural households were organised into advanced cooperatives or collectives.

Local Party cadres won favour for organizing cooperatives, while poorer peasants pushed for full collectivisation as a further redistribution of income and wealth benefited them. In the collectives, the rent portion of cooperative income (that is, the portion accruing to land shares invested in the cooperative) was abolished and all personal income depended on labour alone. Therefore, poorer peasants who had contributed little land would gain against the better-off peasants who had contributed relatively larger land holdings. The continuing contradictions concerning land use within cooperatives could be solved by collectivisation. So long as any private ownership of land was maintained, peasants would be reluctant to allow their own land to be used in disadvantageous ways (for example, flooded for irrigation), while their right to withdraw or sell their land interfered with its full integration into cooperative use. Finally, it is thought that the larger scale, smaller numbers, and lack of property income in collectives were conducive to greater government control of agriculture – very attractive in the eyes of the state.

In 1979, there were 53 300 communes, which were divided into 699 000 brigades and 5.154 million production teams. A production team usually consisted of a village, with about 150 persons on average per team. Most farming was done by a team, whereas larger-scale work was done by a brigade.

Commune authorities under the authority of the central government determined what to produce. An assigned quota of the output had to be delivered to the government procurement department at a centrally fixed procurement price, while remaining output was left for distribution to commune members. Members earned income in money and in kind proportional to the number of work points earned, which equalled the number of days the team worked.

However, some aspects of the market economy were evident even in this period. Between 1958 and 1978, some farmers had small, private plots and some rural markets existed where agricultural products were traded. There were even some spot rural markets.

One point to note is that a major objective of the central procurement of agricultural goods was to provide adequate supplies of essential food products to urban residents under a system of rationing, including grain, vegetable oil, meat, sugar and cotton cloth at low prices. The 'urban bias' is an enduring characteristic.

2.3   External Sector and Trade

China's international trade rose steadily throughout the 1950s to reach some 9% of GDP in 1959. China imported producer goods, such as machinery and rolled steel, while exporting raw and processed agricultural goods, textiles and minerals. Between 1950 and 1961, the Soviet Union accounted for about 45% of imports, of which one-quarter was complete industrial plants and 16% was other machinery and equipment. About 27% were financed by credit from the Soviet Union, permitting China to run a trade deficit with the USSR from 1950–1955, tapping into Soviet savings to supplement Chinese investment at a crucial point.

During the period of readjustment (1963–65) following the Great Leap Forward, international trade underwent a profound change. Trade policy was deeply affected by the post-Great Leap Forward crisis, which reduced both export and import capacity due to the immediate food crisis, leading China to begin importing food grain in substantial quantities for the first time since 1949. Among other effects, this caused China to discontinue the imports of producer goods. Exports declined by over 30%, imports by 44% between 1959 and 1962.

There was also a break with the Soviet Union, which caused a rapid shift in the direction of trade away from the Soviet bloc and toward the West and Japan. This shift turned out to be a long-term trend, where trade with the USSR fell from 70% of total Chinese trade in 1959 to 53% in 1962 and to only 20% by 1970. Depression in international trade continued until the early 1970s when the US changed its policy, though relations with the Soviet Union never quite mended.

2.4   Investment

The main priority of achieving industrialisation was through increasing investment. In addition to external sector policies, as mentioned before, the central government also used the national budget to channel resources into investment. State budget revenues rose rapidly during the 1950s, both absolutely and in relation to GDP, constituting about 22% of GDP in 1952 and rising to 29% in 1957. State revenues were able to rise due to state enterprise profits which by the end of the 1950s constituted more than 60% of total government revenue. Both the policy of keeping industrial goods prices high relative to wages and salaries, and the automatic growth of depreciation allowances as capital stock increased, contributed to a rate of gross capital formation that compared favourably with that of Japan in the 1930s, when that nation was at a comparable level of development.

2.5 Fiscal Policy

This system of revenue collection enabled the ambitious investment programme to be financed without excessive inflationary pressures. It mostly affected consumer goods, especially luxury goods, which discouraged their use and expedited the state's policy shift towards investment. The resulting simplification of the tax structure made the system progressively less bureaucratic and thus less costly to run. However, with the state leading investment, enterprises were sidelined and this contributed to their inefficiency. Enterprises did not keep their profits, so did not increase them; they merely transferred the costs of inefficiency to the state via reduced profits and taxes.

2.6 Labour

The chief organs for administering employment policy were the Labour Bureaux, established at the provincial and municipal levels in May 1950. Their principal duties related to unemployment, welfare, and the mediation of labour disputes in the private sector.

In 1949, total non-agricultural employment was around 26 million. Of this, industry and construction employed 3.3 million. By 1952, this figure nearly doubled to reach 6.3 million, again reflecting the shift toward industry and away from consumption.

The Chinese government had inherited a sizeable amount of urban unemployment (4 to 12.5 million in 1950). The government at first assumed that the problem would be solved by economic growth, but soon realised in 1954 that the problem was both long term and structural.

The weak demand for labour, which contributed to the persistence of unemployment, was due in part to the capital-intensive nature of the First Five Year Plan. But the Plan also influenced labour supply, by building expectations of high-paying jobs in industry and thus encouraging rural-urban migration, a principal contributor to unemployment throughout the 1950s. Urban wages, for instance, rose 143% from 1949 to the end of the First Five Year Plan, whereas rural income increased by less than half that amount (69%). It was not only income that was affected, but also job security and social insurance. After the Labour Insurance Regulations were promulgated in February 1951, urban workers received medical, disability and retirement coverage, while rural workers had rather meagre private, cooperative and state relief resources.

The first of China's wage system reforms occurred in 1950, one year after the Communist Revolution. It was aimed at transforming the food supply system of wartime communism into a wage system. Under the reformed system, government and military officials and employees in the newly established state-owned enterprises began to receive cash salaries and compensation according to job titles and ranks. The second wage reform in 1956 was part of an overall plan to nationalise the economy. The aim was to regulate wages for an expanded workforce in both the state and collective sectors. Salary standards were patterned after the Soviet model and centrally regulated according to regions, occupations, industries, sectors (state or collective), level of management of enterprises (central or local), and characteristics of workplace, for example, technology and size. The core of this wage system was a complex structure of salary standards for more than 300 occupational classifications.

This system of labour allocation and administratively determined wages remained largely intact until the re-emergence of urban unemployment, which will be discussed in the sub-section 2.8, where the pre-reform period is reassessed.

2.7   Cultural Revolution Economic Policies

It is worth reflecting on the economic policies of the Cultural Revolution. The impetus for, and the consequences of, the Cultural Revolution will not be discussed here, as the period certainly cannot be explained in economic terms alone. Instead, the focus will be on one of the main economic policies that arose from it: self-reliance or *zili gengsheng* ('regeneration through one's own efforts'). This principle urged the full utilisation of labour and skills to establish an industrial system in China. Due in part to the break with the communist USSR, there was a rejection of foreign methods in favour of indigenous approaches suited to Chinese conditions, a phrase still often heard today. Also, with a drying up of Soviet credit, there was a belief that domestic savings should be relied upon to finance the capital accumulation that drives growth.

Although applicable to a much greater set of issues, self-reliance may be understood as a strategy of import substitution designed to produce a comprehensive industrial base. One of the rationales has to do with learning and motivation. Regardless of the size of a region's static comparative advantage in agriculture, its prospects for harnessing science and technology and achieving long-term economic development depend on mastering the know-how of manufacturing.

A gauge of the extent of the inward-looking orientation of the Chinese economy is the ratio of foreign trade to GDP (imports plus exports). For the period 1952–74, this has been estimated at around 6%, similar to the Soviet Union at that time, but well below those of industrialised capitalist economies. However, this varied throughout different time periods. Trade grew in the 1950s when China benefited from close economic ties with the USSR. In the 1960s, after the break with the USSR, trade stagnated. In the first part of the 1970s, China turned outward again. During 1970–1973, the real value of trade with non-centrally planned economies increased by an estimated 78%, more than twice the 36% growth in gross national product (GNP) over the same period.

Trade can be consistent with self-reliance. During the late 1960s, China continued to build up its productive capacity to make up for the goods that it had previously imported from the Soviets. Industrial output grew by an average rate of 9–10% per annum. However, during the 1970–1973 period when trade grew much faster than GNP, imports may have contributed to self-reliance by strengthening weaknesses in China's own industrial capacity and overcoming bottlenecks in the domestic economy. Imports were concentrated in a few industries, notably fertiliser, petroleum refining, petrochemicals, ferrous metallurgy, and electric power, for instance.

2.8 Reassessment

Despite the high levels of investment and rapid growth, the Chinese economy at the end of the 1970s produced standards of living which were not much better than those of the 1950s. In the crucial category of grain consumption, average per capita food grain availability in 1977 was similar to that of 1955. Average grain consumption in the rural population for 1978–80 was actually lower than in 1955–57; whereas it was slightly higher for urban areas.

Within the state sector, the freeze of wages after 1957 and the entry of new workers onto the lowest rungs of the wage structure caused the average wage to fall 17% in real terms between 1957 and 1977. But, a large increase in the labour force participation rate – from 30% of the urban population in 1957 to 55% in 1980 – enabled the average per capita income of wage earners to increase by 62% in real terms during that period However, a lack of 'non-productive' investment led the already cramped housing space of 4.3 square metres per urban resident in 1952 to decline to 3.6 square metres in 1977.

However, China did score many economic and technological triumphs. It created a machine-building industry, launched satellites, became a nuclear power, built large ships, and even synthesised insulin. But these advances did not translate into an improvement in living standards or significantly affect productive efficiency. Most of China's industrial growth had come from increases in productive factors, especially fixed capital, rather than via the efficiency of inputs. Even the growth in labour productivity was achieved mainly by increases in the amounts of physical capital per worker (the capital-labour index grew from 100 in 1952 to 373 in 1978). Part of the explanation lies in the structural shifts towards more capital-intensive, heavy industries, which were later reversed.

This is the crux of the problem of 'imbalance' that required 'readjustment'. However, another part is due to structural and systematic factors, stemming from deficiencies in the system of economic organisation, planning and management. A reassessment of the structural imbalances and systematic flaws – flaws in the planning, management, and incentive systems giving rise to imbalances – followed. This tension became a principal theme of the new economic strategy that marked the start of market-oriented reforms announced at the Third Plenum of the Eleventh Central Committee in December 1978.

To compound matters, the problem of high urban unemployment reappeared in 1978. In 1979, the urban unemployed were thought to exceed 10 million or some 10% of the estimated non-agricultural labour force of 104 million. Before 1976, unemployment was largely avoided, by such means as some 20 million urban residents being sent to the countryside after the Great Leap Forward. Their return likely contributed. For instance, the 17 million youths who were sent out to the countryside from 1966 to 1976 were urban residents.

Also, job allocations were handled by the state labour bureaux, which were responsible for placing school-leavers, demobilised soldiers, youth returning from the countryside, and released convicts. The burden on the already disorganised state apparatus resulted in many job-seekers spending long periods of time 'waiting for work'. Enterprises were forbidden to recruit workers and individuals could not seek jobs in compliance with the state's goal of providing full employment. This commitment resulted in general overstaffing (a form of 'disguised unemployment'). This problem was exacerbated by the continuing gap between urban and rural incomes which resulted in an oversupply of labour at existing wages. The numbers were dependent to some extent on administrative suppression of the movement of labour through prohibition of rural-urban migration via the *hukou* or household registration system. Other contributing factors included the favoured sector in China's development strategy being heavy industry, which is capital-intensive.

Therefore, high urban unemployment, stagnating levels of food consumption, deteriorating urban housing conditions, falling real wages, widespread rural poverty and sluggish productivity growth – all despite rapid economic growth as conventionally measured – may be viewed as the impetus for market-oriented reforms undertaken in 1978 and marked the start of the reform period.

3. POST-1978 REFORM PERIOD

Since then, China has been a remarkably successful economy after its adoption of market-oriented reforms some 30 years ago. Figure 2.1 shows China's real GDP growth has averaged over 9% per annum from 1979 to 2008. Even in the midst of the worst economic crisis for nearly a century, China registered growth of 8.7% in 2009, as a result of large stimulative spending by the government.

Figure 2.2 shows the rapidity with which China has propelled itself to become the world's third largest economy at market exchange rates, and the second largest when adjusted for purchasing power parity (PPP). It accounts for a share of global GDP that is second only to the United States and it is growing more quickly than other major economies (Figure 2.3). It is also the most populous nation, a leading destination for foreign direct investment (FDI), and one of the largest global traders. Concomitantly, it is a developing country with a per capita GDP that only recently exceeded $1000 and has significant numbers of people living in poverty. Despite its

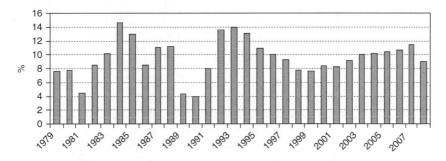

Source: *China Statistical Yearbook,* various years.

Figure 2.1   China's real GDP growth, 1979–2008

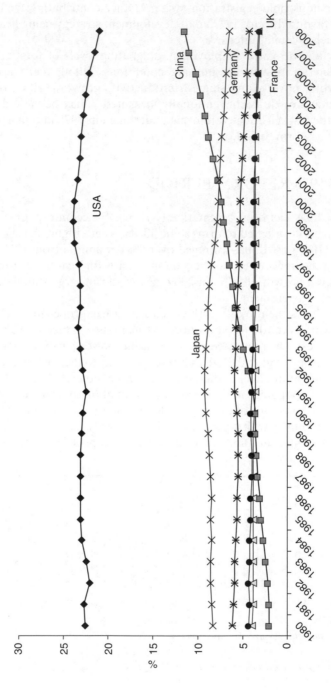

Source: IMF.

Figure 2.2   PPP-adjusted share of global GDP, 1980–2008

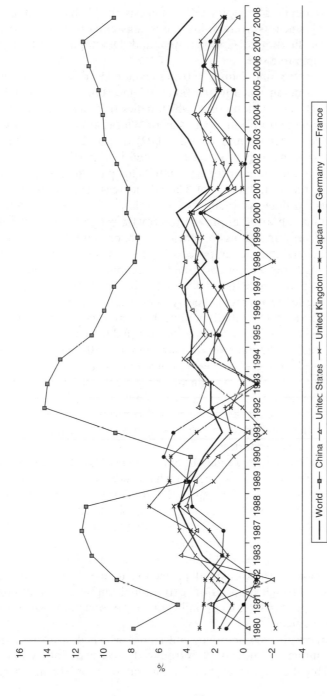

Source: IMF.

Figure 2.3 Real annual GDP growth of major economies and the world, 1980–2008

aggregate size, China's per capita GDP suggests that it has substantial growth potential, since its average income is substantially below that of Organisation for Economic Co-operation and Development (OECD) countries of comparable size.

It is often observed that China's strong economic growth for nearly three decades has taken place in the midst of uncertain property rights and arguably high transaction costs, which defies the usual depiction of efficient markets in the traditional (Coasian or Walrasian) economic sense (see, for example, Jefferson and Rawski 2002). Its gradualist approach to transition from central planning has resulted in a partially reformed economy within a communal property state. This particular path raises questions about the foundations of China's increasingly decentralised economy and its ultimate sustainability.

With a rapid liberalisation approach to growth, property rights would be established quickly and allow for efficient exchange, in theory. By contrast, China's incremental reform process has left it with ill-defined property rights and high transaction costs, and yet economic growth has been rapid. This chapter will argue that the so-called 'institutional innovations', which allowed the state to create property rights without a change in ownership from public to private, had an appeal in a gradualist reform path. Then, as decentralisation increased, the state created further contractually defined rights, such as the joint venture laws in the 1980s, which likewise extended incentives and granted legal protection to foreign investment without requiring widespread private property rights to be established. Finally, as the economy grows increasingly complex due to liberalisation, legal reforms enabled the market to be more decentralised and developed, such as through the creation of regulatory agencies, for instance, which enables capital market formation.

Membership of the World Trade Organization (WTO) also introduced elements of international economic law, which speeded up legal reforms and further decentralisation. In turn, the resultant economic growth increased the need for more laws and regulation. This process has culminated in an evolutionary framework in China that is not dissimilar to that of other economies when they undertook corporate sector development under an initially underdeveloped legal system, but has distinct elements, such as the eventual need to extend protection to the de facto private property created through decades of institutional innovations and contractually desired property rights initially granted to foreign investors and eventually Chinese firms.

Figure 2.4 traces the major policy milestones which first created the informal institutional reforms that introduced incentives into China's economy and highlights the eventual adoption of more formal legal

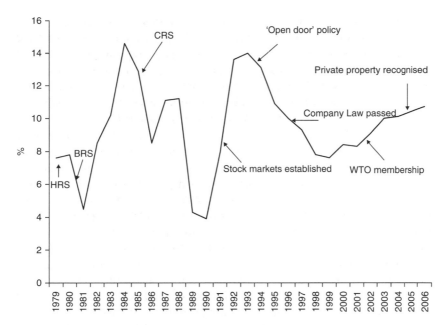

Source: *China Statistical Yearbook,* various years, and author's assessment.

Figure 2.4   Real annual GDP growth and policy milestones

reforms. The 'institutional innovations', which were informal institutional arrangements that gave profit incentives to farmers, state-owned enterprises (SOEs) and even local governments, are highlighted respectively as the Household Responsibility System (HRS) in 1979, which lasted until 1984, the Budgetary Responsibility System (BRS), starting in 1980, the Contract Responsibility System (CRS), which began in 1981 and lasted until the late 1980s, alongside direct lending by state-owned commercial banks (SCBs). The more formal institutional forms that China adopted to incentivise economic activity included the 'open door' policy, which gave foreign investors the legal entities of joint ventures (JV) as vehicles for their investment, that took off in 1992; the creation of the two stock exchanges in Shanghai in 1990 and Shenzhen in 1991; as well as the passage of the Company Law in 1993 that heralded the era of legally defined corporations and the restructuring of the state-owned sector into shareholding companies; and finally, membership of the World Trade Organization in 2001, which introduced international economic laws into China and ushered in a period of rapid regulatory forms and agencies, such as the China Banking Regulatory Commission (CBRC). Finally, China recognised private property in its Constitution in 2004 and gave equal protection to private and public property in 2007, heralding an era of more formal, legal rights into its property ownership system. Certainly, this is an overview of the institutional reforms in China and there are numerous other policy initiatives that took place. Some of the main ones will be discussed in this chapter, which seeks to understand the interplay between laws – including international trade rules – institutions and growth in China.

Therefore, this chapter argues that institutionally and contractually defined rights were sufficient to support China's economic growth, as they suited the gradualist transition approach, since private property rights were not essential in the early part of the reform process. As China becomes increasingly marketised, there are limits to using informally defined rights and an increased need for explicit legal reforms. These contractually and institutionally defined rights have the additional advantage of not relying on formal mechanisms for enforcement, as they are not clearly rooted in the Chinese legal system, but can be enforced informally through social and business relationships or sometimes through contractually defined measures such as binding arbitration. In other words, villagers know the implicit ownership of farmland, while foreign investors are aware that their rights are defined in the contract and disputes are settled outside of formal litigation. For instance, although subject to the Chinese legal system, Chinese-foreign joint ventures are often entered into with trusted parties and sometimes externally enforced through international arbitration procedures.

This section will proceed in three parts. The first is a review of China's economic reform strategy and why institutional innovations appeared to enable China's rapid growth in the early stages of reform. This is followed by an evaluation of China's creation of certain forms of property rights which became more formalised during its transition. Finally, the chapter assesses the implications of this approach for China's growth prospects and global integration, including the influence of international laws and rules.

3.1   China's Approach to Economic Reform

China's approach to economic growth must be viewed within the context of its status as a transition economy that is also a developing country. China has been in transition for 30 years from a centrally planned economy which followed Soviet-style heavy industrialisation for a time, toward becoming a marketised economy. China adopted its reforms gradually or incrementally during this period. By so doing, it has phased in market forces into an administered economy, but without a fundamental transformation into a privately owned economy.

   Economic reform in China is a partial reform strategy, which has been characterised by institutional innovations and regional experimentation (see, for example, Qian and Xu 1993; Fan 1994). Reform began in the countryside and early successes were seen in the creation of township and village enterprises (TVEs) in rural areas. TVEs injected industry and market orientation into the rural economy, which was endowed with abundant and surplus labour. Further, the Household Responsibility System gave residual ownership to farmers so that they could earn a return on their effort within a framework of the communal ownership of land. These reforms reorientated national saving to households, injected incentives into an economy that did not recognise private property and reallocated the essential factor of labour to more productive enterprises. Output grew rapidly in the early 1980s, as seen in Figure 2.1, leading to the observation that China's growth began in the countryside (Riskin 1987).

   When these measures were seen to be successful, China introduced further reform into urban areas in 1984, encouraged by the experiments in the countryside. Managers in state-owned enterprises were granted more autonomy and allowed to retain a portion of profits by means of a further institutional innovation known as the Contract Responsibility System. Wage reform introduced a performance element into pay (Yueh 2004). Urban reforms further bolstered the status and income of urban residents, who had been favoured in the administered economy (Knight and Song 1999). Urban residents enjoyed an 'iron rice bowl' and social security provision provided by the *danwei* or work unit which was not available to rural residents. The 'urban bias' had enabled China to undergo industrialisation as discussed in the previous section and the favourable treatment of urban residents maintained stability, which is a critical element of a gradualist transition path.

   Indeed, stability is essential in maintaining a 'dual track' transition. In allowing enterprises to sell part of their output at market prices, the authorities must be able to control the sale of goods to the administered part of the market in order to implement a partial liberalisation strategy (Murphy et al. 1992). However, at the same time, China sustained a degree of decentralisation that permitted experiments to take place so that market-oriented reform could be introduced without affecting the economy as a whole (Qian and Xu 1993). This approach further allowed the authorities to adapt in a practical way to changing circumstances rather than follow a prescribed plan of reform.

   The final prong of China's reform approach is the 'open door' policy. China created Special Economic Zones (SEZs) initially in southern coastal provinces, which were essentially export-processing zones that were open to international trade and foreign investment (Lardy 1998). The introduction of market forces into SEZs allowed the government to experiment with a limited degree of opening up. These measures began in 1979, but did not take off until 1992 when Deng Xiaoping took a tour of the earliest SEZs in Fujian and Guangdong. Since then, China has created further forms of SEZs, such as Free Trade Zones and High-Technology Development Zones (HTDZs), which are geared to attracting foreign investment in technology sectors and promoting research and development (R&D). The SEZs gave foreign investors a degree of legal protection that was not enjoyed by Chinese enterprises, and was sufficient to induce significant amounts of inward FDI into China in spite of an otherwise poor legal system. China has been transformed from an economy with an export-to-GDP ratio of 15% in 1990 to an impressively open 30% by the year 2000. Within the span of a decade, China reached the global market share of the East Asian 'tiger' economies at the peak of their export-led growth.

Some of the elements of China's reform strategy are outlined in the next section to gain an understanding of the gradualist approach to economic transition, before the chapter analyses the incentives inherent in this approach that stimulated growth within an underdeveloped, domestic formal institutional framework increasingly subject to global forces – both market and rule-based.

3.2 'Gradualism' and Initial Conditions

It is thought that a 'big bang' approach was not desired by China on account of reasonable economic conditions at the time of the first adoption of reforms (Riskin 1987). 'Gradualism' was preferred to the more radical reform programmes, which were similar to the rapid introduction of market forces termed 'shock therapy' by the Eastern European and former Soviet Union (EEFSU) economies. In contrast, the EEFSU countries in the late 1980s accepted a 'shock therapy' package, again under terms particular to their circumstances (notably, the lack of authority of the central government). The ability to adopt gradualism or radical change could depend on the extent to which the economy had stagnated and declined at the time of reform. The lower is the growth potential of the old system, the stronger are the incentives and the will to pursue radical reform.

Gradualism is further related to initial conditions and economic structure. It is more likely to be successful in an underdeveloped and under-industrialised economy with a large rural surplus labour force. Rural incomes had been falling compared to the urban population in China. The pre-existence of a declining sector, such as agriculture, results in a population of people who possess a strong demand for opportunities and who will also constitute a new labour force.

Thus, there are two main conditions that permit an incrementalist reform approach to be successful. First, China started its reforms before the state sector was in drastic decline, so that heavy subsidies were not needed, contrary to the situation of former Soviet firms in the late 1980s. Second, the start of rural reform and accompanying liberalisation of private economic activity in the presence of a large rural labour surplus generated growth rapid enough to outpace the speed at which subsidies to SOEs were increasing.

Further, stability is required to provide sufficient control over the economy so that quantity ceilings can be maintained and goods are sold at both administered and market prices (Murphy et al. 1992). Otherwise, all firms would rush to sell at market price and the market track would overwhelm the administered track. And, on the eve of reform, the state sector must be sufficiently viable so that the requirements of continuing transfers from the state sector do not exceed the growth in the non-state sector.

In all of these respects, the gradualist transition path, along with favourable initial conditions, laid the groundwork for China's incremental reform of incentives and introduction of institutionally defined incentives.

3.3 Experimentation and Coordination Structures

Much of the innovation and many of the advances that occurred in the process of reform were less by design and resulted more from the Chinese government's pragmatic flexibility. Some of the changes under a gradualist approach were due less to planning, but are more accurately characterised as adjustment to practical circumstances. For example, one of the key steps in starting the reform process was the advent of the Household Responsibility System. It was banned in 1979, but accepted when it became widely practised by rural residents.

Generally, the Chinese government approach can be described as 'no encouragement, no ban' (Naughton 1996). Experiments encompassing different reform programmes at various governmental levels were encouraged, including the creation of SEZs. SEZs were specially designated areas in which export-oriented companies were permitted to flourish and become foreign-invested in restricted locales, such as Shenzhen. Special treatment was further given to different regions and local initiatives were respected.

It has been suggested that one reason for this success has been the form of coordination found in China (see Qian and Xu 1993). M-form structures of coordination are based on minimal interdependence among regions or industries, so that experimentation in one area can be completed without its success or failure causing disruptions elsewhere. U-form organisation is characterised as 'top-down' because of more interdependence and thus experimentation could affect the whole system. M-form is thought to be more conducive to experimentation and heterogeneity among units makes experimentation less applicable in U-form hierarchies as in the Soviet Union. China was perhaps characterised by the former, as a result of much decentralisation that preceded the reform period, which accounts for the success of experiments in heralding further reforms.

3.4   The Theory of Partial Reform and 'Dual Track' Transition

As a result, a process characterised as one of partial reform was adopted, in which some markets were liberalised and permitted to sell output at market prices, but also required to sell to state firms at administered prices. This 'dual track' system has been extended to cover almost all economic transactions. Although the reforms were not accompanied by immediate privatisation of ownership, the resulting arrangements generated new forms of economic organisation. The most important was the creation of a parallel non-state sector to the state one. Much of China's dynamic growth can be attributed to the non-state sector, consisting of private and semi-private enterprises, including community-owned rural industrial enterprises, Chinese-foreign joint ventures, and individual businesses. The appeal of this approach is in part to honour 'implicit contracts', arising from expectations under a socialist system where jobs and welfare are maintained by the state. This transition path reduces market efficiency and instead reflects vested interests, as unemployment is not created and social security provision is not disrupted. The gain from the maintenance of such distorted incentives is that resistance to reform is reduced. Although not perfectly efficient, the introduction of profit incentives was essential in fuelling the 'dual track' system and the forms that such incentives took are the subject of this chapter's investigation.

3.5   'Easy-to-Hard' Reform Sequence

With decentralisation of decision-making powers to local governments and increased autonomy given to enterprises, there were a number of problems generated by this reform strategy. The gradualist approach is in actuality an 'easy-to-hard' reform sequence. It addresses the easy problems first and leaves the hard ones until later (Fan 1994). A radical approach would do the opposite: the aim would be to maximise efficiency gains and minimise the implementation costs of reform. However, restructuring may be easier with the gradualist approach. If a gradualist transition strategy is not geared toward introducing rapid and complete marketisation, but is concerned with implementing reform and overcoming opposition, then it has the tendency to leave the difficult issues unresolved. However, restructuring may be easier with the gradualist approach as it minimises the political costs of reform. Different conditions could produce a different optimum sequence.

4. CREATING PROPERTY RIGHTS

For rural residents, SOEs and multinational corporations, China's introduction of incentives took the form of 'institutional innovations' and contractually defined rights, such as those which created the corporate JV vehicles for foreign investors. By gradually building institutions that were not an overhaul of the communal property system and therefore did not jeopardise the implicit social contract and stability of a gradual transition, these new economic entities did not herald a transformation of China's property rights system, but were nevertheless sufficient to establish profit motives within an imperfect formal legal structure. However, the limits of these institutional innovations and contractually defined rights were apparent as the market became increasingly decentralised and more formal institutions seemingly required.

4.1 The Institutional Innovations

China does not have a system of formal property rights conventionally defined and only recognised the existence of private property in March 2004, when the concept was included in its Constitution. Yet, China's phenomenal growth has taken place through the creation of residual claimant rights in its partially marketised economy, notably, for example, the Household Responsibility System for farmers implemented to great success in the late 1970s and early 1980s, and the Contract Responsibility System, instigated in the mid 1980s for SOEs.

In the rural economy, at the start of reform in 1979, the Household Responsibility System created a system of effective residual claimants in the rural areas. Farmers were given incentives to share risk with the state by retaining some returns from their labour above what they are to remit to the state. Rural township and village enterprises were also subject to a two-tiered compensation structure whereby profits could accrue to the labourers in the rural industry so long as sufficient remittances or transfers went to the state. This system was extended in a qualitatively different manner to urban areas and to foreign investment in the form of contractually defined rights.

Second, China's 'dual track' transition, in which one part of the market was liberalised while another was kept under administrative control, depended on the creation of rights to retain returns from the marketised part of the economy. A 'dual track' approach that did not create incentives for the risk-averse actors beholden to the principal or state in a transition economy would not have been feasible. In other words, prior to this 'institutional innovation', collectivisation meant that there was little incentive for farmers to produce output, as their work points were allocated on the basis of a day's labour irrespective of effort. The creation of these implicit property rights can be likened to a sharecropping system where there is a residual ownership right to instil incentives while not granting outright property ownership to the farmers. This process of creating and defining some form of property rights shaped and explains China's successful use of a gradualist or incrementalist approach to marketisation. With this change in incentives, output increased tremendously and 1984 witnessed a bumper crop (Riskin 1987).

The evidence of growth stemming from these incentives is notable, as China's real GDP growth in this early 1980s period averaged over 9%, agricultural output was high, and rural industrialisation helped remove surplus labour from the farms (Riskin 1987). Whereas the HRS refined the incentives facing households and is often called an 'institutional innovation', the creation of TVEs through permitting this corporate form is a more striking example of how China created a new institutional form whose parameters were defined by policy and not by private ownership or outright transfer of the ownership to individuals. Yet, the reliance of the Chinese rural workers on this newly recognised institutional form was sufficient to instil market-driven incentives, and a significant part of China's growth in agricultural productivity and the rural economy can be traced to both the HRS and decollectivisation (Lin 1992; Huang and Rozelle 1996).

Decentralisation and institutional innovations within the state sector were also important. Decentralisation has occurred in almost all areas of decision-making in production, pricing, investment, trade, expenditure, income distribution, taxation and credit allocation. The main institutional innovations were the Budgetary Responsibility System, the Contract Responsibility System, and permitting direct borrowing (Riskin 1987). Since 1980, under the BCS, the central government shares revenues (taxes and profit remittances) with local governments. For local governments which incur budget deficits, the contract sets the subsidies to be transferred to the local governments. Fiscal decentralisation further gave scope for regional experimentation, another key element to China's gradualist path, as it permitted increased market-oriented activity, while limiting the possibility of instability from arising given the nature of China's semi-federal structure (Qian and Xu 1993).

The CRS in 1981 permitted SOEs to pay a fixed amount of taxes and profits to the state and retain the remainder (Koo 1990). In principle, so long as the SOEs deliver the tax and profit remittances specified in the contracts, they are free to operate. This resulted in increased production of SOEs in the 1980s through the reorientation of incentives of managers (Groves et al. 1995). However, the decline of SOEs by the 1990s illustrates that the limit of relying on institutional innovations as 'soft budget constraints' continued to plague the enterprises, despite the positive incentive effects of the CRS (Choo and Yin 2000).

Since 1985, state grants for operating funds and fixed asset investments were replaced by bank loans, the final element of the institutional innovations. Local governments and SOEs are allowed to borrow directly from banks. Six years later, local governments and SOEs were permitted to borrow from household and other institutions. By liberating one 'track' of the dual track system, there was scope for these institutionally defined rights to foster a profit incentive to SOEs and state-owned banks which helped boost output, again without creating private property rights in the ownership of these enterprises and banks.

4.2 Contractually Defined Rights

This system of informal property rights extended to China's treatment of multinational corporations investing and establishing primarily manufacturing facilities. Since the 'open door' policy began and with its take-off in the early 1990s, China has rapidly become one of the world's top destinations for foreign direct investment. For most of the reform period, especially prior to WTO accession, the predominant form of FDI was Chinese-foreign joint ventures, where the Chinese and foreign partners set up either equity or cooperative joint ventures. Equity joint ventures partitioned returns on the basis of the invested capital in the joint venture, while returns were contractually defined in cooperative joint ventures. Both forms of joint ventures, however, were vested essentially in a set of contractually defined rights. The uncertainty that might have been generated by a lack of recognition of private property, such as those held by joint ventures, though, did not seem to serve as a deterrent to FDI. Because of the lack of private property rights in the rest of the Chinese economy, the joint venture laws in some ways provided more protection to foreign-invested enterprises than accorded to Chinese non-state firms, such as *getihu* (sole proprietorships) and other non-state-owned enterprises (Huang 2006).

This system of contractually defined rights was not limited to foreign investment. In 1998, China undertook privatisation of housing, whereby the housing formerly allocated through work units was sold off at preferential prices to urban residents. By 2001, the housing market was effectively privatised. However, the rights of the owners of the housing were limited to residing in the flat or house for a designated period of time. This contractually defined right is in effect in the form of a leasehold and thus not outright ownership. The expectation of housing owners is that they will have the right to renew their contract and the passage of the 2007 Property Law largely confirms this expectation. Investment, moreover, is high in the housing market despite a lack of comprehensive protection of private property and uncertain land use rights. These contracts also carry enforcement risk; however, the implicit social contract that arises means that should expectations not be fulfilled, there is the possibility of social instability, as has been seen when housing and land have been confiscated by the state for development.

Another example of these contractually defined rights is the corporatisation and effective privatisation of state-owned enterprises through a process of share issue privatisation (SIP), following the lack of success of the CRS in sustaining the profitability of SOEs. Since 1992, many SOEs have become shareholding companies, where ownership is in the hands of shareholders and a portion of the shares are traded on domestic and international stock exchanges.

Corporatisation was intended to effectively privatise SOEs by making them shareholding companies when the institutional innovation of the CRS failed to address the soft budget constraints that plagued the inefficient SOEs. Stock ownership is based on a contractually defined obligation rather than a clear announcement of private property as would be expected with mass privatisation of state-owned enterprises. By corporatising its enterprises and maintaining controls over the tradability of shares listed on the domestic stock exchanges, China has managed to instil profit incentives without a change in ownership.

This was effective in sustaining SOE growth for a while, but it became clear that further reform was needed and a large-scale restructuring (*gaizhi*) programme was undertaken in the mid 1990s that has paved the way for the later effective privatisation of SOEs. One of the consequences of China's form of privatisation is that shareholders require and expect protection of these contractually defined rights, so regulatory agencies such as the China Securities Regulatory Commission (CSRC) was established from 1992, as well as other regulatory agencies such as the China Insurance Regulatory Commission (CIRC) in 1998 and the China Banking Regulatory Commission in 2003.

4.3 Enforcement

China has successfully established a system of contractually defined and institutionally structured rights encompassing the set of so-called 'institutional innovations' – the market-oriented institutional reforms governing households, firms and even local governments – as well as with respect to foreign investors and the domestic non-state sector. This system of institutionally and contractually defined, but arguably informal, property rights stimulated China's impressive economic growth during the reform period, despite the lack of recognition of private property per se and within an incomplete legal system, particularly with respect to enforcement.

In a system of contractually or institutionally created rights, enforcement would seem to be of considerable significance, yet China's legal and regulatory systems lagged, and still lag, behind the set of contractually defined obligations underpinning its economy. Clarke (2003) emphasises the security of property rather than enforcement as important in China, and informal, but still defined by policy or contract, property would be consistent with this view. Indeed, the studies of social capital/networks in China and elsewhere reinforce the notion that socially acknowledged ownership rights are secured through informal enforcement rather than a formal process, reducing the importance of the formal legal system and the effectiveness of its enforcement procedures (Greif 1993; Allen et al. 2005). For instance, Ho (2006) finds that collectively owned land is subject to period division within a village and that these rights to the land are well known, expected and respected, despite a lack of private ownership of land in China. However, the recent reforms to property laws in China will protect these informal rights through formal channels, which perhaps signal the limits to a purely informal institutional framework.

A further possibility for a system of contractually defined rights is that arbitration can be specified as an enforcement mechanism. Although arbitration is not a possibility for all transactions, particularly those related to SOEs, it provides another avenue of specifying a manner of conflict resolution that does not rely on the courts but can utilise an agreed set of terms and laws. China International Economic and Trade Arbitration Commission (CIETAC) is often used by international investors, for instance, and has a better reputation than the Chinese court system.

4.4 The Limits of the Informal System

In the rural economy, although agricultural productivity was stimulated by the Household Responsibility System (Lin 1992), longer-term investments required more certainty. Thus, by the late 1990s, China adopted a land tenure system whereby, instead of regular reallocations of farm land, rural farmers owned leaseholds of 50 years and could plan and invest for the longer term.

Similarly for enterprises, the early success of the CRS was insufficient to stymie the accumulation of non-performing loans in the banking sector that grew throughout the 1980s and 1990s. The 'soft budget constraints' of SOEs, in particular, induced inefficient over-investment, especially as output was stimulated by the CRS and meant that further SOE reforms were needed. The corporatisation policy, coupled with the *gaizhi* or restructuring policy, was enabled by the promulgation of the Company Law in 1993 and the creation of two stock exchanges in Shanghai and Shenzhen in the early 1990s. These formal legal/institutional measures created shares in the SOEs and thus legally defined the ownership of these companies. However, many SOEs were still majority-owned by the state, so the extent of private ownership was limited to a minority holding in the newly listed companies (Du and Xu 2006). Nevertheless, TVEs, as well as private Chinese firms, also took advantage of the greater certainty afforded to legally recognised corporate entities by incorporating in various forms such as limited liability companies (LLCs) and China's growth remained high throughout the 1990s, even as the efficiency of SOEs declined during this period.

Finally, the system of informal institutions never suited foreign investors who required more certain property rights. Thus, the first laws governing corporate forms were passed in the late 1970s and 1980s to create Chinese-foreign joint ventures and in rare cases, wholly-owned foreign-owned enterprises. The JV and foreign enterprise laws contractually defined the rights and obligations of these firms, which provided for a greater level of certainty than those governing other enterprises in China. Even though enforcement of the contractual rights and ensuing commercial contracts were imperfect, the rapid growth of FDI in China attests to the perceived relative security of contractually defined rights even within a markedly communal property system. However, as the market evolved and increased in complexity, the push for an ever growing number of laws to protect the rights of both foreign and domestic firms grew. In the years leading up to, and certainly after, WTO accession in 2001, China passed a large number of laws to govern its markets, including merger and acquisition (M&A) and (an updated) bankruptcy laws in 2002 and 2007, respectively, as well as improved patent laws, to underpin the growing complexity of its economy. In this way, formal legal reforms began to support the predominantly informal institutions that supported China's economy and the interactions between formal/informal institutions and economic development are increasingly evident.

5. ECONOMIC GROWTH AND GLOBAL INTEGRATION

In analysing China's growth model and evidence, the direction of reform points to the need for more formal legal protection as the economy aims to sustain its growth rate and stabilise its integration with the global economy.

5.1 Evidence of China's Economic Growth

The gradualist path in China has resulted in largely extensive growth, perhaps on account of the distance from the technological frontier of the economy. Recall, for instance, the large, surplus rural labour force. China's growth is less associated with gains in real productivity over the reform period and more with increases in factor accumulation (for example, see the evidence cited in Wang and Yao 2003). As an example, surplus labour in the agricultural sector was efficiently re-allocated with the creation of TVEs to absorb rural employment. This is not to discount the improvements gained from introducing market-oriented incentives in the state sector (Groves et al. 1995). However, the bulk of the sparse empirical evidence indicates that China's growth is more similar to the East Asian 'tiger economies' factor accumulation process, which is only associated with small increases in real productivity (see Chow 1994). As extensive growth reaches its limit due to diminishing returns, limits in capacity, slowing growth of population, there is unlikely to be a further growth spurt, especially as China already has high levels of labour force participation. Early growth based on extensive growth is predicted to lead to a dramatic slowdown, which has been seen in other socialist economies such as the Soviet Union between the 1950 and 1970s.

Sustaining economic growth through factor accumulation will be limited due to China's aging population and its already high rates of labour force participation, including for women due to the socialist economy established in the pre-reform era. Therefore, one of the main challenges is to sustain continued economic growth via productivity advances instead. This can be achieved through factor reallocation, such as utilising China's abundant labour more efficiently. However, although there is still much surplus labour in China's SOEs and SCBs, the restrictions on mobility between rural and urban *hukou* holders (the household registration system that controls residency) have resulted in areas such as Guangdong reporting a shortage of millions of workers. A measure of the low degree of mobility in Chinese labour markets is given by Knight and Yueh (2004), who find that 78% of urban residents had only ever held one job in 1999.

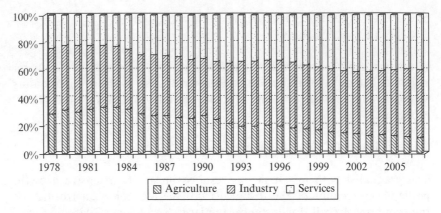

Source: China Statistical Yearbook, various years.

Figure 2.5   Sectoral composition of GDP

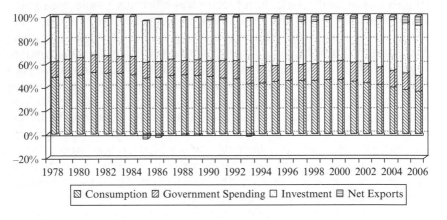

Source: China Statistical Yearbook, various years.

Figure 2.6   Components of GDP

Growth can also come about through the reorientation of the capital stock. The challenge is that China is already industrialised, as seen in Figure 2.5 due to the pre-reform centrally planned economy that instituted industrialisation before 1978; the creation of new capital stock is a challenge, particularly given its underdeveloped capital markets and lack of market instruments to dictate investment in more productive assets, such as the use of interest rates, which were only partially liberalised in October

2004. Figure 2.6 shows the fairly constant level of investment in China and the large role that it plays in generating national income.

Although investment is expected to continue to grow, the need will be to generate investment in R&D and technological advancements rather than increasing real estate construction, for instance. As with many developing countries, China has had low levels of investment in R&D and instead adopts or imitates the technology of advanced economies through foreign investment and capital inflows. This process is well known in development and is termed 'catching up'. At low levels of growth, the rate of growth can thus be substantial.

China appears to be targeting its strategy toward promoting investment in technology sectors, such as the Shanghai-Pudong science park. China's creation of HTDZs and its early focus on joint ventures, frequently accompanied by technology transfer agreements, were intended to serve this purpose. However, although FDI has been impressive in China, it comprises less than 10% of total annual investment and much of it is thought to be accounted for by 'round-tripping', whereby Chinese capital leaves the country and returns to gain benefits as 'foreign' investment. Indeed, the need to improve domestic productivity has led China to become the second largest investor in research and development on a per capita GDP basis in the past few years. The education of scientific personnel and development of infrastructure have accordingly been a focus. Coupled with the access to foreign capital and global markets, China is attempting to increase the technological component of its growth model to sustain a rate of growth that would otherwise begin to slow due to limits on factor accumulation. The emphasis on technology and innovation, in particular, requires further protection of proprietary information and intellectual property, which suggests that growth itself is linked to the creation of more legal rights and better enforcement.

5.2 Global Integration

Turning to China's forays into the global economy, Figures 2.7 and 2.8 show the composition of China's exports and imports divided into several goods and commodity groupings.

What is clear is the dominance of trade in manufactures and telecommunications equipment, which reflects China's place in global production/supply chains. The existence of intra-industry trade, particularly vertical trade, in China suggests a degree of global integration that is consistent with the high degree of foreign invested enterprises which have accounted for more than half of all exports since the mid 1990s (Yueh 2006). The extent of foreign investment further suggests an avenue where China has

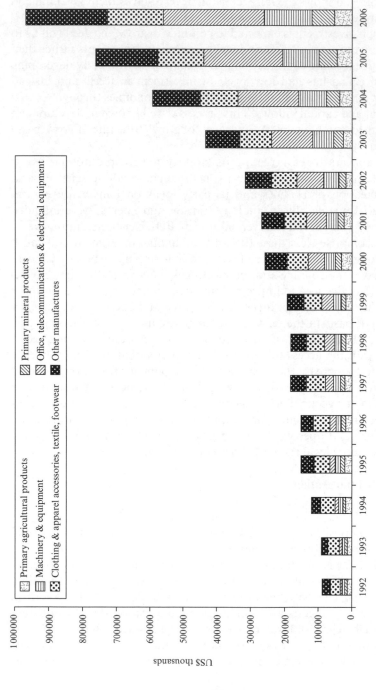

Legend:
Primary agricultural products
Machinery & equipment
Clothing & apparel accessories, textile, footwear
Primary mineral products
Office, telecommunications & electrical equipment
Other manufactures

US$ thousands

Source: UNCTAD.

Figure 2.7 China's exports

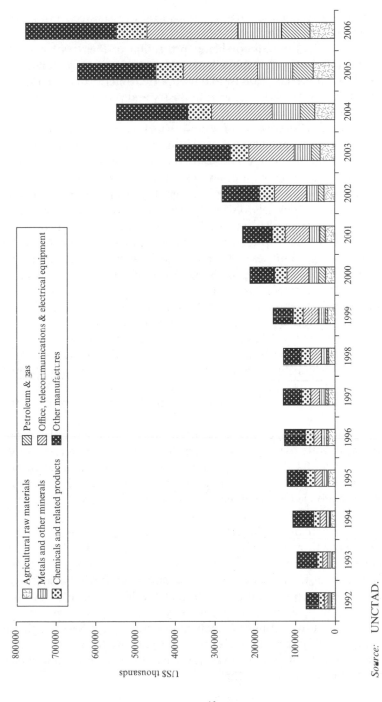

Source: UNCTAD.

Figure 2.8   China's imports

affected global investment patterns and also raises issues concerning the expectations of foreign investors who play a significant role in China's economy and their demands for better protection of their property. On the import side, a further notable feature is the rapid growth of imports of energy and raw materials alongside the imported intermediate manufactured goods that are a feature of intra-industry and processing trade.

In turn, the effect of China's trade patterns on the rest of the world falls into several areas. Countries and sectors which compete with China in producing manufactures will likely become uncompetitive (for example, Chile and clothing manufacturers), but countries which buy from China will gain from lower import prices which increases the standard of living and results in a low inflationary environment (for example, the European Union). Countries which sell to China are likely to experience a growth in exports alongside an improvement in their terms of trade defined as the ratio of export to import prices (for example, Africa and East Asia). By the same reasoning, countries which purchase the same items as China will experience the price effects of China's high levels of demand for energy and raw materials (for example, OECD countries).

The impact of China on other countries will depend on their trade patterns, terms of trade, exchange rates, and domestic productivity, such that not every sector will be uncompetitive as a result. Overall, the net China effect has so far been to contribute to a lower than expected global inflationary environment (Rogoff 2006). However, the reaction of the rest of the world to China's rise has been cautious and there have been some protectionist sentiments in the global economy as countries adjust to the emergence of China.

China's wider economic impact has been varied, but it has indeed contributed significantly to the growth of the global economy as a result of its rapid growth rate. Its global integration further suggests that a slowdown in China will affect global trade and production. Taken together, China's fate is increasingly tied to the global economy, and its prospects will therefore affect the rest of the world as a result.

For China, the main implication of its global integration is to provide a source of growth while it reforms its domestic economy – fuelling the non-state sector in a form of the 'dual track' system. Although arguably its market share of world trade will not increase much further, its integration into global supply chains, including at the higher technology end, will enable China to imitate the technology of developed countries and potentially allow it to continue to catch up in growth rates. Second, global markets provide a source of competition and pressure for increasing efficiency that can help the non-state sector expand while China undertakes difficult reforms in the state sector.

Moreover, since joining the World Trade Organization in 2001, China has become part of a rules-based trading system that exposes it to the best-practice standards of international economic law, perhaps allowing China to leapfrog legal, as well as technological, developments if international norms can aid in the formulation of China's evolving legal reforms to support its increasingly decentralised economy.

In return, China's adoption of international rules and standards serves to ease frictions with its trading partners over the extent of protection of the assets and proprietary information of their multinational corporations. As China for the first time adopts more rules granting market access and guarantees of protection to foreign investors in areas such as portfolio investments as part of its WTO commitments, including the Qualified Foreign Institutional Investors (QFII) scheme adopted in 2002 permitting foreign entities to invest in China's equity market and further intellectual property rights (IPRs) protection with the adoption of the TRIPs (trade-related aspects of intellectual property rights) agreement that is part of the WTO articles, these rules provide benchmarks for foreign investors seeking more certain protection while operating in China's underdeveloped legal system. For its part, China can gain know-how from investments in the services sector, as well as access to more advanced intellectual property which will benefit its economic growth. In other words, China can adopt legal measures commensurate with international best practice to induce more innovation and learning in its economy, even whilst its own legal system is developing and improving to keep pace with its remarkable economic transformation. From 1990 to 2005, there has been a ten-fold increase in patents, a legally protected innovation, since China's 2001 accession to the WTO and adoption of international rules governing intellectual property rights.

Despite the furore over the incomplete protection offered to IPRs, China's remarkably fast development of intellectual property is consistent with an economy that is integrating into a global standard for such protection. Knowing the global standards aids China in developing its IPR regime in a manner which is consistent with international expectations and facilitates the development of intellectual property which is essential to sustain economic growth.

6. CONCLUSION

China has performed admirably since market-oriented reforms were introduced three decades ago. This chapter has analysed the nature of its transition and resultant growth model, which has highlighted the importance of institutions in fuelling reform.

Given the 'easy-to-hard' sequence that characterises China's reform strategy, there are many challenges that lie ahead. The coincidence of the 'hard' issues with an opening of the economy to global trade provides possible ways to grow within the constraints of a partial reform strategy and one that had been characterised by informal institutional innovations. The limits of such reform were felt in the 1990s, and indeed in the 1980s for foreign investors, which led to more formal legal reform, which proved to be sufficient to underpin China's rapid growth. Foremost among its ensuing challenges is to transform a growth model from one that has grown via productivity advances from factor reallocation to one which is fuelled by technological advancement and innovation. This in turn calls for more legal protection and clearly defined property rights in an economy increasingly open to global factors, including international economic law, with its global protection of intellectual property, among other things.

For its part, the effects of China's rise have been felt in the global economy. Countries which have experienced an improvement in their terms of trade have benefited from China's rise, while others have had to contend with declining sectors as a result of China's growth. China's rise has seemingly benefited the global economy, while exerting competitive pressure in a wide range of sectors. Given the openness of the Chinese economy, its own fate is increasingly tied to the health of the global economy, while at the same time, it is affecting the very growth of the rest of the world. Its global integration, therefore, further demands that its institutional structure quickly improves to be aligned with the expectations of the global economy despite its underdeveloped legal system. The adoption of internationally based rules grants more certainty to businesses than would otherwise be expected for an economy at this stage of development and helps to underpin China's fast-growing economy.

In conclusion, this chapter has outlined China's reform approach and focused on the elements of China's transition from a centrally planned to a more market-oriented economy and the importance placed on informal institutions that incentivised economic activity without a transformation of communal into private ownership. However, as reforms progressed, legal and other formal reforms were needed to sustain growth, such that China has developed a corporate law system and increasingly adopted international rules such as those pertaining to IPRs. As China's transition proceeds and its growth model moves more toward one that needs to achieve technological progress and innovation, legal reform will become more pertinent, while in turn, such reforms should support an increasingly decentralised marketising economy. Therefore, although China is often touted as an economy that has grown without having a strong rule of law, it had its own systems of informal institutional innovations and formal contractual rights which served to create the necessary property rights to stimulate market exchange. China's institutional development and evolving legal system can shed some light on how it has managed remarkable growth with an underdeveloped institutional structure – an issue of concern for many developing countries.

NOTE

* See further my chapter 'China's Economic Reforms in the Globalisation Era' (with Justin Yifu Lin and Yang Yao)', Yang Yao and Linda Yueh (eds), *Globalisation and Economic Growth in China*, London: World Scientific Publishing, 2006.

3. Enterprises and agriculture

1. INTRODUCTION

In many respects, the evolution of enterprises was intertwined with agriculture in China's transition and economic development. China achieved industrialisation through the use of 'price scissors' that kept agricultural goods prices low and manufactured goods prices high in order to fuel the urban economy (Knight 1995). This 'urban bias' continued in the reform period and is evident in policies such as the household registration system (*hukou*), which allocates urban and rural residents to their respective geographical domiciles.

On the eve of reforms in 1978, some 80% of China's population dwelled in rural areas and were employed in agriculture, despite the country having only some 6–7% arable land, less than the world average. Industrialisation in urban areas should have exerted strong pressure on the rural populace to migrate to better wages and the generous benefits system provided to urban residents through SOEs when such a social safety net was absent in the rural areas. However, the *hukou* system forbids such migration. When reforms were introduced in 1978 in rural areas, not only was agriculture reformed but rural industry was also created. Township and village enterprises (TVEs) helped to absorb surplus labour from China's low productivity agricultural sector, which also deterred rural-urban migration until much later on in the reform process.

Therefore, the development of TVEs during the reform period is particularly related to the reform of agriculture. In the first two sections of this chapter, both will be discussed. Then, the chapter will turn to SOEs and the final sections will consider the growth of private and foreign enterprises, all in an attempt to assess the efficiency of the crucial enterprise sector in China's ongoing reforms.

2. AGRICULTURE

Pre-reform agricultural productivity showed very little improvement for nearly three decades. Under the commune system, peasants were organised into production teams and brigades, where each team member was assigned work points for a day's labour. The resultant lack of incentives meant that output per labourer in the period 1952–79 only increased from 947 kg to 1063 kg (Xu 1982).

The initial reforms at the end of 1978 were thus geared towards the agricultural sector. The first major agricultural price rise occurred in 1979, almost at the same time as the reformers were deciding to decollectivise. By 1984, the commune system was gradually replaced by the Household Responsibility System (HRS). The HRS created strong incentives for farmers to reduce production costs and increase productivity by allowing them to retain for their own profit output produced above quota (Naughton 2007). Between 1978 and 1983, the government increased the above-quota price so that the payment farmers received for voluntary sales beyond the mandatory deliveries increased by 41% for grain and by around 50% for cash crops (Sicular 1988). By 1981, the time of the second major price increase, less than half of China's farmers had been allowed to dismantle their communes, yet demand for decollectivisation was considerable given the HRS (Lin 1992).

Simultaneously, until 1984, state-run procurement stations purchased all grain sold by farmers at the above-quota price so long as they had already fulfilled their mandatory marketing delivery quota (Sicular 1988). The results were unequivocal. Between 1978 and 1985, agricultural output increased by 67% in under a decade. In part, this was caused by an increase in inputs. But, mainly, it was due to strengthened incentives: productivity (measured as the amount of output for a given amount of inputs) increased by nearly 50%, as compared with the minimal increase in output per worker of 12% recorded for the entire pre-reform period (Lin 1992).

The role of central planning in this programme is worthy of note. By 1984, the state only claimed control over 12 commodities, including rice, wheat, maize, soybeans, peanuts, rapeseed and several other cash crops (Sicular 1988). However, the crops that remained almost entirely under the planning authority of the government still accounted for more than 95% of the sown area in China.

After 1985, market liberalization began in earnest. After record growth in grain production in 1984 and 1985, a second stage of price and market reforms was announced in 1985 aimed at radically limiting the scope of government price and market interventions and further enlarging the role of market allocation. Other than for rice, wheat, maize and cotton, the intention was to gradually eliminate planned procurement of agricultural products; government commercial departments could only continue to buy and sell on the market. For grain, incentives were introduced through the reduction of the volume of the quota and an increase in procurement prices. Even for grain, after the share of compulsory quota procurement in grain production reached 29% in 1984, it fell to 18% in 1985 and 13% in 1990. Correspondingly, the share of negotiated procurement at market price increased from 6% in 1985 and doubled to 12% five years later (de Brauw et al. 2000).

Moreover, the record growth in grain in 1984 and 1985 led to a glut, which drove market prices below state fixed prices and led to a new series of delivery contracts in an attempt to minimise costs (Sicular 1988). This meant that even after the start of liberalisation of output in 1985, the process was still partial and executed in a start and stop manner. For example, after the initial commercialisation of the grain bureau, when grain prices rose in 1988, leaders halted the process.

Despite its halting nature, as the right to private trading was extended to include surplus output of all categories of agricultural products after contractual obligations to the state were fulfilled, the foundations of the state marketing system began to be undermined. For example, in 1980, there were only 241 000 private and semi-private trading enterprises registered with the State Markets Bureau; by 1990, there were more than 5.2 million (de Brauw et al. 2000). Between 1980 and 1990, the per capita volume of transactions of commerce in Beijing urban food markets rose almost 200 times. Private traders handled more than 30% of China's grain by 1990, and more than half of the rest was bought and sold by commercialised state grain trading companies, many of which had begun to behave like private traders (de Brauw et al. 2000).

Over the second half of the decade, agricultural growth was slower, but still averaged 4.5% annually. The slower gains in productivity, though, even with such incentives, were to be expected, given the limited arable land in China. This was exacerbated by comparative advantage shifting against agriculture and toward China's abundant labour, with greater opening up to the global economy. However, even as agriculture declined as a share of GDP from 30% in 1979 to around 10% by the mid 2000s (Figure 2.5), its share of employment remains higher, at some 40–50%. Surplus labour in the rural area remains and was a significant issue during China's developmental process, leading to the impetus to create rural industry alongside agricultural reform.

3.   TOWNSHIP AND VILLAGE ENTERPRISES

Township and village enterprises are widely seen as the engine of China's early growth and an example of the importance of rural industrialisation (Oi 1999). The growth of rural industry has long been closely related to conditions in agriculture and utilisation of the large, rural population. Between 1952 and 1977, rural residents entered non-agricultural activities in three great waves. The first came during the First Five Year Plan, when large-scale urban industrial construction absorbed a large amount of rural labour. The second wave occurred during the Great Leap Forward movement in 1958, when many communes and brigades set up small industries. The third wave occurred in the early 1970s, when the State Council urged that the mechanisation of agriculture be speeded up, thus, factories producing machinery mushroomed.

Restrictions on farmers' non-agricultural activities were greatly relaxed after the Third Plenum of the 11th Central Committee in December 1978, which marked the start of market-oriented reforms in China. Again, shrinking agricultural resources were the initial force behind the development of TVEs. The adoption of the HRS greatly enhanced the production enthusiasm of farmers and increased their income, which provided capital for the development of TVEs. On the other hand, the HRS highlighted the agricultural labour surplus, which encouraged the movement of the labour force from the agricultural to the non-agriculture sector. However, in their early period of development, TVEs were discriminated against by the central government since they were in competition with state-owned enterprises for raw materials and markets. Nevertheless, this sector expanded rapidly under the promotion of local leaders. Shortly after, the Chinese central government realised that setting up rural enterprises to absorb rural surplus labour was a preferable way to solve the rural unemployment problem than allowing rural labour to search for employment opportunities in urban areas.

TVEs are economic units which are either collectively owned or mainly owned and controlled by rural residents. However, in actuality, TVEs are nominally owned by local community citizens and under the direct control of local government leaders. Before economic reforms began in 1979, TVEs, then known as Commune and Brigade Enterprises, were completely subordinated to, and an invisible part of, the People's commune system in rural China. At that time, TVEs were physical entities but not recognised economic units, for example, they had no balance sheets. Assets were moved in or out of a TVE, or even of the community in which it was based, at the will of the community or government authority. Hence, ownership and the entity itself were ambiguous.

TVEs in their early period in the late 1970s depended heavily on financial support from the agricultural sector. Initially, the accumulation of funds for investment in non-agricultural activities was related to the unusual growth of agricultural incomes, which stemmed partly from the growth of agricultural production and partly from procurement price increases that returned industrial profits to agriculture. During this same period, the saving rate of rural residents climbed by seven percentage points. The growth of rural deposits helped expand local banks' supply of funds and fund the development of TVEs.

Conversely, TVEs also raised rural incomes. During 1980–1985, average per capita rural income jumped from 191 yuan in 1980 to 397 yuan in 1985. Combined with the growth in agricultural productivity, the early 1980s alone accounted for half of China's impressive poverty reduction during the 30 year reform period (Chen and Ravallion 2007).

Throughout much of the 1980s and the 1990s, the Chinese government took a series of steps to make TVEs economically recognisable production units run like business enterprises. In 1983, the central government issued a policy document to make clear that the property and assets of the TVEs should be protected, that those who contributed to TVE growth could share the benefits in the form of profit sharing and enhanced wages, and that small-scale family production of some items should be encouraged. In 1984, the 'Horizontal Economic Alliances' policy was established. The role of TVEs was elevated, making them an instrument of the government to achieve agricultural modernisation, absorb surplus labour from agriculture, and alleviate poverty.

This government policy, combined with other shifts in policy, created considerable incentives for TVE growth. The fiscal decentralisation of the early 1980s gave greater decision-making power to local governments and linked fiscal revenue to the career potential of local officials, creating strong incentives for them to promote these enterprises. TVEs were also given privileged access to capital and were helped by massive loans from the state banking system. The Agricultural Bank of China held nearly 80% of all rural deposits and loans, about half of which was provided to TVEs (Brandt et al. 2003).

Under the purview of the Agricultural Bank until the mid 1990s, the township branches of the Agricultural Bank themselves as well as controlled much of the lending. In 1985–86, tight fiscal and monetary policies due to inflationary pressures in the macroeconomy meant that bank loans replaced grants with the goal of making investment decision-making more market-rational. Lower levels of the Agricultural Bank are responsible to the Ministry of Finance but are also responsible to local governments. This allowed provincial authorities to apply pressure to provincial bank branches to extend loans even during periods when the central authorities were urging credit tightening. Capital thus flowed to TVEs ahead of other enterprise forms. Thus, local governments had incentives to ensure that TVEs were profitable, as this generated more local revenues. TVEs were thus explicitly preferred in industrial policy and flourished.

TVEs developed quickly throughout the 1980s and in the early 1990s. By the late 1980s, over 18 million rural enterprises provided employment (sometimes seasonal or part-time) to over 90 million people, some 17% of the national labour force. At that time, their gross value of output was about 21% of the national total. TVEs were fewer than 10% of all enterprises, but accounted for half of rural enterprise employment and three-quarters of the sector's output value. The World Bank estimates show that annual growth rate of TVEs from the mid 1980s to the mid 1990s was about 25%. At the end of 1992, China had 48200 townships and 806000 villages. On average, each township with an average population of 18000 had 8.2 township enterprises with 66 employees per enterprise, and each village with a population of about 1000 had 1.4 village enterprises with 23 employees per enterprise. By 1995, TVEs accounted for approximately a quarter of China's GDP, two-thirds of total rural output, and more than one-third of export earnings.

However, TVEs began to decline for a number of reasons. Notably, there is an issue of ill-defined property rights. The property rights of a collectively owned TVE are assigned to the whole of the legal residents in a community that runs the enterprise. However, due to dispersed ownership rights, it cannot be operated under the direct control of every owner of the firm but has to be operated by the township or village government. Many argue that the de facto owners of collective TVEs are local government leaders as they are the public agents of local residents (Che and Qian 1998; Jefferson and Rawski 1994; Zhu 1998).

The property theory argues that only under well-defined private property rights will an economy operate efficiently. The inefficiency of public enterprises is thus traced to their ill-defined property rights. Weitzman and Xu (1994) argue that TVEs are best viewed as vaguely defined cooperatives with weak property rights. The outstanding initial performance of TVEs appears to present a paradox or challenge for traditional property right theory. It could be that TVEs are basically quasi- or disguised private enterprises (Nee 1996). Or the success of TVEs could be attributed to various factors such as local governments' financial incentives, their relatively hard budget constraints, managerial incentive contracts and market competition (Naughton 1996). The government, in any case, responded by trying to improve the property rights of TVEs.

During the mid 1980s, local governments and firms started experimenting with joint stock ownership. In 1988, the government officially legalised private ownership in the TVE sector. In June 1990, the Regulation on Township and Village Collective Enterprises of the People's Republic of China was issued by the State Council to establish their standing. By 1996, most of the steps taken to protect property rights and provide better incentives in the TVEs were confirmed through legislation, when the country's highest legislative body, the Congress of People's Representatives, passed the TVE Law. The TVE Law states that '[n]o organizations or individuals shall illegally and administratively interfere with the production and operation of a TVE, including changing the individuals responsible for the firm, or illegally take or use the property of a TVE without compensating for it'. It also establishes the principle of simultaneous development of different forms of ownership in the enterprise sector, which eventually led to the development of privately owned firms that eroded the competitiveness of TVEs and also opened the way for them to privatise.

Having started out producing consumer and light industrial goods neglected by SOEs geared towards heavy industry, TVEs' market niche was initially eroded with SOE reforms. As competition intensified from domestic and foreign firms with greater opening up in the 1990s and credit was increasingly hard to obtain, the collectively owned TVE sector shrank and there was a trend toward privatisation. Falling growth rates and deficits came to characterise TVEs.

Also, TVEs were highly geared towards exports. The average annual real growth rate of their exports over the period 1988–99 was as high as 28%, exceeding that of China's total export growth of around 13%. However, after WTO accession in 2001, there was greater competition from foreign firms which contributed to the decline of TVEs. As part of its WTO terms, China lowered its tariffs. Moreover, in 2000 in anticipation of accession, the Law on Wholly-owned Foreign-owned Enterprises was revised. This law now allowed wholly foreign-owned enterprises to sell their own products in China or to appoint other business organisations to sell their products under certain conditions.

Finally, part of the argument for the decline in TVEs mentions the theory that greater competition and diversified ownership forms will likely result in a decline in the position of TVEs. China has instituted a number of policies designed to increase competition. In 1999, the State Development and Planning Commission instituted regulations imposing fines for companies found to have cut their prices below cost or to have offered hidden discounts (Wedeman 2009). Private firms were also accorded greater rights. A 1999 constitutional amendment redefined the private sector. It was recognised that private enterprise plays 'an important part in the economy' and that 'private property rights should be protected'. This was followed by the 2007 Property Law, providing equal protection to private and public property for the first time. The constitutional change also acknowledged that the self-employed, private and other non-public sectors constituted an important component of the socialist market economy, whose lawful rights and interests would be protected by the state. These developments underscore the growing importance of new and private forms of ownership while which TVEs are an opaque hybrid, ultimately defined by collective ownership, which has lost its lustre with the rise of the private sector.

Township and village enterprises were the early engine of growth in China, but have struggled throughout the latter part of the reform period. With the growing employment pressures in urban areas and lagging incomes in the rural sector, there is a renewed attention to rural industrialisation. As the majority of the population still reside in rural areas, the revival of rural industry – perhaps in the form of TVEs – has become a policy priority. Understanding the reasons for their decline and the prospects for rural industrialisation has taken on a new urgency in China. However, as with most developing countries, the challenges of sustaining rural industry are not simple ones to contend with. China's early success with TVEs may be due to the surplus labour in agriculture which became a ready workforce that exploited a niche in consumer goods neglected by the dominant SOE sector. With competition and marketisation, it is not apparent where the competitiveness of TVEs or other rural industries will lie vis-à-vis renewed SOEs and a burgeoning private sector, radiating from urban areas. SOEs are explored next in this chapter.

4. STATE-OWNED ENTERPRISES

State-owned enterprises (SOEs) dominated the Chinese economy throughout the centrally planned period from 1949 to 1978 and in the early part of the reform period. But SOEs suffer from the inefficiencies associated with 'soft' budget constraints, whereby state ownership meant that they were not subject to a 'hard' or actual budget since they demanded their inputs (labour, capital) directly from the state. There was no incentive to minimise costs and instead there was over-investment as SOEs did not have to take account of the actual cost of their inputs. They were also characterised by surplus labour, worsened by their role in maintaining employment levels. As a result, most were loss-making and subsidised by the state, whose aim was to use SOEs not only for production but also as vehicles for delivering social security payments and maintaining full employment. The multiple objectives of SOEs mean that they were not only maximising profits but also aiming to provide employment and social security to the urban population (Bai et al. 2000).

The state funded SOEs directly through subsidies and indirectly through the state-owned banks. This resulted in a significant accumulation of non-performing loans (NPLs) in the banking system, which was itself plagued by the same inefficiencies as state-owned enterprises. This in turn led to inflationary episodes, whereby loose monetary policy was used to fuel credits to the state-owned banks and SOEs (Brandt and Zhu 2000). The government would then rein in those loose policies and impose austerity, which drove the fairly rapid swings in China's business cycles in the mid 1980s, late 1980s and early 1990s, where GDP growth would fall from over 10% to some 4% from peak to trough in a matter of months (see Figure 2.1).

There was an evident need to reform the SOEs. Since market-oriented reforms began in 1978, a profit-sharing and bonus payment scheme was introduced in a few selected SOEs and extended to all of them by 1983. Under the profit-sharing scheme, instead of remitting their profits to the state, state-owned enterprises gained the right to retain a modest share of total profits. From 1979 to 1983, enterprises were allowed to draw a specified percentage (usually less than 10%) from their total profit if major targets were fulfilled (Naughton 2007). In the mid 1980s, reformers moved to a pattern of progressive profit sharing, in which, in addition to a fixed base retention, the enterprise retained a specified percentage of the increase in profit, typically around 20%.

The year 1984 marked the start of the 'dual track' pricing system, which attempted to further incentivise SOEs. Under the 'dual track', the government allowed state enterprises to sell output in excess of quotas. The Chinese term *shuangguizhi* refers to the co-existence of a traditional plan and a market channel for the allocation of a given good. It implied a two-tier pricing system for most goods; a single commodity had both a (typically low) state-set planned price and a (typically higher) market price (Naughton 2007). Under the dual pricing regime, firms, including SOEs, were allowed to buy and sell at the market price once they had fulfilled their plan responsibilities. The principle of the dual price system was to induce enterprises to face market competition without causing sudden disruption to the planning mechanism (Hay et al. 1994).

After the initial period of experimenting with profit sharing in state-owned enterprises, the Contract Responsibility System (CRS) was also created in 1984. The CRS provided for profit contracting, in which each firm would contract to remit a fixed amount of profit, and any profit earned above the contracted level was kept almost entirely by the enterprise. By the end of 1987, about 80% of the large and medium-sized SOEs had adopted the Contract Responsibility System, and by 1989 almost all SOEs had adopted this system (Choo and Yin 2000).

The retained profit could be used for three purposes: investment, contributions to the enterprise's welfare fund, and bonus payments to employees. The proportion of retained profits allocated to bonus payments could exceed 30%. The amount of bonus payment to any individual worker or group could not be more than three times their basic wage. This restriction was relaxed from 1985 onward, but a tax was introduced on additional bonuses above the threefold limit. The autonomy to award a bonus to employees was a major breakthrough in the Chinese wage system. In the past, employees were guaranteed a fixed salary according to their political position and length of service in the firm and such a wage system did not reflect individual effort. Thus, shirking and lack of discipline were widely observed. Under the new system, the amount of bonus paid to individuals would depend on how well each had fulfilled their production and profit targets; hence, employees would have incentives to work harder in order to receive larger bonuses.

Before 1986, the forms of the contract were simple, but they became more complex later on. Some state-owned enterprises and urban collectives used the contract form 'two guarantees and one link', which implied that the enterprise was required to pay taxes and hand over the shares of profit to the state, but also had to have funds available for investment in technical upgrading and thus at the same time to link the total wage bill to economic performance. The 'three guarantees and one link' contract additionally required an enterprise to guarantee the growth of the firm's fixed assets.

How these CRS contracts worked was that the government or its representative bureaux delegated the managerial tasks of an SOE to a manager (or a group of managers) with specific targets stipulated in the contract. The manager was to fulfil the targets and was in turn motivated by the imposition of a bonus or penalty according to the performance of the firm. If the realised profit exceeds the profit target, subject to certain restrictions on fixed capital depreciation and total wage payment, the manager can share the above-target profit with the government at a rate fixed by the contract. However, if the target is not met, then the manager must pay a penalty. The penalty is either fixed or an amount proportional to the difference between the target and realised profit, or the performance bond is forfeited. The penalty is usually no more than half of the manager's annual salary. While the managerial contract commits the manager to a bonus as well as a penalty, the latter is not often strictly applied. If the profit target is not met, the manager will almost certainly blame external factors, such as poor market conditions, and bargain with the monitoring government bureaus to soften the penalty.

The reform of SOEs in the 1980s was generally regarded as successful as it increased the autonomy of state-owned enterprises and the incentives for their managers and workers (see, for example, Groves et al. 1995). Most studies of total factor productivity (TFP) growth during the 1980s found positive growth rate among the SOEs. For example, Jefferson et al.

(1992) found TFP growth of 2.4% for state-owned enterprises and 4.6% for collective enterprises, respectively, from 1980 to 1988.

However, the widely observed phenomenon of the 'soft penalty' undermined managerial incentives and resultant firm performance (Choo and Yin 2000). Importantly, due to output being incentivised while budget constraints remained 'soft', the CRS did not impose market discipline on the cost side and SOEs continued to require subsidies even as managers responded by increasing production. By the early 1990s, an estimated two-thirds of all SOEs were loss-making (Fan 1994). The continual support given to SOEs fuelled an ever-worsening non-performing loan problem in the banking system, which is associated with macroeconomic instability and had led to dramatic collapses in other transition economies. Therefore, in 1994, the contract responsibility system was abandoned and replaced by the next stage of SOE reform, corporatisation.

By creating shareholding companies out of SOEs, corporatisation could be viewed as the start of share issue privatisation (SIP), a form of privatisation that is thought to be less destabilising than others such as mass privatisation. However, in China, it was not the aim of the government to privatise, but rather to instil more market incentives through creating clearer property rights, thought to be achievable through shareholding but not the CRS. The centrepiece of corporate law, the Company Law, was adopted in 1993 and came into effect the following year. It provided a framework for ownership that could include restructuring SOEs to convert them into corporations. SOEs were transformed into limited liability and joint stock companies by means of corporatisation (*gongsihua*). Within the large and medium-sized enterprise sector, by 2001, the number of industrial SOEs fell to nearly one-half of the 15 533 firms that had existed in 1994 (Jefferson and Su 2006). Mirroring the precipitous decline in SOEs during this period, the number of shareholding enterprises increased rapidly from less than 1000 to nearly 6000.

A further part of this shift away from old ownership forms came in December 1994 when the State Council proposed a pilot scheme termed the *zhuangda fangxiao* or 'grasp the large and release the small' policy. 'Grasping the large' meant that a small number of large state-owned enterprises in industries viewed as strategically important for the government to control, including petroleum, metallurgy, electricity, military industry, and telecommunications, were restructured and eventually placed under the supervision of a newly created entity, State-owned Asset Supervision and Administration Commission (SASAC). Other relatively large SOEs, although not clearly destined for lasting government control, were also not liquidated or privatised outright. Rather, these companies were converted to joint stock corporations, some shares in which were sold to workers and managers, while others were made available for purchase and trading by individuals on the Shenzhen, Shanghai and Hong Kong stock exchanges.

Notably 'letting go of the small' did mean permitting provincial and lower-level governments dispose of their loss-making SOEs. Between 1995 and 2000, some 82% of a total of 59410 small- and medium-sized SOEs, which together accounted for about 33% of the overall SOE sector output, underwent restructuring, involving direct privatisation.

This process, called *gaizhi* (change of system), however, ended up affecting most SOEs. Conversion was not limited to small enterprises. During the period from 1997 to 2001, the number of large and medium-size SOEs declined from 14811 to 8675, while the number of large and medium-sized shareholding enterprises increased from 1801 to 5659 (Jefferson and Su 2006). The government, therefore, retained some but not all of the large SOEs.

In 1999, the Decision of the Central Committee of the Communist Party of China on Major Issues Concerning the Reform and Development of State-owned Enterprises was adopted which fleshed out the policy of 'Strategic Realignment of the State-owned Economy'. According to this decision, China had to complete this strategic realignment by 2010 and decide which sectors the SOEs should try to enter and which they should exit. With the exception of a few key sectors, such as 'industries that are crucial to national security', 'industries that are natural monopolies or oligopolies', 'industries that supply public goods and services' and 'pillar industries and backbone enterprises in high and new technology sectors', the state was to reduce its activity or withdraw altogether from competitive industries.

By the end of 2001, 86% of all SOEs had been restructured (Garnaut et al. 2005). This took various forms, including internal restructuring, corporatisation and public listing of shares, sale, lease, joint ventures and bankruptcy. Among the surveyed mid- and large-scale SOEs that were restructured, 13% had gone out of business through bankruptcy or debt-for-equity swaps, 28% were sold or leased out to private owners, 27% introduced employee shareholding, 20% went through internal restructuring, 8% went through ownership diversification, including public offerings and private placement to outside investors, and the remaining 4% became joint ventures. In more than 70% of these cases, *gaizhi* involved the transfer of at least a portion of ownership from the state to private hands (Garnaut et al. 2005). This resulted in the first large-scale unemployment in urban areas. Layoffs began to surge in 1995, and in the four-year period from 1996 to 1999 an average of 7 million workers were laid off annually, exceeding 50 million employees between 1993 and 2004 (Dong and Xu 2008).

The government kept a firm grip on 100 central and 2600 local, large SOEs. At the Third Plenary Session of the 16th Central Committee in 2003, the Decision on Issues Regarding the Improvement of the Socialist Market Economic System was adopted to remove some of the obstacles to privatisation that still existed. The 'shareholding' system was to replace state ownership as the mainstay of public ownership. This was to be a mixed form of ownership, involving the state, collectives and the non-state sector. Even when the state was involved, it was no longer considered necessary in certain circumstances for it to have an absolute majority of the shares.

Public listing of SOEs in the domestic stock exchanges was another crucial part of corporatisation. Some large- and medium-sized SOEs were transformed into publicly listed firms on the domestic stock market during the 1990s. Initially, the vast majority of China's publicly listed companies were formerly state-owned or state-controlled firms, mostly large ones.

The creation of stock markets in 1990 (in Shanghai) and 1991 (in Shenzhen) indeed furthered the SOE reform process by listing the newly created shares, enabling these enterprises to raise finance on capital markets. Market discipline through movement in stock prices was also expected since investors would reward or shun stocks. However, China's stock exchanges are far from typical.

The initial boom in the number of listed companies on the stock exchanges and in the value of shares issued came in 1993. In that year, there were 183 listed companies, mostly former SOEs, and the stock issued and sold that year amounted to 9.6 billion Yuan. By 1997, there were 745 listed companies and the stock issued and sold that year was 26.8 billion Yuan. At the end of 2000, there were about 1080 firms listed on China's two national stock exchanges (see Table 3.1). Almost all these firms are former SOEs. The market capitalisation of the bourses made them among the largest in Asia. From 2001, restrictions were relaxed and non-SOEs gained access to the stock markets.

The bourses were run by administrative dictate with quotas allocated to provinces for initial public stock offerings (IPOs), which tended to result in the better ones being chosen since the next year's quota depended on this year's firm performance (Du and Xu 2009). However, as with the SIP process generally, this was not wholesale privatisation. The state and legal persons (other SOEs) controlled some two-thirds of all shares, with only one-third of the listed shares being tradable. Also, the listing tended to be of subsidiaries of major SOEs, for example, CNOOC Ltd. is 70% owned by CNOOC, the national oil company. Together, this meant that the Chinese state had effective control over the listed firms. With low liquidity, the benefits of market discipline were not realised.

Table 3.1 The number of listed companies and market capitalisation in Shanghai and Shenzhen Stock Exchanges, 1990–2006

	Number of listed Companies			Market capitalisation (100 million RMB)	
	Shenzhen	Shanghai	Total	Shenzhen	Shanghai
1990		8	8		12.34
1991	24	8	32		29.43
1992	77	29	106	48.97	558.40
1993	120	106	226	133.53	2206.20
1994	135	171	306	109.04	2600.13
1995	237	188	425	94.86	2525.66
1996	362	293	655	436.45	5477.81
1997	413	383	796	831.11	9218.06
1998	463	438	901	887.97	10625.90
1999	463	484	947	1189.07	14580.47
2000	514	572	1086	2116.00	26930.86
2001	508	646	1154	1593.16	27590.56
2002	508	715	1223	1296.54	25363.72
2003	505	780	1285	1265.27	29804.92
2004	536	837	1373	1104.12	26014.34
2005	544	834	1378	933.41	23096.13
2006	579	842	1421	1779.15	71612.38

Source: China Securities Regulatory Commission.

This led to a change in the view of ownership of listed firms. During most of the 1990s, the limit on the private ownership stake in China's listed firms stood at one-third. In 1999, the Ministry of Finance permitted state-owned shares to be reduced to 51%. In 2000, the government decided to abandon the quota system and let the market determine which firms can go public. The first non-quota IPO appeared in 2001. Following on from this, in 2002, the China Securities Regulatory Commission (CSRC) announced guidelines for takeovers and mergers of listed companies. This applied to foreign firms, though the largest stake a group of foreign investors could hold in a Chinese company was 10%. However, this decision has seen increasing quantities of state-owned shares being sold to non-state entities, including, since 2002, qualified foreign-based institutional investors (QFII) such as Goldman Sachs, Deutsche Bank and Merrill Lynch.

The Chinese government was often deliberate in targeting these well-known institutional investors, noting that they were 'strategic partners' designed to bring knowledge of corporate governance techniques with them. Some of the larger investors were given seats on the board, such as Goldman Sachs with the float of ICBC, one of the four large state-owned banks. However, control remained with the Chinese side and foreign banks were limited to holding minority equity stakes.

Thus, there was still a need for reform. In 2005, the Chinese authorities announced the gradual floating of non-tradable state-owned shares for all domestically listed companies. All listed companies were required to propose a reform plan to transfer the status of non-tradable shares and to develop a compensation package for existing tradable shareholders, comprising flexible combinations of cash, warrants and bonus shares. The central purpose of this reform is to convert non-tradable shares to tradable shares at a price acceptable to minority investors. Progress has been slow as shareholders were reluctant to see their shares diluted, but large SOEs such as Baosteel are gradually moving ahead.

Despite the intent to make listed firms truly private and allowing for greater privatisation in general, the government showed its hand regarding the end result of the various SOE reforms. In 2006, SASAC announced that it would maintain controlling positions in some crucial SOEs (the so-called 'national champions'). These sectors included armaments, power generation/distribution, oil/petrochemicals, telecommunications, coal, aviation and shipping. SASAC's goal is to maintain 'between 30 and 50 internationally competitive conglomerates with intellectual property and famous brand names'. This is also the culmination of the 'going out' policy which began in the mid 1990s to create Chinese multinational corporations. The dual listings of SOEs in international bourses as well as domestic ones and the gradual relaxation of capital controls led to outward forays by Chinese firms in the 2000s.

Therefore, in conclusion, Table 3.2 shows the result of the SOE reforms. Since 1998, loss-making SOEs have more than halved, while the output and value-added of the sector have more than doubled. Profits have increased more than ten-fold in less than a decade. Examining the increase in fixed assets and falling employment in SOEs, the restructuring process has increased investment and shed surplus labour. The remaining SOEs are more efficient, employ fewer workers and produce more output.

The relatively steady share of SOEs in GDP in the 2000s and the emergence of SOEs among the leading Chinese multinational corporations all point to the continuation of a state-owned sector in China. With some of the large SOEs in energy and infrastructure, state ownership would not be out of line with other countries. But China must also contend with the legacy issues of central planning and the implicit continuation of 'soft' budget constraints. In other respects, there are signs of continuing privatisation via SIP and public listing, including on international stock exchanges. SOEs are likely to remain in China; the question is at what cost if they are maintained for political or ideological rather than economic reasons.

5. PRIVATE FIRMS

The standing of privately owned firms in China has always been less than certain during the reform period as it clashed with the notion of communal property inherent in much of the early economic reforms. However, by 2007, private firms in China were better established, though most are small and medium-sized enterprises (SMEs), which still suffer from insecure property rights protection, credit constraints and the lack of a level playing field with respect to SOEs.

In 1987, the 13th Congress of the Chinese Communist Party (CCP) recognised the 'private economic sector' as a necessary supplement to the state sector, whilst in 1988 the Constitution was amended to acknowledge the private sector as a 'complement' to the socialist public economy that is allowed to develop 'within the limits prescribed by law', indicating a somewhat grudging acceptance of the role of private sector. In June of that year, the Provisional Regulations on Private Enterprises were passed, which legitimized sole proprietorships, partnerships and limited liability companies with eight or more employees. However, the regulations allow only a limited class of persons to form such enterprises: farmers, the urban unemployed, retired persons, etc. The regulations, in a sense, view private

Table 3.2 Main financial indicators for SOEs, 1998–2004

Year	Number of enterprises (units)	Loss-making enterprises (units)	Gross industrial output value (million RMB)	Value added of industry (million RMB)	Total assets (million RMB)	Original value of fixed assets (million RMB)	Total liabilities (million RMB)	Total profit (million RMB)	Average number of employees (10000 persons)
1998	64737	26289	33621	11076	74916	47913	35648	525	3747
1999	61301	24001	35571	12132	80471	53146	49877	997	3394
2000	53489	18223	40554	13777	84014	57294	51239	2408	2995
2001	46767	16858	42408	14652	87901	61782	52025	2388	2675
2002	41125	14865	45178	15935	89094	64521	52837	2632	2423
2003	34280	12081	53407	18837	94519	69701	55990	3836	2162
2004	35597	11112	70228	23213	109708	76599	62005	5453	1973

Source: China Statistical Yearbooks, 1996–2006.

business formation as a supplementary activity undertaken by those outside the primary urban socialist economy.

The absence of a basis in law hindered the development of the non-state economy during the first decade of reform. Clarke et al. (2006) note that legal obstacles were evident even in places like Wenzhou, where the private economy enjoyed strong local political support and extensive social networks. Furthermore, private enterprise owners felt they had no recourse when they encountered contract disputes, since courts were unwilling to recognise their claims (Lubman 2002).

By 1997, the Communist Party's 15th Congress recognised the private sector as an 'important' (not just supplemental) component of the economy. Amendments to the Constitution in 1999 went further and began to legitimise private ownership. Significantly, the Economic Contract Law of 1993, together with the Foreign Economic Contract Law, was replaced in that year by a unified Contract Law, designed to cover contracts by individuals and enterprises alike, regardless of ownership or nationality. Under the unified Contract Law of 1999, natural individuals – not just legal persons – can enter into legally enforceable contracts.

In 2001, President Jiang Zemin announced that private entrepreneurs could become Communist Party members. Further constitutional amendments in 2004 provided that the 'non-publicly owned' sector was not only permitted but encouraged, which gave more rhetorical protection to private property. Finally, the Constitution was amended on 14 March 2004 to include guarantees regarding private property ('legally obtained private property of the citizens shall not be violated'). This was the first time in PRC history that the legal status of private property was officially endorsed by the Party, leading eventually to the Property Law of 2007, which gave equal protection to public and private property.

However, despite the constitutional amendment in 2004 protecting private property rights, the Party is struggling to create fair market conditions for private firms. There is reason to believe that it will be a long time before private firms acquire equal status with other types of firms, such as state-owned enterprises and foreign-funded firms which had been privileged in a number of respects (Huang 2006). Private firms in China not only experience political and social discrimination, but must also deal with the lack of a level playing field. State-owned enterprises continue to enjoy preferential status in obtaining bank loans and other key inputs (Brandt and Li 2003). The 2008 Anti-Monopoly Law exempts SOEs from many of its provisions, for example.

Despite these obstacles, entrepreneurs and *de novo* private firms are rapidly growing, especially in the 2000s, motivated by the various legal reforms and greater opening of the market. Private as well as state-owned firms have increased exponentially and some are expanding overseas. Firms like handset maker, Ningbo Bird, have taken market share from the likes of Nokia and Motorola in the 2000s. The first global commercial M&A deal was when TCL purchased Thomson of France in 2004. Others soon followed, including Lenovo's deal with IBM and failed attempts such as by Haier for Maytag. Chinese SOEs had invested overseas in energy and commodities to secure supplies for the past couple of decades, but the start of commercial outward investments marked a maturation of private firms. A later chapter will focus on the determinants of entrepreneurship in China's particular institutional environment and investigate the various challenges faced by those starting their own businesses in an attempt to grasp how this important sector will evolve.

6. FOREIGN FIRMS

At the second session of the Fifth National People's Congress in July 1979, The Law on Joint Ventures using Chinese and Foreign Investment was adopted, granting foreign investment legal status. This landmark piece of legislation marked the official opening to foreign investment, and reflected the importance granted to foreign direct investment at the very start of the reform period. Over the past 30 years, foreign invested enterprises were welcomed but closely governed. In the initial stages, FIEs were restricted to Chinese-foreign joint ventures in an attempt to enable the Chinese to learn from the more advanced foreign firms by working side by side. Later on, particularly after WTO accession, wholly-owned foreign-owned enterprises (WOFEs) began to outnumber JVs as controls were relaxed and the nature of FDI changed from being predominantly in production toward allowing more in the retail sector, so that WOFEs such as foreign retailers began to establish themselves in China.

In its initial phase, a by-product of this law was the Chinese government's establishment of four Special Economic Zones in the southern provinces of Guangdong and Fujian that are near to Hong Kong and Taiwan. Special incentives, such as preferential tax policies, were offered to FDI in these SEZs. The State Council also awarded rights of autonomy in foreign trade to these provinces and, in 1980, set up four Special Economic Zones in Shenzhen, Zhuhai, Shantou and Xiamen. In 1984, the concept of SEZs was extended to another 14 coastal cities, all of which were designated Economic Trade and Development Zones (ETDZs). Hainan Island became a province and, in 1988, the fifth and largest SEZ. After the central government granted preferential treatment to the first 14 coastal cities, 24 inland cities lobbied for the same privileges. In 1988, the State Council announced that the number of open coastal cities and counties would be expanded to 284 and encompass a population of 160 million.

Also, in 1985, 'development triangles' were created in the Yangtze River delta near Shanghai, the Pearl River delta in Guangdong, the Min Nan region in Fujian, Liaodong and Shandong peninsulas, and the Bohai sea coastal region bordering Tianjin were also opened to foreign investors. In 1990, the Pudong district of Shanghai was designated as a new development zone to lead development along the Yangtze River. This opening up process led to a scramble for further development, particularly following Deng Xiaoping's southern tour in 1992 that marked the take-off of FDI in China.

The primary purpose of SEZs was to promote international trade by creating essentially export-processing zones, while a later form known as Economic Trade and Development Zones aimed at developing import substitution capacity. ETDZs reflected a desire to promote foreign investment in some of the major centres of the domestic economy, rather than concentrating in peripheral zones. Preferential and lenient policies enabled SEZs to attract FDI.

The SEZs enjoyed both privileged political and fiscal status, which granted them exceptional authority and resources in implementing market-driven economic policies denied to other segments of the economy. For instance, the SEZs were normally placed under the direct control of the mayor or vice mayor. This not only guarantees the zone a favourable allocation of government resources, but also facilitates quick decision-making at the municipal level. Special Economic Zones were also granted independent fiscal authority (*yiji caizeng*), which enabled them to collect tax revenues and assume fiscal responsibility.

Due to these institutional arrangements, foreign firms located in the SEZs enjoyed tax benefits and access to well-developed infrastructure and facilities at very low cost. Red tape associated with applications for and licensing of investment, plant establishment, imports and exports were reduced so that foreign firms could start and run their projects with minimal bureaucratic fuss. These benefits, together with an abundant low-cost labour supply, created an attractive investment environment for foreign firms.

However, China's underdeveloped legal system was a source of uncertainty for foreign firms used to much clearer property rights. Thus, in 1985, the Foreign Economic Contract Law was passed. This statute covered contracts between Chinese entities and foreign parties, and was geared towards developing a separate regime to govern foreign firms. It was the first law governing contracts for any enterprises in China and preceded any comparable company law for domestic firms – the latter did not come into effect until the 1990s.

This more flexible regime was expanded by a large increase in activity in 1986, which saw a raft of more favourable regulations and provisions used to encourage FDI inflow. In 1986, the Law on Wholly-owned Foreign-owned Enterprises was passed. This statute allowed for the first time an enterprise organised under Chinese law to be wholly owned by one or more foreign investors, with no Chinese equity participation. However, numerous restrictions applied that limited the approval of WOFEs since learning via Chinese-foreign joint ventures was still preferred.

Also in that year, the State Council promulgated the Provisions of the State Council for the Encouragement of Foreign Investment. These so-called 'Article Provisions' provided foreign joint ventures with preferential tax treatment, the freedom to import inputs such as materials and equipment, the right to retain and swap foreign exchange with each other, and simpler licensing procedures. Additional tax benefits were offered to export-oriented joint ventures and those employing advanced technology. The government also attempted to guarantee further the autonomy of joint ventures from external bureaucratic interference, to eliminate many 'unfair' local costs, and to provide alternative ways for joint ventures to balance foreign exchange. Privileged access was provided to supplies of water, electricity and transportation (paying the same price as state-owned enterprises) and to interest-free RMB loans.

Then in 1988, the Law on Chinese-foreign Cooperative Joint Ventures was passed, which allowed for a joint venture with more flexible features than the Law on Chinese-foreign Equity Joint Ventures. Finally, the Corporate Income Tax of Foreign-invested Enterprises in 1991 formalised some of the tax breaks.

Thus, China's FDI policy took off in the spring of 1992, when Deng Xiaoping toured China's southern coastal areas and initial SEZs. His visit renewed fervour among local governments for the creation of SEZs. In order to rein in the rampant expansion of local special zones, the State Council promulgated a circular stating that only those special zones designated by the central and provincial governments could legally operate. A two-level approval system was established based on this circular. The central government granted a more privileged status to the newly established Pudong new district in Shanghai and approved 18 national ETDZs, including Beijing, Shenyang, Hangzhou and Chongqing. Meanwhile, it shut down as many as 1000 zones, set up without the proper approval of the central and provincial governments.

The results were remarkable. China quickly became the leading destination for FDI among developing countries in the world, registering some $40 billion per year during the 1990s and 2000s. It even began to rival the

United States and United Kingdom for inward FDI due to its cheap and abundant labour force.

Nevertheless, the restrictions placed on FIEs, even after WTO accession in 2001, meant that foreign firms continued to find it difficult to operate in China. FIEs have produced more than half of Chinese exports since the mid 1990s, reaching over 60% in the 2000s and exceeding 80% in high-tech goods. However large their presence may be in export-oriented SEZs, their penetration into China's domestic market remains limited. Although China has committed to opening large swathes of its domestic market – particularly services – as part of its WTO commitments, FIEs face numerous non-tariff barriers that limit their presence in China.

Their early contribution was to provide foreign exchange earnings and employment for surplus rural migrant workers and they continue to do so. Moreover, FIEs were a source of know-how and learning for Chinese firms, either formally through technology transfers or informally through working with foreign managers. They were also a source of growth in China's 'dual track' transition as part of the non-state sector that enabled the gradual reform of state-owned enterprises and provided competition during the transition. For its part, China offers to foreign firms the fastest-growing economy in the world, with a rapidly expanding middle class, particularly in urban areas. With greater opening up and marketisation to come, FIEs ranging from Rolls-Royce to MacDonald's will constitute an important sector in China. The final chapter will return to assessing China's FDI policy in order to gain an understanding of how China can be characterised as an 'open' economy and yet is also known for having fairly strict controls on foreign investment and in the export and import sectors.

7. CONCLUSION

As with growth generally, institutional and some legal reforms character-ise the trajectory of enterprises and also agricultural development in the reform period. Agricultural reforms in the early 1980s, alongside rural industrialisation – primarily TVEs – paved the way for later reforms of urban-based SOEs. China's enterprises have undergone dramatic trans-formations as the economy moved from one characterised by SOEs under central planning to one notable for an increasingly complex set of corpo-rate forms, not only for state-owned but also for non-state firms, including foreign ones.

SOEs dominated China's industrial output until the rise of TVEs in the early 1980s. In response, in the mid 1980s, SOEs were reformed and granted managerial incentives to increase output. However, without the cost side being addressed, SOEs were inefficient and became a troubling source of non-performing loans in the banking system. By the early 1990s, SOE reform moved into a phase termed corporatisation which transformed many of these enterprises into shareholding or joint stock companies. With the creation of the two domestic stock exchanges, some also became publicly listed. Formalised by the Company Law in 1993, SOEs underwent a form of share issue privatisation, which was much more gradual than the mass privatisation undertaken in other transition economies. The 'grasp the large, let go of the small' policy retained the large SOEs and privatised the small ones. Then, the *gaizhi* or restructuring policy speeded up during the mid 1990s and large-scale layoffs appeared for the first time. By the 2000s, SOE share of GDP stopped declining and the large and arguably more profitable companies had ambitions to be not only national but also global players.

TVEs had a less complex trajectory. As SOEs reformed and private firms emerged, collectively owned TVEs lost their niche and competitiveness such that many became privatised since the 1990s. They joined the growing rank of private firms. Private firms struggled and continue to do so in China, but they gradually appeared in the 1990s as a result of liberalisation of ownership and particularly that of the consumer goods market in the late 1980s and early 1990s. Credit constrained still by a system that gives precedence to SOEs, private firms face numerous obstacles to growth. However, recent measures permitting M&A have even produced commercial firms from China which are active on the global stage.

Finally, foreign firms have evolved from being primarily joint ventures producing for export to wholly foreign-owned enterprises selling in China's domestic market. Numerous restrictions still apply and market access remains limited, but foreign firms now operate more freely than before. The competition that they introduce is in turn beneficial to Chinese firms. Areas such as intellectual property and China's incomplete legal system pose challenges, but the rise of the immense middle class makes China a strategic market as well as a location for global production.

In summary, China's reform process has been rather unique and the path is arguably unfinished as SOEs retain a foothold in not only the domestic but also increasingly in the global economy. How the government manages the legacy issues of 'soft' budget constraints as well as formulating the kind of market structure consistent with an economy underpinned by a rule of law will be crucial for China's continuing development.

4. Labour*

1. INTRODUCTION

Productivity advances drive long-run economic growth, and a crucial factor is labour productivity. The productivity of labour in China was of marginal relevance in the pre-1978 period when the labour market was administered and wages were centrally determined and detached from effort (Knight and Song 2005). However, the picture has changed dramatically in the post-1978 reform period due to numerous labour market reforms as well as radical changes in ownership structure whereby state-owned enterprises (SOEs) have lost their previous dominance and a much more competitive market has evolved, driven not only by the rise of private firms but also by the forces of globalisation. Urban residents were shifted from protected lifetime jobs in SOEs to seeking work in a labour market, increasingly characterised by private and foreign firms as well as competition from rural-urban migrants who had previously been segregated from urban areas.

Key labour market reforms included liberalising wages to better reward productive characteristics such as human capital, as well as increasing job mobility to permit better matching between worker and employer characteristics, leading to a more competitive labour market (Knight and Yueh 2004). Loosening labour market controls and the need for migrant labourers to work in newly created export industries have led to what has been called 'the greatest migration in human history'. An estimated 200 million rural-urban migrants have moved from the countryside to the cities during the past two decades, tearing down the urban-rural divide in employment. Finally and crucially, the aim of these reforms is ultimately to increase labour productivity – an important determinant of economic growth. Whether through improvements in human capital or reforms of SOEs, labour market reforms are a key part of increasing productivity in China, which underpins long-run economic growth. Therefore, this chapter will cover key labour market reforms, including reform of wages, as well as analysing the nature of the emerging labour market. It will conclude with an assessment of changes in labour productivity as a result of these reforms. These reforms, very much in line with the theme of the book, are institutional in nature. Reforming wages and the closed nature of employment, as well as loosening migration controls, were all policy measures intended to change the structure of the labour market to promote greater productivity to support China's economic development.

2. EMPLOYMENT AND WAGE REFORMS

As part of the economic reforms in urban areas which were intensely implemented after 1984, within the labour market, significant changes occurred, including granting more discretion to enterprises for wage-setting and permitting the retention of profits. Before the 1980s, state labour agencies exercised a virtual monopoly over the allocation of urban labour (see, for example, Bian 1994). Governmental planning, rather than the market, dictated the supply of and demand for labour. Allocations to enterprises were aimed at avoiding unemployment. Job assignments were made without much reference to the needs of enterprises or the characteristics of workers. The initial job assignment was crucial as the first job was typically the only job, the so-called 'iron rice bowl'.

When reforms started in the mid 1980s, the state monopoly of labour allocation was replaced by a somewhat more decentralised system. Central and local labour authorities continued to plan the labour requirements of state and large collectively owned enterprises and remained responsible for the placement of college graduates. However, labour exchanges began to be established for the registration of job vacancies, job placements and training. By the 1990s, recruitment quotas for state enterprises were abolished and firms were by and large allowed to choose their employees.

In the latter part of the 1990s, attempts to resolve the problem of inefficiency in the state sector discussed in the last chapter included downsizing and layoffs of workers by a quarter or more within five years (1997–2001). This was a drastic change from the official policy of full employment. *Xiagang* workers are laid-off workers who are officially registered as part of their enterprise or work unit, but who do not go to work or receive a wage. They remain on the books of the firm and receive a low income (funded in three parts – by the employer, the local government and the unemployment insurance scheme), but do not have to attend work. *Xiagang* employees retain their status for three years, or for less if they were recruited by another registered urban employment unit. They are registered as *xiagang* by their work unit and are officially entitled to minimum income support, although they often do not receive any such support in practice.

This classification was newly created as part of the five year restructuring programme of reforming inefficient SOEs begun in 1997. These

Table 4.1   Changes in the urban labour market, 1994–2000

	1994	2000	Increase 1994–2000	2000 (1994 = 100)
Registered urban unemployment:				
million	4.76	5.95	1.19	125.0
% of urban labour force	2.8	3.1	0.3	110.7
Xiagang employment:				
million	1.58	9.11	7.53	576.6
% of urban labour force	0.9	4.7	3.8	522.2
Total urban unemployment:				
million	6.34	15.06	8.72	237.5
% of urban labour force	3.7	7.8	4.1	210.8
Total urban employment:				
million	184.13	212.74	28.61	115.5
Employment in urban units:				
million	152.59	116.1	−36.46	76.1
% of total urban employment	82.9	54.6	−28.3	65.9
Migrant employees of urban units:				
million	13.72	8.97	−4.75	65.4
% of employment in urban units	9.0	7.7	−1.3	85.6

Source: National Bureau of Statistics and Ministry of Labour and Social Security, *China Labour Statistical Yearbook*, 1995 and 2001.

layoffs epitomise the reforms in the labour market from the mid to the late 1990s related to labour market and wage reforms. The dramatic changes in the urban labour market during this period can be seen in Table 4.1. Registered urban unemployment was very low in 1994 (2.8% of the urban labour force) and redundant workers (not classified as unemployed) negligible (0.9%), but it was notable by 2000. Moreover, there are other forms of unemployment not captured by official statistics, including those who are classified as 'youth waiting for work' and even those willing to take early retirement at unreasonable ages such as in a person's mid thirties. Some are simply considered 'not in post' or *ligang*, defined as taking a long vacation without pay. Also, the unemployment rate only pertains to urban areas and refers only to urban workers, as rural-urban migrants are not classified, so their being out of work is not registered.

The Chinese urban labour market is, in short, characterised by many imperfections. Increased competition with the move to a more market-oriented economy should be associated with more variation of wages with productivity if accompanied by appropriate reform of the wage structure. It is also underdeveloped in that workers still face some restrictions on moving from one city to another on account of the household registration system (*hukou*), which gives rise to frictions and low mobility that hamper the functioning of supply and demand in matching of workers to jobs. Both of these – reform of wages and employment – will be discussed in sections 2 and 3 of this chapter.

2.1 Reform of Wages

There were two waves of wage reforms prior to 1978, discussed in Chapter 2. The third wave consisted of three sets of reforms promulgated in 1985, 1992 and 1994, followed by the most recent overhaul of the wage structure which was implemented between 1996 and 2000. These wage reforms apply to state-owned enterprises and collectively-owned enterprises, but not to private or foreign-owned enterprises. Government agencies and non-profit institutions – the other large employers in the Chinese economy – are also subject to a different wage system. The latter categories are free to set their wages within the confines of the Labour Law.

In 1985, the Ministry of Labour (MOL) determined that the budget to be allocated for wages would be linked to the economic performance of SOEs and collectively-owned enterprises. It was to be measured by enterprise profitability or a combined indicator of economic returns. The indicators vary by region and reflect local economic conditions, such as unemployment, the consumer prices index and regional growth. The goal was to provide profit-oriented incentives. Under the previous system, these enterprises turned over all profits to the state and paid workers with wages redistributed by the state. Except for a small amount of bonus funds linked to limited above-quota output, there was little incentive to be profitable. With these reforms, however, wage budgets were linked to an enterprise's profitability and performance. Basic wages and profit quotas were projected from an enterprise's performance for the previous three years and the firms were allowed to retain, after taxes, above-quota profits for investment in plant capacity, employee welfare programmes, 'floating' salaries (that is, bonus-type, temporary salary increases), salary increases and bonuses. These incentives appeared to have stimulated profit-oriented behaviour in state-owned enterprises initially (see, for example, Groves et al. 1995).

In 1992, the State Council issued a circular stating that enterprises were permitted to set their internal wage structure within the confines of the overall wage budget established by the government. There were two methods available to enterprises. The first was that wages would be linked to enterprise performance. If the wage bill exceeded the governmental standard wage bill implied by the aggregate positions established by the Ministry of Labour, the enterprise must pay a Wage Adjustment Tax of 33% to the Department of Taxation. The government's standard wage is not the same as the minimum wage, which for Beijing was 420–430 RMB per month in late 2000. The standard wage, for instance, was 800 RMB per month for an office worker and varied by occupation and region. The second method was for the enterprise to propose a wage budget and then submit it for approval to the Ministries of Labour and Finance, which then considered the proposal in the context of the consumer price index and local wages. The primary difference was that if an enterprise chose the latter method, it was not liable for the Wage Adjustment Tax. These policies were designed to ensure that profits accrued to the state, but also that profit-oriented incentives were maintained.

Beginning in 1994, enterprises that were publicly listed companies, that is, companies which had issued shares that were listed on one of the two stock exchanges in China (Shenzhen or Shanghai) were permitted to set their own wages subject to two standards. The first was that the growth rate of total wages must be lower than that of after-tax profitability, and the second was that per capita wage growth was to be lower than labour productivity growth. In addition, the Ministry of Labour suggested to enterprises that wages were set not only according to occupation and rank, but also based on skills and productivity. Of the estimated 100 000 SOEs, approximately 40 000 had issued shares and set wages under this regime. Non-stock enterprises were still subject to the previous system.

Finally, there was an overhaul which was part of the Ninth Five Year Plan in 1996. Previously, there had been six components of the wage in enterprises: the basic wage, bonuses, benefits and subsidies, overtime wages, supplementary wages and an 'other' component, primarily based on hardship. These categories have been replaced by two components of wages, fixed (*guding*) and variable (*huo*). The fixed portion includes the basic wage, seniority wage, insurance (medical, unemployment and pensions), and a housing fund. The system of allocated housing was largely abolished around 1998 and replaced with a housing fund. A deduction from an employee's pay cheque was paid into the fund and matched by the enterprise. The variable portion includes bonuses, based on both individual productivity and enterprise profitability. Enterprises continue to pay for training and other in-kind compensation, such as firm outings and gifts of daily goods. The standard work week was designated as 40 hours, with 50% overtime pay at weekends and 300% overtime pay on national holidays, such as Lunar New Year, for hourly workers. These reforms were intended to create a more market-oriented wage structure, transforming the labour market.

2.2   Rewarding Labour

The result of these reforms is a labour market that has been fundamentally transformed from one where the plan dictated pay to a burgeoning labour market where individual productivity is rewarded. Using two large-scale household data sets from urban China (China Household Income Project (CHIP) surveys), where these reforms have primarily taken hold, this section estimates the changes in wage determination in the 1990s. These cross-sectional data sets will be used to investigate the effects of the major reforms on the urban wage structure of the 1990s by analysing the components of annual income and the rewards to both productivity and non-productivity-related characteristics in the two periods.

Briefly, the households in both data sets are drawn from a sub-sample of the National Bureau of Statistics (NBS) of China annual household income and expenditure survey. Both are original, representative urban surveys which include detailed information on wages and income for individuals. Eleven of the 30 provinces of China are included in the 1995 data set, while the 1999 urban survey covers six provinces and 13 cities. In 1999, the provinces are Beijing (chosen to represent the four cities that are independently administered municipal districts), Liaoning (to represent the north-east), Henan (to represent the interior), Gansu (to represent the north-west), Jiangsu (to represent the coast) and Sichuan (to represent the south-west). The capital of each province is chosen as a city within the sampling frame – a total of three cities are chosen in Sichuan and Henan and two in each of the others except Beijing. There are 6594 households and 21 697 individuals in the urban portion of the 1995 data set, and 4557 persons and an average of 3.24 persons per household in the 1999 survey.

Table 4.2 provides a comparison of the components of income for 1995 and 1999 for the working-age urban population in China. In 1995, mean income is 6033 RMB. Annual average income is 19% higher for men (6689 RMB) than for women (5413 RMB). Wages comprise about 80% of total income. Bonuses are the next substantial part, constituting 13–14%, and a slightly larger component of earnings (approximately 17%). Subsidies are 11% on average. Self-employed income contributes less than 1% of annual income, while other earned income constitutes 6% or so. Property income is a small portion of income, between 1–2%, which is unsurprising given that a private housing market was not established until the late 1990s. Transfer income, on the other hand, which includes pensions and gifts, is approximately 6% of income. For women, however, it is 8% of total annual income, while it is merely 4% for men. As women have an earlier official retirement age than men (55 as compared with 60), this disparity might be reflected in pensions.

Table 4.2   Mean annual income and components for the working-age urban population, 1995 and 1999 (in RMB and % of total income)

Category of Income (sub-category)[1]	Men in the 1995 sample (N = 6438)	Women in the 1995 sample (N = 6814)	Total for the 1995 sample (N = 13252)	Men in the 1999 sample (N = 1347)	Women in the 1999 sample (N = 1415)	Total for the 1999 sample (N = 2762)
Annual Income	6689 (100%)	5413 (100%)	6033 (100%)	8574 (100%)	6026 (100%)	7267 (100%)
Wages	5556 (83.06%)	4277 (79.01%)	4898 (81.19%)	6375 (74.35%)	4119 (68.35%)	5218 (71.81%)
Bonus	941 (14.07%)	727 (13.43%)	830 (13.76%)	522 (6.08%)	292 (4.85%)	404 (5.56%)
Subsidy	999 (14.93%)	814 (15.04%)	904 (14.98%)	317 (3.69%)	187 (3.10%)	250 (3.44%)
Laid-off subsidy	–	–	–	76 (0.88%)	89 (1.48%)	83 (1.14%)
Other income from work unit	370 (5.53%)	300 (5.54%)	334 (5.52%)	110 (1.28%)	103 (1.72%)	107 (1.47%)
Self-employed income	40 (0.60%)	31 (0.57%)	36 (0.60%)	668 (7.8%)	176 (2.93%)	416 (5.73%)
Other employee income	51 (0.76%)	32 (0.59%)	41 (0.68%)	58 (0.68%)	40 (0.66%)	49 (0.67%)
Other income from Work	137 (2.05%)	79 (1.46%)	107 (1.77%)	276 (3.21%)	210 (3.48%)	242 (3.33%)
Second job income	29 (0.43%)	11 (0.20%)	20 (0.33%)	44 (0.51%)	19 (0.31%)	31 (0.42%)
Property income	111 (1.66%)	77 (1.42%)	94 (1.56%)	121 (1.41%)	93 (1.54%)	107 (1.47%)

Table 4.2 (continued)

Category of Income (sub-category)[1]	Men in the 1995 sample (N = 6438)	Women in the 1995 sample (N = 6814)	Total for the 1995 sample (N = 13252)	Men in the 1999 sample (N = 1347)	Women in the 1999 sample (N = 1415)	Total for the 1999 sample (N = 2762)
Transfer income[2]	258	448	356	284	865	582
	(3.86%)	(8.28%)	(5.90%)	(3.32%)	(14.36%)	(8.00%)
Pensions[3]	65	280	176	176	690	439
	(0.97%)	(5.17%)	(2.92%)	(2.05%)	(11.46%)	(6.05%)
Gifts received	96	64	80	72	77	75
	(1.44%)	(1.18%)	(1.33%)	(0.84%)	(1.27%)	(1.03%)
Asset sales	13	4	8	2	0.16	0.95
	(0.19%)	(0.07%)	(0.13%)	(0.02%)	(0.00%)	(0.01%)
Hardship Subsidy (1995)/ Unemployment benefits (1999)	0.16	0.11	0.13	2	14	8
	(0.00%)	(0.00%)	(0.00%)	(0.03%)	(0.23%)	(0.11%)
Income in kind	96	70	83	17	11	14
	(1.44%)	(1.29%)	(1.38%)	(0.20%)	(0.17%)	(0.19%)

Notes:
[1] The selected components do not sum to 100%, as not all components are included and some are sub-components (in italics). It is also the case that those who take a pension are not the same individuals who earned a wage, for instance, which would also cause the percentages of the components of income not to add up vertically to 100%.
[2] Transfer income includes pensions, price subsidies, support for the elderly, child support, income from gifts, survey income, asset sales, unemployment benefits, minimum living benefits, and other hardship subsidies. We show the largest categories in the table.
[3] There is a notable gender difference in pensions as we include women who have retired at the official age of 54, in an attempt to maintain comparability with men who have an official retirement age of 59.

Sources: China Household Income Project, urban survey, 1995 and 1999.

Turning to the 1999 urban sample, mean income is 7267 RMB. As in 1995, there is a significant gender earnings gap. For men, mean income is 8574 RMB, while it is 6026 RMB for women. Table 4.2 shows that wages constitute the major share of annual income (over 70%). Work-related income (for example, self-employed income and other employment income) comprises over 80% of total income. Wages are surprisingly a lower percentage than in 1995, leading to the conclusion that there is more secondary income in 1999, as total earned income is similar. There is more unemployment and *xiagang* in the population, which would be reflected in less earned income from the primary job. There is also more self-employment in 1999; the mean value of that income is about 5% of total annual income, a five-fold increase from four years before. Transfer income is similar for men in 1999 as compared with 1995, but for women, it is greater. As early retirement is a popular way of downsizing SOEs, it is perhaps likely that women have been expected to retire earlier than the official retirement age and thus they received more pension income in 1999, relative to 1995, and a higher mean transfer income as a result.

On the whole, the components of income changed considerably between 1995 and 1999. Although earned income still constitutes nearly 80% of annual income in 1999, there are more diverse sources of earnings, such as from self-employment, when compared with 1995. Moreover, surprisingly, bonuses are a smaller portion of total income in 1999, as are subsidies and income in-kind. Estimating the determinants of income for these two years will allow for a better understanding of the changes in the urban wage structure.

Earnings functions (alternatively termed earned income) are estimated for the two samples, first using ordinary least squares (OLS). The focus is on wages, so there is potential sample selection bias in that those individuals who did not work for pay are not observed. To correct for sample selection, those who report annual income but no earned income are excluded from the estimation (see Heckman 1979). A probabilistic model (probit) accompanies the earnings function by predicting entry into wage employment using a relevant exclusion restriction. The exclusion restriction is an instrument that is correlated with entry into wage employment but unrelated to earnings, so that the selection bias can be corrected. Correspondingly, the income function is now found by using maximum likelihood estimation (MLE). The results of these estimations are reported in Tables 4.3 and 4.4. Both tables report results for the two cross-sections of data using non-selection corrected OLS and selection-corrected MLE. As noted, the latter corrects for inconsistency introduced by sample selection bias; both include robust standard errors. The probit estimations in the first column render the predictors of entry into wage employment,

*Table 4.3　The determinants of earned income for employed individuals in
　　　　　urban China, 1995*

Dependent variable: Log of annual earned income	Coefficient (t-statistic)		
	Probit	Corrected MLE	Uncorrected OLS
Constant	1.0259	5.9030	6.3440
	(1.185)	(42.611)***	(45.457)***
Personal Characteristics:			
Male	0.0998	0.1331	0.1304
	(1.024)	(13.350)***	(13.088)***
Age	0.0488	0.1050	0.0818
	(1.156)	(16.052)***	(12.911)***
Age squared	−0.0008	−0.0014	−0.0011
	(−1.536)	(−17.549)***	(−14.556)***
Communist Party member	4.6682	0.1004	0.1037
	(−)	(8.223)***	(8.472)***
Productive Characteristics:			
Years of education	0.0302	0.0437	0.0424
	(1.343)	(15.579)***	(15.184)***
Years of employment experience	0.0287	0.0200	0.0219
	(2.825)***	(10.910)***	(11.825)***
Occupation	0.0463	−0.0280	−0.0293
	(2.044)**	(−6.308)***	(−6.615)***
Exclusion Restriction:			
Have children in the household	−0.6602	−	−
	(−4.231)***		
Provinces:			
Beijing	0.2520	0.2614	0.2553
	(0.633)	(7.645)***	(7.503)***
Shanxi	4.5034	0.2621	0.2626
	(−)	(9.782)***	(9.778)***
Liaoning	0.0706	0.1962	0.1970
	(0.245)	(5.393)***	(5.411)***
Anhui	−0.2429	−0.1414	−0.1420
	(−1.029)	(−3.747)***	(−3.782)***
Henan	−0.1305	−0.3649	−0.3665
	(−0.460)	(−9.939)***	(−9.949)***
Hubei	−0.2445	−0.0544	−0.0522
	(−1.186)	(−2.289)**	(−2.193)**
Guangdong	4.4828	0.0531	0.0586
	(−)	(1.697)*	(1.877)*
Sichuan	−0.2337	−0.2060	−0.2071
	(−1.208)	(−6.004)***	(−6.033)***

Table 4.3 (continued)

Dependent variable:	Coefficient (t-statistic)		
Log of annual earned income	Probit	Corrected MLE	Uncorrected OLS
Yunnan	4.4686	0.1381	0.1389
	(–)	(4.910)***	(4.919)***
Gansu	4.4744	0.1925	0.1946
	(–)	(5.880)***	(5.974)***
Inverse Mills Ratio	–	−0.0269	–
		(−2.676)***	
R^2	–	–	0.2355
Pseudo R^2	0.1840	–	–
$X^2 (18)$	163.89***	–	–
Wald $X^2 (17)$	–	2933.07***	–
F(17, 5976)	–	–	171.43***
Number of observations	12016	11943	11943

Notes:
1. Mean value of logarithm of annual earned income is 8.3313 with a standard deviation of 0.5074.
2. *** denotes statistical significance at the 1% level, ** at the 5% level, and * at the 10% level.
3. Omitted dummy variables are: female, non-Communist Party members, and Jiangsu province.
4. Heteroskedasticity-consistent robust standard errors adjusted for clustering at the household level are computed.
5. The exclusion restriction of the presence of any children under the age of 18 was also tested, and the presence of a young child under the age of 13 in the household performed better.
6. Wald chi-squared values are computed because of the lack of the assumption of homoskedasticity in the error terms.

Source: China Household Income Project, urban survey, 1995.

including the significance of the exclusion restriction, and correspond to the MLE results in the second column. The final column presents the OLS results for comparisons of robustness.

First and promisingly, the returns to education increased slightly during this period. A year of education is associated with a 4% increase in income in 1995, but increases by over 25% by the end of the decade (5.5% income premium in 1999). This is good news for a developing labour market in which it is hoped that wages are better linked to human capital, captured in years of education attained. The income premium associated with age declined from approximately 10% to 3% from 1995 to 1999, with not much

Table 4.4   The determinants of earned income for employed individuals in
             urban China, 1999

Dependent variable: Log of annual income	Coefficient (t-statistic)		
	Probit	Corrected MLE	Uncorrected OLS
Constant	1.7579	7.4042	7.2676
	(1.375)	(21.420)***	(21.347)***
Personal Characteristics:			
Female	−0.2618	−0.1977	−0.2094
	(−2.002)**	(−8.060)***	(−8.670)***
Age	−0.0766	0.0328	0.0354
	(−1.112)	(2.077)**	(2.267)***
Age squared	0.0013	−0.0005	−0.0005
	(1.378)	(−2.459)**	(−2.628)***
Communist Party member	0.3984	0.1577	0.1645
	(1.467)	(4.858)***	(5.086)***
Productive Characteristics:			
Years of education	0.1069	0.0559	0.1645
	(3.755)***	(10.712)***	(11.672)***
Years of employment experience	0.0302	0.0130	0.0143
	(2.013)**	(3.989)***	(4.494)***
Ownership sector of employer	0.1261	0.0891	0.0960
	(2.499)**	(5.763)***	(6.405)***
Exclusion Restriction:			
Have children in the household	0.3771	–	–
	(2.521)**		
Cities:			
Beijing	−0.1617	0.5762	0.5691
	(−0.483)	(8.369)***	(8.405)***
Shenyang	0.1089	0.0972	0.0978
	(0.294)	(1.411)	(1.444)
Jinzhou	−0.2486	0.0477	0.0362
	(−0.728)	(0.600)	(0.473)
Nanjing	0.3701	0.4902	0.4934
	(0.783)	(7.782)***	(7.936)***
Xuzhou	−0.1525	0.2840	0.2783
	(−0.423)	(4.043)***	(4.004)***
Zhengzhou	−0.7835	0.0746	0.0088
	(−2.505)**	(0.893)	(0.108)
Kaifeng	−0.2685	−0.2655	−0.2765
	(−0.781)	(−2.955)***	(−3.109)***
Pingdingshan	-0.1197	0.2537	0.2505
	(-0.338)	(3.299)***	(3.311)***

Table 4.4   (continued)

Dependent variable: Log of annual income	Coefficient (t-statistic)		
	Probit	Corrected MLE	Uncorrected OLS
Chengdu	−0.1367	0.0950	0.0868
	(−0.381)	(1.256)	(1.170)
Zigong	−0.0666	−0.1755	−0.1800
	(−0.183)	(−2.174)**	(−2.236)**
Nanchong	0.1284	0.0797	0.0832
	(0.328)	(0.988)	(1.047)
Lanzhou	−0.1814	0.1267	0.1144
	(−0.0529)	(1.430)	(1.304)
Inverse Mills' Ratio	–	−0.5010	–
		(−9.2868)***	
R^2	–	–	0.2942
Pseudo R^2	0.1741	–	–
X^2 (21)	98.82***	–	–
Wald X^2 (20)	–	740.91***	–
F(20, 1239)	–	–	42.63***
Number of observations	2383	2322	2322

Notes:
1. Mean value of the logarithm of annual income is 8.8468 with a standard deviation of 0.6840.
2. *** denotes statistical significance at the 1% level, ** at the 5% level, and * at the 10% level.
3. Omitted dummy variables are: male, non-Communist Party members, urban collective sector, and Pinliang.
4. Heteroskedasticity-consistent robust standard errors adjusted for clustering at the household level are computed.
5. Not all variables are reported for the sake of brevity.
6. The exclusion restriction of the presence of any children under the age of 18 was also tested, and the presence of a young child under 13 in the household performed better.
7. Wald chi-squared values are computed because of the lack of the assumption of homoskedasticity in the error terms.

Source: China Household Income Project, urban survey, 1999.

change in the age squared term. This suggests that the administered wage structure with salaries highly linked to age may be beginning to experience some erosion. The return to employment experience declined over this period, leading to the conclusion that the 2% income premium reaped in 1995 is now close to 1% per year of employment experience in 1999. As most workers in the samples have held only one job, so that employment experience is largely synonymous with tenure (see Knight and Yueh 2004), this suggests a decrease in seniority pay rewarded for tenure, which is consistent with the interpretation put forward for the decline in rates of return to age.

The results also indicate that the wage profile is flatter in 1999 than in 1995. Calculated from the coefficients on the age and age squared variables for each set of estimations, the approximate peak wage of annual earnings is at 47 or 48 years of age in 1995, while it peaks at a younger age in 1999. This provides further support for the interpretation that wage reforms over this period decoupled the link between age and seniority pay in favour of more reward at earlier periods in a worker's career if warranted, something previously prevented by administrative scales.

Finally, of the important characteristics of employment, occupation and the ownership sector are both significant. Occupation in the 1995 estimation centres on the distinctions between non-manual and manual workers. Manual workers earn less income when compared with non-manual workers. In 1999, the distinction of ownership of the employer is a more prominent issue leading to the introduction of this control variable. There is a positive wage premium associated with employment in private enterprises.

Two important characteristics in the urban labour market which are not related to productivity but are significant indicators of the wage structure are gender and Communist Party membership. The coefficients on the gender dummy variables unambiguously indicate that the gender wage gap increased in 1999 as compared with 1995. Table 4.3 shows that the coefficient on the male gender dummy variable is 0.1331, which suggests a positive income premium for being male, whereas Table 4.4 shows a larger negative coefficient on the female gender dummy variable of –0.1977. Converting the coefficients on the dummy variables into figures, the disparity in income for men and women has grown from 14% to 18% over this four-year period. This is disturbing, as earned income was largely (although not completely) equalised in the administered labour system. With increasing discretion over pay by management, there seems to be an increase in discriminatory pay on the basis of gender.

A final variable of interest is Communist Party membership. The income premium granted for being a Party member increased from 11% to 17% between 1995 and 1999. This is initially surprising, but may indeed be consistent with a labour market in development. The increased premium suggests that informal associations may be important in a labour market moving away from an administered structure towards one in which managers exercise more discretion in paying wages. The better one's informal connections, as proxied by Communist Party membership, the more rewards in terms of income. There are many other interpretations of this result, including the predominance of Party members in exercising pre-eminence in budding private enterprises and otherwise translating their membership into economic advantage.

Finally, the disparities among provinces remain. Individuals in Beijing continue to enjoy an income premium that is higher than any other area. Poorer areas, such as Shenyang and Liaoning, hard hit by the restructuring of SOEs, fared badly during this period.

A note on labour force participation from Tables 4.3 and 4.4 is that being female decreases the chances of entering into wage employment in 1999, while there was no gender difference evident in 1995. This is a significant finding for a labour force that has been characterised by high participation by women (approximately 83% in 1995 versus 68% in 1999). But women were disproportionately laid off during the *xiagang* era as seen in the lower 1999 labour force participation rate.

Consistent with the other conclusions from the earnings functions, years of education are significantly associated with better chances of being employed in 1999, while there was no effect in 1995. This provides further support that possessing human capital improves both earnings and the chances of employment in a more market-oriented labour market. Years of employment experience continue to be important in selection into wage employment in 1999, as in 1995.

Wage reforms have resulted in greater rewards for human capital, particularly education, which suggests that the labour market is increasingly moving towards a market-based system. However, it is also the case that non-productive traits such as gender are also significant, indicating potential discrimination in the labour market which is a well-known, if unfortunate, occurrence in competitive labour markets. Wage reforms have transformed the Chinese labour market. The next section turns to labour mobility, another important facet of a developing labour market.

3. LABOUR MOBILITY

During the period of central planning, China had an administered labour system where urban labour was allocated bureaucratically. Labour mobility was not permitted, either across cities or across employers within a city, so that one's first job was often one's last. The relationship between a worker and his or her *danwei*, that is, work unit, was close and pervasive; the enterprise provided lifetime employment and was the source of welfare, which was termed the 'iron rice bowl'. Hence, labour mobility or labour turnover in urban China was low.

Labour market reforms in the 1990s led to workers acquiring more rights to move from one employer to another. However, voluntary mobility continued to be impeded by the employer-specific provision of social welfare, services, such as pensions, medical care and housing, which were gradually being privatised.

A labour market in transition from a planned to a market-oriented system experiences increased mobility from a low level. Initially, involuntary mobility results from enterprises discarding surplus labour and producers adjusting to market demand and prices. As the transition progresses, the proportion of voluntary quits increases as individuals move to jobs that better match their productive characteristics and reflect expanding activities. Urban China is arguably in the first stage of this transition because labour mobility has risen recently from very low levels. In developed economies, mobility in labour markets is characterised by long-term employment relationships, with most new jobs ending early, and the probability of a job ending declining with tenure (Farber 1999). The labour market in urban China may exhibit only the first of these characteristics.

The rate of job mobility is likely to be inversely related to the length of job tenure. Table 4.5 reports the length of tenure, that is, job duration, in China and in various other countries, ranked by average length of tenure.

Table 4.5   Average and median job tenure for select countries

Country	Average tenure (years)	Median tenure (years)	Distribution of tenure (percentage)	
			Under 2 years	Over 20 years
China (urban residents)	19.9	19.0	5.6	45.5
Poland	17.5	17.0	5.7	43.9
Japan	11.3	8.3	23.6	21.4
Germany	9.7	10.7	25.5	17.0
United Kingdom	7.8	5.0	30.3	9.4
United States	7.4	4.2	34.5	9.0
China (migrants)	4.5	3.0	39.2	1.3

Notes:
1. The data relate to 1995, except for the US (1996) and China (1999).
2. The tenure of migrants in China is measured from the time of entry into the urban labour market.
3. For both urban residents and migrants, the data for China on the distribution of tenure include those with two years of tenure, which slightly biases upwards both figures.

Sources: OECD, 1997 and China Household Income Project, urban survey, 1999.

Chinese urban residents are at the top of the list, having the longest average tenure at 19.9 years while Chinese rural-urban migrants are at the bottom, having the shortest at 4.5 years. The figures for median tenure and for the distribution of tenure show almost identical patterns. Poland, the other transition economy for which data are available, is closest to Chinese urbanites, followed by Japan. The European countries occupy intermediate positions and the United States, with its flexible labour market, is closest to Chinese migrants. It is therefore important to separately analyse and investigate the reasons for the relatively long job tenure of urban residents and the relatively short tenure of rural-urban migrants. An overview of migration in China is first provided in the next section as a preface to the analysis.

3.1 Economic Migration

In China, urban residents have traditionally been protected against labour market competition from rural-urban migrants. Over the period of urban economic reform – beginning in the mid 1980s and accelerating in the 1990s government allowed rural-urban migration to increase in order to fill the employment gap when growth in labour demand outstripped that of the resident labour force in the urban economy. However, as the reform process gained pace and controls were lifted, it is plausible that migrants and urban residents increasingly competed.

During the period of the communes and central planning, the movement of labour in China was tightly controlled and restricted. During the period of economic reform and transition to a market economy, rural-urban migration became important, reflecting a growing urban need for migrant labour, but also a weakening in the power of the authorities to control labour. Despite their greater freedom, it remains difficult for rural workers to acquire urban registration (*hukou*) and thus permanent urban residence. Government attempts to maintain continuing control over the 'floating' population of temporary rural-urban migrant workers. Generally, migrants have been permitted only in the 'residual' urban wage jobs not wanted by residents. These tend to be the lowest wage, lowest skill, least pleasant jobs (Knight et al. 1999). Although rural households thus have a strong economic incentive to send workers out to the cities and towns, migrants are still at a considerable disadvantage in the urban labour market by comparison with urban workers, with respect both to job opportunities and to terms and conditions of employment.

Permanent migration is controlled through the *hukou* registration system. A *hukou* confers legal rights to be resident in the locality and to share the resources of that community. In the case of cities, it involves rights to a package of benefits, and in the case of villages it involves rights to land for farming and housing. The *hukou* system has been preserved over the years but its effectiveness has declined. It has become possible for a rural person to buy a *hukou* in a town or small city, although restrictions on settlement in a large city remain tight.

In some developing countries in Asia and Africa, the system of 'circular' or 'oscillating' migration can be a voluntarily one, especially when permanent migration would involve the loss of land rights (see, for example, Hugo 1982; Cordell et al. 1998). In China, village land is generally allocated on a rent-free, contract basis, so implying that withdrawal from the village can involve an opportunity cost. However, temporary migration in China is hardly voluntary. The combination of the security provided by access to land, the cost of withdrawal from the village, the relatively low income from farming, the lack of security in the city, and the difficulties of urban settlement means that for many rural households the best available option is to send out a migrant on a temporary basis. The evidence for China suggests that the removal of restrictions on urban settlement would result in faster urbanisation. For instance, a survey of rural-urban migrants in the mid 1990s found that, if a satisfactory job could be secured, 78% would like to work in it as long as possible; 90% of the sample would like their family to join them either immediately or when a long-term well-paid job was found; and 70% wanted an urban *hukou* (Knight and Song 1999: 295). China has indeed witnessed a process of increasing urban settlement, albeit still constrained, made difficult and often unofficial.

There is evidence that city governments have pursued these regulatory policies in order to protect their residents. For instance, regulations in various cities across China excluded workers without local *hukous* from a range of occupations and required employers to obtain permits for hiring such labour (Solinger 2004). Jobs were classified into three types: urban *hukou* jobs, rural migrant jobs, and jobs open to all, but with urban workers receiving preference. City labour bureaux also imposed quotas on the number of migrants that each enterprise could employ. The restrictions were sensitive to the state of the city labour market, being tightened if unemployment among city residents rose. It is to be expected, therefore, that migrant employment would be curtailed as a policy response to rising urban unemployment in China, but would be relaxed as and when labour market conditions permitted. For instance, during the period of the *xiagang* policy, there were numerous protests by laid-off workers, especially the many who did not receive their income support, and this induced the government to introduce the so-called 'putting out fires' fund to placate them, and rein in rural-urban migration.

The demand for migrant labour first emerged and developed in the coastal region, especially in Guangdong and in the Special Economic Zones (SEZs), where foreign investors were encouraged to produce for export. This fast-growing and fast-privatising region has a large proportion of migrants in total employment, a high proportion is female, and migrants are able to move higher up the job ladder. For instance, the migrant density in Shenzhen – neighbouring Hong Kong – was as high as 35% in 1995, and the proportion of migrants who were skilled manual or non-manual employees no less than 32% (Knight et al. 1999). Given indications of labour shortages and rising wages for migrants in the private sector of this, the most dynamic region, it is likely that migrants are less a threat to, and thus more able to compete with, urban residents than in other parts of China.

3.2 Differential Job Mobility

During the reform period, only the temporary migration of rural people is normally permitted. Generally, migrants are employed on short-term contracts. Rural *hukou* holders are discriminated against in accessing housing and social services like education and health care, so deterring them from settling in the cities. A pattern has emerged in which migrants spend brief periods in urban employment, engaged on one or two short-term contracts, and then return to their rural homesteads. This pattern is changing only gradually as more migrants attempt to bring their families to the, still inhospitable, cities. In these circumstances, employers have little incentive to train their migrant workers. Therefore, labour mobility among rural-urban migrants may be too substantial to promote efficient human capital formation.

Before the policies concerning employment in the Chinese urban labour market were loosened, urban *hukou* workers were favoured by placement in good jobs, that is, permanent, secure 'iron rice bowls', while migrants were discriminated against and restricted to bad jobs, that is, jobs that were temporary and had little job security and few non-wage benefits. Institutional arrangements ensure that jobs held by urbanites last longer than jobs held by migrants. The rate at which jobs turn over is the reciprocal of job duration. Hence, the rate at which vacancies occur for good jobs, and thus for urban workers, is less than the rate of vacancies for bad jobs, and thus for migrants. Therefore, in any period, the mobility rate of urban workers is less than that of migrants.

Using the same 1999 household survey discussed earlier, this hypothesis is investigated. The most notable feature of the labour market in the late 1990s is a general lack of mobility. As many as 78% of respondents had only one job and a further 16% had two jobs. Thus, only 6% had three or more jobs. No fewer than 74% of current employees with 30 or more years of employment experience were still in their first jobs. For the select minority of workers who changed jobs, the average length of their completed tenure was 5.5 years. For the urban sample as a whole, the average length of first job tenure, including incomplete tenure, was 21.3 years. Considering only current job tenure, that is, omitting completed jobs, the average length was 16.6 years. Allowing for future tenure in continuing jobs, the predicted duration of completed tenure for the sample as a whole would be extremely long.

The analysis of migrants is based on workers in a sample of rural-urban migrant households, that is, households that establish residence in the survey cities but retain their rural *hukou*. Because they live in resident households, these migrants are unlikely to be representative of all rural-urban migrants. Migrants who leave their rural homesteads and come to the cities on their own to work temporarily, often living with other migrants at their workplaces or in dormitories, are likely to be underrepresented in the NBS survey. The mobility rate of this group is likely to be higher than that of migrants who establish urban roots. Regarding mobility, the migrants appear to be similar to the urban workers. As many as 77% had only one job, another 10% had two jobs, 7% had three jobs, while only 6% had more than three jobs. However, these similarities are misleading. For urban workers, the data consider the period since entry to the labour force, but for migrants, the data refer to the period from entry into the city labour market only. Thus, the average length of employment experience of urban workers is 22.8 years, whereas the average length of city employment experience of migrants is 5.9 years. This difference is due partly to migrants being younger, that is, 28.6 years of age compared with 38.4 years, and partly to migrants not coming to the city immediately when they entered the labour force because most were engaged in rural household economic activities.

The average completed employment duration of migrants is 2.2 years; it is lowest for migrants in their twenties, at 1.3 years and highest for those in their fifties, at 4.1 years. The first job tenure, including incomplete spells, averages 5.0 years; the average length of the current job tenure is 4.5 years. Each of these tenure figures requires careful interpretation. First, briefly employed migrants are more likely to be unsuccessful and may have returned to the village. Second, predicting the length of incomplete spells is difficult because it may be misleading to double the length of the average current tenure from 4.5 to 9.0 years, as would be appropriate for a steady-state process. If migrants are more welcomed as urban residents, they will remain at their workplace longer than in the past. Nevertheless, even the figure of 4.5 years is high by comparison with the conventional wisdom about migrant employment tenure in China. Examining migrants and urban residents with comparable labour market experience of less than six years, migrants have a mobility rate of 0.1230, which is almost twice as high as that of urban residents at 0.0689. Even by 1999, when the 'iron rice bowl' no longer existed, entering urban residents had distinctly lower mobility rates than migrants with comparable amounts of urban employment experience.

The data also revealed that the use of social networks in job search increases the mobility rate for urban residents, especially if it is voluntary. Having larger social networks and more connections improves employment prospects through learning about jobs, receiving referrals to jobs, and having the relationships that facilitate job moves in an administered labour system. Those with more human and social capital have more opportunities, which may be reflected in greater mobility. Factors that reduce significantly the involuntary mobility rate are being a non-manual worker, working in the state sector, and being a Communist Party member. Each of these characteristics provides relative protection against job loss. In addition, age increases the involuntary mobility rate so that older workers are more likely to be laid off.

For migrants who have located their current job by a referral through a social network, mobility is reduced significantly, implying longer job duration. None of the factors relevant for urban residents could explain their mobility decisions. In summary, the determinants of the mobility of urban workers can be well explained by observable characteristics in a household survey, but the mobility of migrants appears to depend on unobserved variables, for example, rural household characteristics, short-term contracts coming to an end, or luck.

Therefore, mobility is low for urban residents in China, but perhaps too high for rural-urban migrants. The reasons have to do with China's institutional policies favouring urban residents and discriminating against migrants, even though the latter has begun to change. In the 2000s, the central government eased the restrictions on migration and made it easier for migrants to settle in urban areas, including allowing the children of migrants to attend school. However, fiscal decentralisation and the pressures of unemployment on local governments have caused the implementation of these reforms to be patchy. Overall, job mobility is low in China – except for migrants, but is rising due to the lifting of restrictions and better matching of employees with jobs that suit their skill set. The next section investigates whether labour productivity has increased in the aftermath of these reforms in the 1990s.

4. LABOUR PRODUCTIVITY

This section examines labour productivity in the 2000s, after the reforms of the late 1980s and 1990s. The culmination of wage and employment reforms, loosening labour market restrictions, and increasing competition is to achieve greater value-added in output per worker. Using a national enterprise data set, this supposed outcome will be assessed.

4.1 Factors Affecting Labour Productivity

Labour market reforms have included liberalising wages to better reward productive characteristics such as education, as well as increasing job mobility to permit better matching between worker and employer characteristics, leading to a more competitive labour market, as discussed earlier. As mentioned in earlier chapters, ownership reform has also progressed significantly throughout the reform period. From state-owned enterprises dominating GDP to accounting for less than half of China's output by 2005, China's economy is therefore increasingly characterised by private sector competition. Moreover, the 'open door' policy culminated in membership of the World Trade Organisation (WTO) in 2001, which heralded a period of global integration and market opening, which again results in greater competitive pressures.

These changes are hypothesised to influence labour productivity in the following ways. The value of marginal product (VMP) of labour is equal to the wage in a competitive labour market, which is a far cry from the administered wage system of China, where compensation depended on age and seniority, among other factors, all of which were unrelated to effort (Yueh 2004). Reform of the labour market better aligns VMP, which is the product of the marginal product of labour (MPL) and the price of the good (P), with the wage: $VMP = MPL \times P$. Therefore, by liberalising wages to match effort, MPL should be raised as a result of rewarding the effort exerted in producing output. Also, reforms to increase the flexibility of labour markets during the 1990s began to propel workers to move to firms which better match their skills and thus improve productivity. This stands in stark contrast to the lifetime employment system that resulted in over-manning and surplus labour, which reduced productivity, as labour, like other factor inputs, is subject to decreasing returns. Reforms geared towards a more competitive labour market would thus increase labour productivity.

As the $VMP = MPL \times P$ equation further suggests, wages are not only determined by effort, but are a function of MPL together with the price of the good. When prices are administered, then demand for, and the quality of, a good do not matter as in a competitive market and thus would stifle labour productivity if wages are kept down despite higher MPL by a state-run product market. The rise of the non-state sector in China foretells of increased competition in which markets would better respond to the forces of demand and supply. Competition may well drive down prices as well as increase them, but market forces rather than administrative ones would operate to appropriately reward firms.

Factor and product market reforms, therefore, play a notable role in increasing labour productivity. Labour productivity is also influenced by the reform of the market for the other factors of production, notably, capital. With over-investment common in SOEs that seek their funding from the state or state-owned banks and the continued presence of the state-owned sector, the capital-to-labour (K/L) ratio is inefficiently high. By reforming the industrial sector and reducing obsolete capital, labour becomes more productive as K/L falls. The relationship is evident in the alternative formulation of VMP, which is the marginal revenue product (MRP) of labour, a more precise measure in less than perfectly competitive markets where price does not necessarily equal marginal revenue (MR): $MRP = MPL \times MR$. The marginal revenue of a firm depends on its productive efficiency and the demand conditions that it faces for its goods. A firm would only hire more workers if the value of the additional output from the worker was warranted by the marginal cost to the firm of that output. MRP, as with VMP, in turn determines wages and therefore the rewards to the marginal product of labour. A firm's capital stock, as well as its industry conditions, would shape its revenue and cost curves.

It follows that labour productivity is further determined not only by factor inputs but also by the technology and efficiency of the use of its workers and capital. A firm with lagging technology will be less efficient than one with more advanced production capabilities, affecting its cost curves and therefore the productivity of its workers. Chinese firms and firms from developing countries which lag behind the know-how of competitors from more advanced economies will have lower labour productivity than otherwise comparable firms. Globalisation and the incursion of foreign firms directly into the domestic market, as well as acting as competition in the global economy, will expose these differences, while at the same offering an opportunity for Chinese companies to become exposed to, learn from and even obtain the technological know-how of those firms. This mechanism of learning from technology embodied in foreign capital is well-known and forms the basis for the theory of 'catching up' often discussed in economic growth models (see, for example, Solow 1956).

4.2 Measuring Labour Productivity

Little research has focused exclusively on the determinants of labour productivity in China, though many studies have examined the factors influencing firm total factor productivity (TFP), including those impacting on the productivity of labour. Kraay (2006), using a panel of firms from 1988–92, investigates the role of exports on labour productivity and finds a positive and significant influence. Jefferson et al. (2000), using an NBS data set covering the period 1980–1996, similarly find large increases in labour productivity, particularly for the 1990s, and notably for SOEs during this period, which they attribute to the large-scale layoff policy (*xiagang*) over the latter period. Jefferson and Su (2006) explore the sources of China's growth, including aspects of labour productivity, using an NBS panel data set of large and medium sized enterprises (that is, those with sales over 5 million RMB) from 1995–2004. They conclude that there is evidence of improved allocative efficiency from labour moving out of agriculture and between industrial and ownership sectors which reflect productivity advances.

Another strand of the literature views labour productivity in comparative perspective. Over the period 1952 to 1997, Wu (2001) concludes that China's comparative labour productivity increased from about 3.0 in 1952 to 7.6 in 1997 (USA = 100), showing a significant gap with the U.S. even after three decades of reform. Jefferson and Su (2006) likewise focus on China's international productivity gap and estimate that China's labour productivity must increase by some six-fold before it achieves a GDP per capita that is one-quarter that of the US. Although they find evidence that industries in the coastal regions are already nearly one-quarter of those in the US by the early 2000s, the rest of China lags behind.

The conclusion across these studies emphasises the importance of productivity in driving China's economic growth. Whether in comparative or internally comparative perspective across China's regions, assessing the factors which increase labour productivity will shed light on the reforms which have contributed to China's growth.

The primary data set used in this section is a national firm-level survey. The survey pertained to 2005, which was then matched by China's NBS to their annual enterprise survey to create a panel from 2000 to 2005. The questionnaire was designed by an international research team (including the author), and carried out by NBS with support from the World Bank. The survey was conducted in the summer of 2006 on 1268 firms in 12 cities (province in parentheses): Beijing (municipality), Changchun (Jilin), Chifeng (Inner Mongolia), Dandong (Liaoning), Hangzhou (Zhejiang), Shijiazhuang (Hebei), Shiyan (Hubei), Shunde (Guangdong), Wujiang

(Jiangsu), Xian (Shaanxi), Zibo (Shandong), Chongqing (municipality). The survey data was then matched to the enterprise panel and is a representative sub-sample of that large-scale data set. The National Bureau of Statistics takes considerable care with their annual enterprise survey such that the figures match data obtained independently by the Chinese tax authorities.

Figures 4.1 and 4.2 show China's labour productivity in comparative perspective and over time relative to 1980 when it started market-oriented reforms. Using information from the International Labour Organization (ILO), Figure 4.1 in particular shows the extraordinary gains in labour productivity in China since then. Gains in GDP per worker in manufacturing were steady and comparable to international increases until the early 1990s when China's 'open door' policy took off. After that, whilst other major economies experienced a nearly tripling of productivity and India improved more modestly, China's productivity levels increased nearly seven-fold. The productivity leader nevertheless remains the USA, which is evident in Figure 4.2. China is around one-eighth as productive as the leader, although its gains are much faster than the richer country. By 2005, as seen in Table 4.6, China's GDP per worker in the broader economy as well as in manufacturing was still modest relative to other comparably sized economies due to its low level of development, which contributes to its cost advantage. However, it has had faster labour productivity growth even against a similarly poor country such as India, which contributes to China's faster overall GDP growth.

Turning to the data used in this chapter, Table 4.7 provides measures of the levels and growth rates of labour productivity. According to the standard computation, value-added is the sum of profits, profit taxes, wages and additional labour compensation (insurance and welfare payments). The value-added measure was deflated by the Ex-factory Price Index of Industrial Products, while the capital stock was deflated by the National Price Index for Investment in Fixed Assets (NBS 2006). Table 4.7 shows that average annual real value-added per worker was 50 259 RMB over the period 2000–2005, with an annual average growth rate of 4.77%. This is in line with other raw estimates of labour productivity growth during the reform period, which have been around 4–6% (for example, Jefferson and Rawski 1994). The pattern is echoed in the average profit per worker, growth of which was around 6% for the period. Measured in terms of sales per worker, the real annual average growth rate is an impressive 13.5%. Although somewhat imprecise as a measure of labour productivity, the sales measure indicates that real output per worker has grown rapidly over the period 2000–2005, while growth in profits and value-added has slowed. This suggests that margins are becoming tighter.

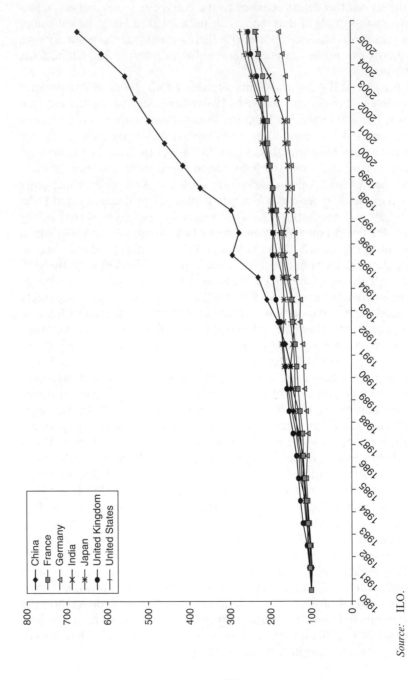

Source: ILO.

Figure 4.1 GDP per worker in manufacturing (1980 = 100), 1980–2005

94

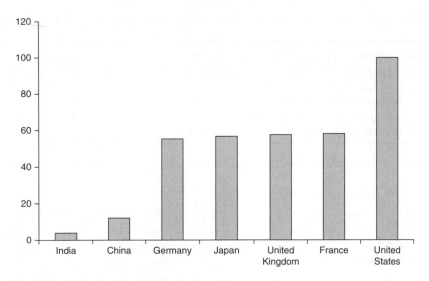

Source: ILO.

Figure 4.2   Comparative labour productivity (USA = 100), 2005

Table 4.6   Labour productivity in comparative perspective, 2005

Country	GDP per worker (1990 US$ at PPP)	GDP per worker in manufacturing (1997 US$ at PPP)
India	2421	4089
China	5772	12642
Germany	19477	57849
Japan	21979	59281
France	22099	60835
United Kingdom	22412	60235
United States	30519	104606

Source: ILO.

China's industrial sector has also changed dramatically over the past few decades, particularly as seen in the diverse ownership structures of enterprises in the 2000s, which have implications for labour productivity. Since the *gaizhi*, or restructuring policy, of the 1990s, the non-state sector has increased its presence in China's economy, accounting for ever larger shares of industrial output. The non-state sector comprises of privatised

Table 4.7   Levels and growth rates of real labour productivity, 2000–2005

Average value-added (VA) per worker (RMB)	50 249
Average annual growth rate of VA per worker	4.77%
Average sales per worker (RMB)	373 768
Average annual growth rate of sales per worker	13.54%
Average profit per worker (RMB)	2032
Average annual growth rate of profit per worker	6.33%

Note: Values are only reported for those firms with four years or more of data (n = 4090).

SOEs, private Chinese firms and foreign invested enterprises (FIEs), such as Chinese-foreign joint ventures (JVs) and wholly-owned foreign-owned enterprises (WOFEs). FIEs can be further disaggregated into those from Greater China (Hong Kong, Macau and Taiwan) and other countries. Since the establishment of the two stock exchanges in Shanghai and Shenzhen in the early 1990s and the more recently permitted overseas listings, a number of firms have become publicly listed (*gufen*) companies. Given the diversity, ownership sector and listing are controlled for before any interpretations are made of the drivers of labour productivity.

Table 4.8 provides firm-level information on value-added, employees, capital stock and the wage bill for the different types of enterprises. It shows that mean value-added per firm is highest for JVs from countries other than Greater China and lowest for private Chinese firms, although WOFEs from other countries have the highest median value, whilst the lowest remains that of private Chinese firms. Mean number of employees is highest in SOEs and lowest for private firms, while the median gives a similar picture, but tie for the largest with Greater China WOFEs. Capital stock is highest for SOEs measured in means, but greatest for other WOFEs when measured in medians, which is less prone to skewness in the data. Private Chinese firms continue to have the lowest values among the different ownership types in both mean and median. Finally, the firm mean wage bill is highest in SOEs and lowest in private firms. But, when measured in medians, Greater China WOFEs have the highest wage bill, while Chinese firms have the lowest. Firm characteristics indicate that private Chinese firms tend to be the smallest in terms of labour and capital, as well as value-added, while the privatised SOEs are only slightly larger.

Table 4.9 provides information on average firm characteristics per worker: value-added per worker, capital stock per worker or the capital/labour ratio, wage bill per worker, hourly wage and the average number of hours worked per week. Value-added per worker – the typical measure

Table 4.8 *Average firm characteristics*

Firms		Value-added (in RMB)			Employees (number)			Capital stock (in 100 RMB)			Wage bill (in 100 RMB)		
Ownership type	N	Mean	Standard deviation	Median	Mean	Standard deviation	Median	Mean	Standard deviation	Median	Mean	Standard deviation	Median
SOE	470	47078	118475	8773	1071	2189	320	117606	316789	16955	23134	108439	3472
Privatised SOE	175	11081	24127	4268	266	335	172	20421	62664	6497	3047	5124	1200
Private firm	370	6702	11510	3203	184	214	117	12665	25808	4745	2076	2930	1115
Greater China JV	64	22975	54190	9753	519	1198	269	40569	59081	13486	8285	19436	3717
Other JV	99	55335	137210	14448	825	1910	283	105412	287332	23476	21089	77185	5351
Greater China WOFE	41	28657	46897	12344	888	1362	320	64765	93148	22170	15081	26207	5606
Other WOFE	41	37007	75847	109863	707	1310	280	91480	195711	297780	11693	21244	5137

Notes: Eight firms did not indicate their ownership type and are omitted.

Table 4.9 Average firm characteristics per worker

Firms	N	Value-added per worker (in RMB)			Capital per worker (in RMB)			Annual wage bill per worker (in RMB)			Hourly wage per worker (in RMB)			Average working week (in hours)		
Ownership type		Mean	Standard deviation	Median	Mean	Standard deviation	Median	Mean	Standard deviation	Median	Mean	Standard deviation	Median	Mean	Standard deviation	Median
SOE	470	44844	61245	26378	94490	256425	56741	13637	10215	11246	6.10	3.18	5.28	42.9	5.9	40
Privatised SOE	175	41816	51648	24561	71031	123777	36503	11089	6537	9688	4.41	1.50	4.17	46.1	6.5	48
Private firm	370	42363	47728	26419	72327	89465	44060	11315	8113	9800	4.61	2.44	4.40	47.1	7.3	48
Greater China JV	64	54990	65591	34669	115044	190531	53107	17819	14019	14131	6.16	3.02	5.26	45.4	7.1	44
Other JV	99	87603	112056	57525	155933	241601	81624	22313	20389	16670	6.60	3.33	5.56	42.8	5.6	40
Greater China WOFE	41	56533	108963	27201	116560	268357	59824	17019	8859	14476	5.22	2.06	4.72	46.1	8.0	44
Other WOFE	41	44844	61245	26378	160755	184121	109149	18794	10570	16522	6.22	4.75	5.56	44.2	7.9	40

Notes: Eight firms did not indicate their ownership type and are omitted.

Table 4.10 Human capital of labour force

	Share of workers with secondary education (%)	Share of workers with higher education (%)	Share of managers with higher education (%)
SOE	64.1	19.9	44.4
Privatised SOE	63.7	16.4	28.5
Private firm	59.0	17.8	33.7
Greater China JV	63.8	27.7	47.3
Other JV	62.2	22.5	16.3
Greater China WOFE	68.3	23.8	23.8
Other WOFE	55.0	27.1	51.8
Average across firms	61.9	19.8	40.3

Note: The human capital of the labour force is estimated based on bands reported by personnel managers. The questions asked for the shares of employees and managers with secondary or higher education with a choice of responses as follows: (1) 0–20%, (2) 20–40%, (3) 40–60%, (4) greater than 60%. The average share is computed taking as the average the mid-point of each band, for example, 20–40% is computed as 30%. As the maximum value is 0.8 or 80%, this is an under-estimate. This is counterbalanced by the lower band, for which 10% is estimated for estimates of 0 20%.

of labour productivity – is highest in JVs from other countries in both average measures, while the lowest is privatised SOEs, again both in terms of the mean and the median. The raw descriptive information indicates that FIEs all have higher labour productivity than Chinese firms, with SOEs at about the same level as private Chinese firms on average. Capital per worker is also uniformly higher for FIEs than Chinese firms, while SOEs have more capital per worker than other Chinese firms. The largest capital-to-labour ratio is found in WOFEs from other countries. Foreign firms have more capital invested, as compared with private Chinese firms, which tend to be credit constrained, and SOEs, which find it easier to access cheap capital via bank financing from the state-dominated banking system. The wage bill per worker is also higher for FIEs, though the hourly wage for SOEs exceeds that of WOFEs from Greater China and is broadly in line with FIEs rather than domestic firms. Of the FIEs, WOFEs from Greater China pay the lowest hourly wage and have the second highest hours in a working week (46 hours). The most hours worked per week on average are in private Chinese firms, while SOEs and other JVs have the shortest working week (around 42 hours). The median values provide a similar picture, with longer hours worked in Chinese firms as compared with FIEs.

Table 4.10 provides some measures of the labour force's human capital (the share of workers with secondary and higher education and the share of managers with higher education), again for the different ownership types. Across all firms, some 62% of workers have secondary education, with more educated workers found in Greater China WOFEs and the least educated in other WOFEs. In terms of higher education, the proportion falls considerably to some 20% across all firms, with the lowest level found in privatised SOEs and the highest in Greater China JVs. FIEs have, on average, more educated workers than private Chinese firms. The picture is more varied when considering the share of managers with higher education. Across all firms, around 40% of managers have higher education. The lowest proportion is found in JVs from other countries, while the highest proportion is in WOFEs also from other countries. SOEs have higher shares than other Chinese firms, though all Chinese firms have more educated managers than FIEs, except for WOFEs from other countries.

The data also show the percentage of firms which are listed on domestic or international stock exchanges. The average is just under 5% of all firms, with SOEs having the highest proportion at over 12%. The lowest share of listings is found in private Chinese firms, privatised SOEs and Greater China WOFEs. Among FIEs, more WOFEs from other countries are listed than other ownership types.

Finally, most firms either do not export or export less than 1% of their output. Across firms, the average export share is 11.5%, with WOFEs from other countries exporting more than other types of FIEs and SOEs exporting a greater proportion of their output than other domestic firms. Greater China WOFEs have the smallest share of exports in their total output, while private Chinese firms also export just a fraction more of their output. Both types of firm appear to be producing for the domestic Chinese market, while other WOFEs, SOEs, and both types of JVs export a greater share of their products.

4.3   Estimating Labour Productivity

Turning from the descriptive data, Table 4.11 reports the estimates of labour productivity. The trend growth rate for labour productivity is high. Estimating from the year dummies, the trend is around 5.7% per annum, indicating a strong rate of labour productivity growth that is roughly commensurate with the raw estimates.

When measures of human capital are added to the estimation in column (2), the result is that the attainment of secondary education by workers has an insignificant effect on labour productivity, but higher education has a significantly positive effect for both workers and managers. Labour

Table 4.11   Determinants of labour productivity

Dependent variable: value-added per worker	Baseline (1)	Human Capital (2)	Competition (3)	Globalisation (4)
Employment	−0.1335***	−0.1291***	−0.1022**	−0.1234*
Capital	0.2559***	0.2193**	0.2434***	0.4562***
Explanatory variables:	*Year dummies*	*Year dummies (included)*	*Year dummies (included)*	*Year dummies (included)*
	2001: 0.0867***	Secondary education of workers: −0.0743	Perceived competition by firm: −0.1017**	Technology transfer agreement signed: 0.4523*
	2002: 0.1717***	Higher education of workers: 0.2328***	NERI Marketization Index: 0.0807***	Export share of total firm output: 0.0986***
	2003: 0.1798***	Higher education of managers: 0.1280***	Share of private sector in provincial output: 0.4086***	Provincial exports as a share of provincial GDP: 0.1212***
	2004: 0.2084*** 2005: 0.2837***	*Regional labour markets* Coastal provinces: 0.3092*** Western provinces: −0.0373		
Constant	2.9539***	3.5034***	3.3366***	2.2383***

Notes: Dependent variable is in logs, as are the employment, capital and education variables. Omitted variables is the central region in column (2). In column (3), the perception of competition measure is ranked from 1–3 with 1 as the most and 3 as the least competitive. The NERI Marketisation Index is compiled by the National Economic Research Institute of China (NERI) and the most recent period available, 2000–2002, is used (http://www.neri.org.cn/special/200407neri.pdf). The NERI Index is scaled between 1–10 based on aggregating and weighting five measures: (1) role of government, (2) economic structure, (3) inter-regional trade, (4) factor market development and (5) legal framework. The share of the private sector in provincial industrial output is measured from 2000–2005. In column (4), technology transfer agreement is a dummy variable that equals 1 if the joint venture signed such an agreement and zero otherwise. Share of exports in firm output is the log of total exports as a ratio of total output of the firm. Provincial export to GDP ratio is also measured. Exports are converted from US$ into RMB at average exchange rates for the relevant year. In all of the dynamic panel system GMM estimations, the Sargan tests suggest the exogeneity of the instruments, while the autocorrelation test for serial correlation in the structure of the error terms cannot reject AR1 but can reject AR2, so the lags are taken from $t-2$ for the endogenous factor inputs. Significance is denoted as: *** $p < 0.01$, ** $p < 0.05$, * $p < 0.1$.

productivity is also found to be lower in the central region than for the others. This is the region with the lowest returns to secondary and higher education, as well as to each year of education. The coastal region, with the most competitive labour market, is found in the estimations to generate the largest improvements in labour productivity relative to the omitted category of the central region, whereas there is no significant difference between the western and central regions. These estimates indicate that labour market reforms resulting in more competitive labour markets have the expected effects on labour productivity in firms which locate in these regions.

Increasing the human capital of workers, specifically the proportion with higher education, by 1% will result in a 23% improvement in labour productivity. Similarly, increasing the share of managers with higher education by a comparable amount will improve labour productivity by nearly 13%. Locating in the coastal provinces with more competitive labour markets will raise labour productivity by 36%, as compared with locating in the interior or western regions. All of the measures suggest that more competitive labour markets generate greater labour productivity.

When measures of competition are introduced in column (3), similarly significant influences on labour productivity are evident. For instance, greater perceived product market competition by the firm's managers increases value-added per worker. Firms which perceive that they are in competitive markets are more productive, lending support to the notion that competition improves productivity. This conclusion is supported by the provincial-level measures of the extent of competition, such as the Marketisation Index compiled by the respected China National Economic Research Institute (NERI), as well as by the share of private sector output in a province.

No measure is perfect in capturing the extent of competition, but the estimations using various proxies are consistent and support the hypothesis that greater market development increases labour productivity. Moving an increment on the perceived competition variable is associated with a 10% increase in labour productivity, while an incremental move in the NERI Marketisation Index induces an 8% improvement. Increasing the share of private sector output in total provincial output by 1% will generate a 41% increase in labour productivity.

Finally, a notable event in the 2000s is China joining the WTO in 2001, although greater opening up and global integration had occurred significantly throughout the 1990s, leading up to accession. Exposure to global markets is likely to improve efficiency due to the greater competitive pressures and potential to learn from the practices and more advanced knowhow of international firms. Adding in these measures, both the extent of exporting by a firm or the province proves to be significantly positive in increasing labour productivity.

Globalisation does not solely refer to exports. The other side of the equation is long-term capital flows of FDI, primarily in the form of JVs or WOFEs. For some years, China's FDI policy was geared at attracting foreign capital which had more advanced technology. As such, China exerted considerable control over FDI through soliciting and approving investments that could help its firms upgrade and move up the value chain. Therefore, although it became less common after WTO accession when FDI controls loosened, some JVs included technology transfer agreements, whereby the foreign partner transferred technological know-how to the Chinese-foreign entity as part of the JV agreement. This is a rare measure of the direct transfer of technology often assumed to be embodied in FDI that could generate productivity gains in developing countries. By including this variable, whether such technology transfer agreements are valuable in improving labour productivity in China can be investigated.

Of the 163 Chinese-foreign joint ventures covered in the survey, some 26 had signed technology transfer agreements. These agreements are signed at the time of the formation of the JV, so should not be endogenous with respect to current firm performance. The average age of such JVs is around 8.7 years, indicating establishment in 1996–1997, which is the same mean age as JVs which did not sign technology transfer agreements. The oldest JVs were formed in 1979 at the start of market-oriented reforms. As Guangdong is included in the survey and it was one of the earliest provinces to open up right at the start of reform, the data capture the earliest to the latest JVs to receive technology transfers, the latter being in 2005. The mean value of the agreement was 14.39 million RMB, with the largest contract worth 400 million RMB. Interestingly, the Chinese side often insisted on these transfers as they were presumed to be less costly than licensing the same technology, given the monopoly pricing of intellectual property. Thus, around 43% of such agreements were bundled as part of the capital investment in the JV without payment of an additional consideration, supporting the favourable position of obtaining technology via this route instead of via the open market. Around one-fifth (21.1%) of firms reported producing new products with the technology obtained in these transfer agreements.

The results indicate that the signing of a technology transfer agreement increases labour productivity in a firm by nearly 57%, making it the largest contributor to productivity gains amongst the variables investigated in this section. The other globalisation variables also reveal an association between exports and labour productivity. The global factors hypothesised to improve value-added per worker therefore also receive support.

Labour productivity in China grew well during the 2000s, and at a pace that has been higher than in the 1990s when growth in value-added per worker was closer to 4–5% on average, whilst the current rate is nearer 6%. The increase is the outcome of significant labour market reforms during the decade of the 1990s, building on wage reforms from the 1980s. The estimations show that labour reforms that reward productive characteristics and more competitive and open markets were all positive contributing factors.

5. CONCLUSION

There remain many restrictions on labour mobility and imperfections in the urban labour market, but significant progress has been made in the past two decades. The urban labour market is undergoing reform and the wage structure is becoming more reflective of labour productivity. There are signs that China is experiencing the increased efficiency of more productivity-related wages, but also the deficiencies of permitting discretion in pay. Labour mobility is alternatively too low and too high for urban workers and migrants. Here institutional changes again impact on the extent of job matches and voluntary mobility that characterise a well-functioning labour market.

Trend productivity growth measured in terms of value-added per worker has been a strong 5.7% per annum from 2000–2005. The hypotheses that labour market reform, competition and globalisation result in increased labour productivity are supported. Improving higher education for workers and managers would improve productivity. This is consistent with high levels of secondary educational enrolment in China as compared with much lower levels of attainment of tertiary education. In the first 30 years of reform, secondary education returns have improved, as have the productivity of workers. At this stage of development, higher education is more important.

Perhaps the largest factor influencing labour productivity, though, is whether a Chinese-foreign joint venture has signed a technology transfer agreement. By signing such an agreement, labour productivity is boosted by around 57%. Not distinguishing joint ventures which have signed such agreements from those which have not, therefore, could confound the productivity gains from FDI and under-estimate the importance of China's selective policy towards foreign investors.

The findings suggest that capital infusion embodying technological know-how, as well as market-oriented reforms in factor and product markets, have made significant contributions to improving labour productivity in the 2000s. In particular, China's policy of obtaining technology as part of forming JVs appears to be successful in improving labour productivity. Labour productivity is a key factor in China's continuing growth prospects. Obtaining technology, as well as encouraging competition and further labour market reforms aimed at higher education, would be fruitful. Sustaining China's development will therefore require attention to maintaining the momentum of its market-oriented reforms as its firms seek to increase their value-added per worker, which will induce longer-term growth effects if the improvements take the form of sustained productivity enhancements.

NOTE

* See further my 'Wage Reforms in China during the 1990s', *Asian Economic Journal*, 18(2), 2004, 149–64; 'Job Mobility of Residents and Migrants in Urban China' (with John Knight), *Journal of Comparative Economics*, 32(4), 2004, 637–60; 'Competition or Segmentation in China's Urban Labour Market?' (with John Knight), *Cambridge Journal of Economics*, 33(1), 2009, 79–94; 'How Productive is Chinese Labour? The Contribution of Labour Market Reform, Globalisation and Competition', University of Oxford, Department of Economics Discussion Paper No. 418, December 2008.

5.   Entrepreneurship*

1.   INTRODUCTION

Entrepreneurship and self-employment start-ups are important drivers of growth, particularly for an economy such as China where partial marketisation relies on the rapid development of the non-state sector in the transition from central planning, as discussed in Chapter 2. China's gradualist reforms are associated with a high degree of market imperfection where many sectors are still controlled by the state and private economic activity tends to be characterised by a great deal of uncertainty as a result.

Moreover, China is a developing country where there are numerous information-related obstacles which can impede obtaining credit and starting a business. In developing countries, self-employment is challenging due to imperfect credit markets, supply chains, and product markets (Banerjee and Newman 1993). The literature on what determines entrepreneurship focuses on institutional factors, such as credit constraints (Blanchflower and Oswald 1998) and individual traits, such as a more positive attitude toward risk for those who choose to enter into self-employment or start small- and medium-sized enterprises (Rees and Shah 1986). Both sets of approaches would support the importance of a number of characteristics that foster entrepreneurship, including social networks, motivation and having the drive to achieve economic gain, as well as attitudes toward taking risks.

Moreover, China has traditionally had a cultural and historical emphasis on interpersonal relationships or *guanxi*, which informs business dealings both within and outside of China. This suggests that networking is possibly an important factor in determining non-state sector development, alongside the other noted traits such as having drive and a willingness to accept risk. Networking and developing interpersonal connects or *guanxi* were found to be important under the administered economy as well (see, for example, Bian 1994). Thus, China is a transition economy and developing country which has a significant lack of formal institutions in the areas of property rights and other features thought to be crucial for entrepreneurship, such as complete credit markets, certainty in contracting and investment protection. Nevertheless, the private sector has overtaken the

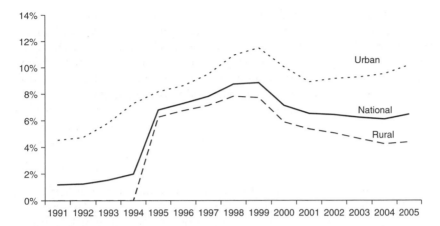

Source: China Statistical Yearbook.

Figure 5.1 Entrepreneurs as a percentage of total employment in China: national, urban and rural areas

state sector in importance even though the system is characterised by an incomplete legal system for protecting private assets, credit constraints upon private enterprises, and regulatory opacity. However, in spite of this context, there is a growing segment of entrepreneurial activity that has propelled China along its gradualist transition path and helped it to achieve remarkable growth rates. Figure 5.1 shows the rapid rise in entrepreneurs during the 1990s and 2000s.

In such an imperfect legal and financial system, it is important to know the characteristics of those who are able to enter self-employment. The dominance of informal and relation-based contracting in China suggests that the elements fostering private sector development are indeed likely to evolve around social networks, as well as other traits associated with managing uncertainty such as motivation or having sufficient drive, but also widely recognised characteristics such as embracing risk. The large-scale restructuring of the late 1990s also resulted in urban unemployment on a significant scale that can be a further factor driving self-employment.

The determinants of entrepreneurship in China, particularly in urban areas, are not particularly well understood despite the growing importance of the private sector. There are a few economic studies of self-employment in both rural and urban China (Wu 2001; Zhang et al. 2006; Mohapatra et al. 2007), as well as a pertinent cross-country survey of entrepreneurs (Djankov et al. 2006). In rural China, education is found to be the key factor in rural farmers leaving the agricultural sector for both self-employment and wage employment (Mohapatra et al. 2007). By contrast, education and Communist Party membership are deterrents in urban areas (Wu 2002). As with most issues in China, there are significant urban–rural differences, suggesting in this instance that rural residents able to move into higher value-added work are the educated ones, while more educated workers in urban areas tend to remain in the institutionally favoured wage employment if possible. Party membership is also found to be a factor that inhibits entrepreneurship, which likewise suggests that the preferred sector in urban China remains the more secure state sector.

In a cross-country survey, the most robust determinant of entrepreneurship was knowing people who had tried entrepreneurship (Djankov et al. 2006). This is consistent with the work on the importance of social networks in China (see, for example, Knight and Yueh 2008). This factor in particular points to the importance of informal relations, which is usually the case, but perhaps more crucially within an imperfect institutional context. Throughout the chapter and by the conclusion, the structural impediments to entrepreneurship will be explored and policy recommendations put forth. As with the other sectors of the economy, self-employment is heavily coloured by the wider legal and institutional set-up. Determining the traits of entrepreneurs who have managed the process will be important and pertinent to informing how reforms can proceed in developing this important segment of the economy.

2.   SELF-EMPLOYMENT AND NETWORKING

China's gradualist reforms are associated with a high degree of market imperfection, where many sectors are still controlled by the state and private economic activity tends to be characterised by a great deal of uncertainty. Moreover, China is a developing country where there are numerous information-related obstacles which can impede obtaining credit and starting a business. Social networks can arise from a need to work within imperfect formal institutions, such as a regime of uncertain property rights, or evolve in the context of community and cultural factors as well resulting from individual preferences (Portes 1998; Frye and Zhuravskaya 2000). It is likely that social networks have both an economic and non-economic function. For instance, social networks can help ease financial constraints and provide needed contacts for operating a business in a partially marketised environment such as China (Oi 1999; Zhang et al. 2006), but also serve a primarily social function with some economic uses (Komter 2005).

The dominance of informal and relations-based contracting in China suggests that the elements fostering private sector development are likely to evolve around social networks, as are other traits associated with managing uncertainty such as motivation or drive, and traditional characteristics such as the willingness to embrace risk. Moreover, China has traditionally placed a cultural and historical emphasis on interpersonal relationships or *guanxi*, which informs business dealings both within and outside of China. This suggests that networking is an important factor in determining non-state sector development in transitioning China.

Self-employment should require many of the same personal traits, such as education, as are needed by employed persons working for a wage, in a transition labour market. However, the self-employed must also contend with the need to obtain credit to start a business and buy inventory, gain access to suppliers and distributors, as well as having the knowledge to navigate the uncertain regulatory and legal environment in China where licences are often required to start a business. Social networks would be useful in all of these respects.

2.1 Credit and Supply Networks

In China, self-employed persons often encounter severe credit constraints due to the credit allocation system which is skewed toward state-owned enterprises (SOEs) (Fan 1994; Lin 2007). Small- and medium-sized enterprises find it difficult to obtain credit and often rely on family and friends, including in the form of remittances from family members abroad, to start a business (Oi 1999). Alternatively, self-employed persons use their social networks to arrange for inventory to be issued without advance payment. Anything which is sold is then split between the vendor and the supplier of the inventory, as with peddlers receiving their goods in advance. The author encountered this type of trust-based relationship in conducting a household survey in China, notably in Liaoning, which has a substantial proportion of heavy industry that was hard hit by the large-scale downsizing of the SOEs in the late 1990s. Access to suppliers and distributors is a significant challenge in a partially marketised economy, and having a social network would facilitate self-employment by helping to overcome such obstacles (see, for example, Wu 2001). With the stagnation of the state-owned sector during this period and the beginning of market liberalisation facilitating the growth of the non-state sector, it is also likely that urban workers began to seek other sources of income and thus became self-employed.

When asked the main reason why the respondent started his or her own business in the 1999 CHIP urban household survey, 37% of the survey respondents said that it was because he or she had the requisite skills and experience, 7% had funds, 11% had real estate, and 17% started a business by joining with relatives. The remaining 27% chose 'other' category. As this was during the period of the *xiagang* policy where there were large-scale layoffs in the SOE sector, it is likely that some became self-employed or more likely small goods peddlers out of necessity. Given the small proportion of the self-employed that started with their own funds, credit is likely to be a constraint that social networks can help with by improving information flows about attaining credit or indeed providing access to credit through personal networks. This figure may be understated since having funds may be a subsidiary reason and respondents were limited to one response. Having real estate in China suggests a social network because all urban land is state-owned and land/buildings were only beginning to become privatised in the latter part of the reform period. Those who had the resource of real estate would likely have had the connections to attain such an asset. This finding supports the argument that one of the motivations for entering self-employment is having overcome credit constraints.

2.2 Navigating an Uncertain Institutional Environment

China has an imperfect legal system with a great deal of regulatory complexity (Chen 2003, Clarke 2003). In such an environment, having the contacts and know-how to obtain a licence would be important. Oi (1999) considers *guanxi* the operational code for getting things done in China. Indeed, licences and permissions are needed not only for starting a business but also for the transport of goods at the city and provincial levels. A social network would help in this instance. Interpersonal relationships would also reduce the costs of enforcement in such a system where trusted individuals are preferred in the absence of an effective legal system (see, for example, Yang 1994; Yan 1996; Kipnis 1997). Networking would increase information flows and reduce the transaction costs of starting a business.

The second most important reason for starting one's own business reported in the survey was the opportunity to join relatives, as well as knowing others who were also entering entrepreneurship. This is consistent with the self-employment literature which emphasises the importance of knowing friends or relatives who are entrepreneurs (see, for example, Blanchflower and Oswald 1998; Djankov et al. 2005) and joint ownership with relatives would ease a number of obstacles. Starting a business with relatives and others who have done it before supports the contention that networking can assist in navigating an uncertain institutional environment if the self-employed person knows others who have knowledge of how to conduct business in an uncertain context, such as helping to obtain licences to operate. Joining with relatives also reduces the transaction costs of enforcement should problems arise. Thus, networking should help with self-employment in urban China.

The above factors suggest the importance of social networks and where they might perform an economic function. This chapter will therefore investigate whether social networks are a significant determinant of self-employment and will hypothesise that having a social network is important in the choice to become self-employed in urban China. It may well be that some people are more entrepreneurial in that they have greater drive or willingness to embrace risk. This can be measured separately in some segments of our data set to see if networks still have an effect if these often observed traits are accounted for.

3. CHINA'S ENTREPRENEURS

The 1999 CHIP survey discussed in the last chapter is used in the estimations. Although the survey was not designed to be a study of entrepreneurship, the detailed information on income, employment and personal characteristics allows for investigations of entrepreneurs in urban China. As such, those who are entrepreneurial but did not start their own firm or become self-employed but would rather work in other firms are not measured in this survey. Again, the total sample size of the 1999 survey is 4500 urban households and around 9000 working-age individuals. The survey covered six provinces and 13 cities. Given the breadth of the survey, there is no need to attempt to normalise the sample as with smaller-scale data typically used in studies of entrepreneurship.

The questionnaire includes both household and individual-level responses. There are 359 individuals in the sample who report that they are self-employed and started their own business. This sample constitutes nearly 4% of all urban workers. This definition would preclude those entrepreneurs who work in formal employment or run privatised state-owned enterprises or joint ventures or the like. There are certainly entrepreneurs who are not self-employed and perhaps run privatised state-owned enterprises, but the data do not permit an investigation of those individuals; only of those who report themselves as self-employed in starting their own firms. However, starting privately owned firms is an important element of transition and economic development and our survey does allow us to explore the traits of those who start their own businesses in urban China.

There is no information on the size of these firms, but there is some limited information on profitability. Most respondents did not answer this question in the survey, perhaps because it is phrased as reporting on the profitability of an 'enterprise' and the common conception of an enterprise

is a state-owned enterprise (SOE). Of those who did answer (30% of the
sample of the self-employed), only 5.6% reported themselves as having
made a 'high profit' that year. The majority (62.9%) reported 'marginal
profit', while the remainder declared that they were making a loss or on
the verge of bankruptcy.

3.1   The Traits of Entrepreneurs

Figure 5.2 and Table 5.1 compare the traits of entrepreneurs and non-
entrepreneurs (or the wage-employed). The reported figures are conditional means of the differences between the two groups.

3.1.1   Personal traits

There are no significant differences in the mean age of entrepreneurs as
compared with non-entrepreneurs nor in their years of education attained
or marital status. The difference in years of employment experience is
notable. Entrepreneurs have on average a decade less experience than
non-entrepreneurs. The likely interpretation of this question in the context
of China is experience in paid employment, as the lifetime employment
system or 'iron rice bowl' was only gradually dismantled, starting in the

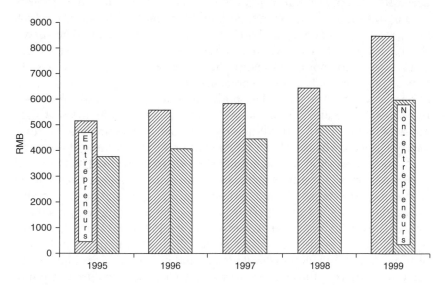

Source: China Household Income Project.

*Figure 5.2   Annual income of entrepreneurs versus non-entrepreneurs,
1995–1999*

Table 5.1   Differences between entrepreneurs and non-entrepreneurs

Personal characteristics	Entrepreneurs	Non-entrepreneurs	Significance of mean difference
Age	36.2	37.2	Insignificant
Years of employment experience	12.9	22.6	***
Experienced layoff	26.6%	19.2%	***
Years of education	9.2	9.4	Insignificant
Gender	55.7% male 44.3% female	49.7% male 51.3% female	***
Marital status	83.4% married	84.2% married	Insignificant
Communist Party member	6.2%	17.7%	***
Social network (size)	8.2	6.4	***
Socio-economic background			
Father's education (years)	5.4	5.2	Insignificant
Mother's education (years)	6.0	5.9	Insignificant
Father is Party member	26.5%	34.2%	Insignificant
Mother is Party member	8.7%	10.8%	Insignificant
Father is self-employed	3.9%	2.8%	Insignificant
Mother is self-employed	1.7%	1.8%	Insignificant
Father is non-manual worker	22.3%	28.4%	Insignificant
Mother is non-manual worker	8.1%	13.7%	**
Income and attitudes			
Annual income (RMB)	9526	7429	***
Average income (RMB), 1995-1998	6474	5365	***
Main considerations when choosing a job[1]			
Wage level	3.6	3.6	Insignificant
Social security provision	3.2	3.3	Insignificant

Table 5.1   (continued)

Personal characteristics	Entrepreneurs	Non-entrepreneurs	Significance of mean difference
Job stability	3.3	3.5	*
Work condition	2.7	2.8	Insignificant
Being able to learn skills	2.9	2.9	Insignificant
Job dignity	2.0	2.1	**
Have the importance of the following factors that influence household income changed compared with before?[2]			
Education	2.3	2.2	*
Political status	2.1	2.1	Insignificant
Rank of work unit	2.1	2.1	Insignificant
Social connections	2.2	2.2	Insignificant
Local urban *hukou* (household registration system)	1.9	1.9	Insignificant
Do you hope that your children will become self-employed?[3]	1.9	2.2	***

Notes:
*** indicates significance at the 1% level, ** at the 5% level, and * at the 10% level in a two-tailed t-test for equality of means.
[1]   Answers are ranked 1–4, with 4 being very important and 0 as unimportant.
[2]   Answers are (1) decreased; (2) unchanged; (3) increased.
[3]   Answers are ranked 1–4, where 1 indicates no and 4 is very much.

Source: China Household Income Project, urban survey, 1999.

mid 1990s, and working in an SOE is what urban residents would consider to be employment experience when answering the question. This would suggest that entrepreneurs have on average around 10 years of experience starting their own businesses which would be consistent with China's liberalisation of its consumer markets in particular in the early 1990s which created an opportunity to start a business in consumer goods. Entrepreneurs are also more likely to have experienced being laid-off during the large-scale restructuring of the mid-to-late 1990s of the SOEs, thus prompting them to start their own business.

3.1.2 Social networks and Chinese Communist Party membership

There are notably significant differences distinguishing the entrepreneurs from the non-entrepreneurs in terms of Communist Party membership and their social networks. Whereas nearly 20% of all employed persons are Party members, only 6% of entrepreneurs are members. If Party members are more likely to be allocated desirable jobs and less likely to be laid-off, then that could contribute to their lesser likelihood of leaving the more secure lifetime employment for self-employment, which is more risky. Finally, entrepreneurs have significantly more contacts in their social networks than non-entrepreneurs. The difference in the conditional mean size of their respective social networks could be important in understanding entrepreneurship. The size of social networks is determined by asking for the reported number of close contacts of an individual in any context, social or economic. The survey question asked: 'In the past year, how many relatives, friends, colleagues or acquaintances did you exchange gifts with or often maintain contact?' The mean size of social network is 6.4 persons and has a reasonable dispersion for non-entrepreneurs. For entrepreneurs, they have on average around two more persons in their networks, giving them substantially larger social networks than non-entrepreneurs.

3.1.3 Socio-economic background

The next set of comparisons is of socio-economic background by examining the differences in family circumstances of both groups. There are no significant differences except for mother's occupation. Fewer entrepreneurs have mothers who are professional or non-manual workers as compared with non-entrepreneurs, though there are no notable differences in the father's occupation or in any other parental characteristic, including whether the parents were themselves entrepreneurs. Given the prevalence of state-owned sector employment in the earlier generation, it is not unexpected that there were few self-employed among the parents. Knight and Yueh (2004) find that 78% of urban residents in the late 1990s were still in their first allocated jobs. The importance of mother's occupation could suggest that entrepreneurs from less established backgrounds were hungrier for success and therefore pursued self-employment.

3.1.4 Income and attitudes

The final set of comparisons is of income and attitudes toward income and work. Entrepreneurs make nearly 30% more than non-entrepreneurs in the survey year of 1999, which is a significant difference in their conditional mean income after controlling for age, gender, education, employment experience, occupation, employment sector, and locale (cities). This is despite more entrepreneurs having experienced being laid-off, which typically reduces income upon re-employment. The survey also included recall data of annual income over the previous four years. When comparing the average income from 1995–98, entrepreneurs made more than 20% more than non-entrepreneurs. The trend confirms that the higher earnings of entrepreneurs are not a one-off phenomenon. Moreover, the maximum earned income for entrepreneurs was RMB 200000, while it was RMB 93780 for non-entrepreneurs. Earning this income is also associated with more variability as the standard deviation of the mean annual income for entrepreneurs was RMB 15480 as compared with RMB 5980 for non-entrepreneurs.

Entrepreneurs and non-entrepreneurs have similar attitudes toward most of the usual job considerations. They both value wages, social securities, learning skills on the job, and good work conditions. However, they differ in that entrepreneurs do not worry as much about job stability or about job dignity. The attitude of non-entrepreneurs is consistent with the administered job allocation system in which the desirable jobs are in the state-owned sector and urban workers would not accept undesirable jobs outside the state sector, leaving room for migrants to enter the labour market, as analysed in Chapter 4. The self-employed are less concerned.

In terms of attitudes toward the factors which affect income, entrepreneurs and non-entrepreneurs are very similar except that entrepreneurs believe more strongly that education is a more important determinant of earnings than before. As entrepreneurs have similar levels of education as non-entrepreneurs but are more likely to have experienced the labour market, this attitudinal measure picks up the general trend of greater reward for human capital in China discussed in the last chapter.

The final attitudinal question asked whether the respondent wished for his or her children to become self-employed. Interestingly, entrepreneurs differed significantly from non-entrepreneurs. Entrepreneurs were less inclined for their own children to become self-employed. This result may pick up the risks and challenges of being self-employed in the transition stage of China's economy, and perhaps also the lingering perception that state-sector employment remains the preferred sector. This is despite the incomes of entrepreneurs being significantly higher than those of non-entrepreneurs.

3.1.5   Migrants

Table 5.2 presents the traits of entrepreneurs further divided into urban residents and migrants, again with conditional means reported to assess the significance of any differences between these groups. All personal characteristics – except for the gender balance between migrant and non-migrant entrepreneurs and the size of their respective social networks – are

Table 5.2 Traits of urban versus migrant entrepreneurs

Personal characteristics	Entrepreneurs (urban residents)	Entrepreneurs (migrants)	Significance of mean difference
Age	36.5	33.3	***
Gender	58.4% male	55.6% male	
	41.6% female	44.4% female	Insignificant
Marital status	78.5% married	92.5% married	***
Education (in years)	10.1	8.0	***
Employment experience (in years)	12.7	9.2	**
Experienced layoff	28.9%	12.9%	**
Communist Party member	5.8%	2.4%	***
Social network (size)	8.2	7.8	Insignificant
Income and wealth (RMB)			
Annual income	8425	11 227	***
Total household net wealth (assets minus debts)	11 778	13 511	Insignificant
Saved funds for family business	8687	5798	Insignificant
Debts incurred for family business	4027	2218	Insignificant

Notes:
1. *** indicates significance at the 1% level, ** at the 5% level, and * at the 10% level in a two-tailed t-test for equality of means.
2. For migrants, years of employment experience in the urban economy are reported.

Source: China Household Income Project, urban survey, 1999.

significant. Whereas the wage-employed have a nearly 50-50 gender mix, some 58% of urban firm owners and 56% of migrant entrepreneurs are male, reflecting a significant male share of business start-ups in China. The sizes of their social networks are not significantly different. However, social networks of migrant entrepreneurs are much larger by an alternative measure which did not specifically ask about maintaining contact, but just asked about the number of relatives, fellow villagers (*lao xian*) – a very important relation in China, and friends or acquaintances that he or she has in the city. The mean size of that network is 14.4 persons, which is inflated by the assessment of the fellow villager category.

Migrant entrepreneurs are around three years younger on average than urban resident entrepreneurs. More (over 90% of) migrants are married, as compared to urban firm owners (79%). There are also significant differences in average years of education. The most educated are the urban entrepreneurs who have completed around ten years of education, followed by the urban wage-employed with nine years and migrants who have eight years.

Unsurprisingly, urban entrepreneurs are also more likely to have experienced being laid-off during the large-scale restructuring of the SOEs during the late 1990s, thus prompting them to start their own business. A smaller proportion of migrant entrepreneurs had experienced layoffs, but that could reflect their exclusion from SOEs and permanent jobs and having had short-term contracts that would terminate rather than result in redundancy.

The final set of comparisons is of income and wealth. There are significant differences in mean incomes, but insignificant differences in wealth and debts as between urban and migrant entrepreneurs. Recall that urban entrepreneurs make around 30% more than non-entrepreneurs, which is a significant difference in their conditional mean income after controlling for age, gender, education, employment experience, occupation, employment sector, and locale (cities). This is despite more entrepreneurs having experienced being laid-off, which typically reduces income upon re-employment. Impressively, migrant entrepreneurs make nearly twice the income of the wage-employed, and 25% more than urban business owners, despite having fewer years of education and facing tougher institutional constraints such as prohibitions on settling in cities. This is all the more impressive considering their annual income prior to coming to urban areas was just RMB 1500 as compared with RMB 11227 earned after migrating, reflecting a substantial increase in income through migration. It is possible that because they are less able to claim the social security support granted to urban residents in urban areas, such as a pension, they are more likely to work hard and seek to earn more income. However, as the conditional mean controls for differences in net assets, which includes measures of in-kind support such as social security for urban residents, it remains a significant difference once net wealth is taken into account.

In terms of measures of wealth, there are no significant differences between the two types of entrepreneurs. Total household net wealth, calculated as assets minus debts, is RMB 20250 for the wage-employed, while it is RMB 11778 for urban entrepreneurs and slightly higher at RMB 13511 for migrants. Unsurprisingly, the entrepreneurs have much more savings geared to their businesses (RMB 8687 for urban residents and RMB 5798 for migrants) as compared to around RMB 2000 that the wage-employed have saved for family businesses. These savings might be geared toward a future family business or it may reflect savings to lend to relatives starting a business. Urban entrepreneurs have the largest share of debt (RMB 4027), as compared with migrant entrepreneurs who owe half of that amount (RMB 2218). Non-entrepreneurs also report debt of around RMB 2000 incurred for family business, which again may reflect family pooling of resources for a future endeavour. It appears that although entrepreneurs are richer than the wage-employed in terms of income, they have less wealth, presumably because their assets are tied up in their businesses in a credit-constrained environment where businesses are funded through own or familial savings.

3.1.6 The secondarily self-employed

In addition to the approximately 4% of all urban workers who are solely self-employed (including migrants), there are another 80 individuals who are both employed and also report themselves to be self-employed, suggesting that they are working for themselves as secondary employment. During the late 1990s when employment was becoming increasingly insecure, this is perhaps not surprising. It is also possible that they are temporary workers and turn to self employment during periods when they are out of work. They constitute just under 1% of all urban workers, so taken together the self-employed (solely and as second jobs) constitute around 5% of all urban workers.

Those who are self-employed as a second job are similar in profile to the self-employed, though they are slightly younger on average, have fewer years of employment experience, and fewer are married. Notably, nearly one-third had experienced unemployment in the previous five years, perhaps explaining why this group seeks out additional income to stave off insecurity in employment. Those who are solely self-employed also have greater experience of layoff, around 27% of the sample. Membership of the Chinese Communist Party provides a stark contrast with urban workers: whereas nearly 18% of employed persons are Party members, only 6% of self-employed are members and 7% of the secondarily self-employed are. If Party members are more likely to be allocated desirable jobs and less likely to be laid-off, then that could contribute to their lesser likelihood of needing self-employment, which is more risky.

3.2 The Determinants of Entrepreneurship

This section now turns to the determinants of entrepreneurship for the two types of self-employment. As outlined above, there are likely to be different characteristics and drivers for those who are self-employed in addition to their paid employment, so the empirical findings separately analyse those who are entirely self-employed and developing China's private sector from the ground level from those who are self-employed as a second job to supplement their income; although it would also be interesting to investigate the motivation of the latter, who take advantage of China's marketisation to develop opportunities. There may be different traits that influence self-employment for the solely self-employed who leave the security of paid employment and enter and start private sector activities. Also, with the high rate of experience of unemployment in this sample, there might also be different determinants for those who entered self-employment after experience of unemployment. As such, these three groups will be assessed separately.

Tables 5.3–5.5 identify the factors influencing the likelihood of becoming self-employed for the three groups, i.e., wholly self-employed, self-employed as a second job, and those who become self-employed after experiencing unemployment. Separate estimations will be undertaken for men and women within each table. The multinomial logit regressions allow for three outcomes: wage-employed, self-employed as a second job and self-employed. The coefficients on the explanatory variables represent an increase or decrease in the probability of self-employment.

The findings of the main sample of the self-employed are generally consistent with studies of self-employment that find that knowing people who are entrepreneurial or having connections increases the likelihood of entrepreneurship (see, for example, Rees and Shah 1986, Djankov et al. 2005, 2006, Zhang et al. 2006). The social network variable is significantly positive and remains robustly so for the entire sample and for the sub-samples of men and women. As seen in columns (3)–(5), a one person increase in the size of a social network will increase the probability of self-employment by 1.9%. It is not a large effect, but if a social network were to be expanded by ten persons, then the probability of self-employment would rise by 19% and so forth.

Amongst the personal characteristics, the significant and negative coefficient on female gender implies that being a woman reduces the probability of self-employment, as do years of education and wage employment experience, as well as Party membership. Age, by contrast, increases the probability. Experience of unemployment in the previous five years also raises the probability of self-employment. This variable was insignificant in columns (1) and (2) before the social network variable was included, suggesting that there was omitted variable bias from not accounting for social networks. If the wrong variables are included, the estimates are inefficient but not biased. In this instance, those who had experienced unemployment are more likely to become self-employed once their social networks are

Table 5.3 *Determinants of self-employment, urban sample, multinomial logit regression (robust standard errors in parentheses)*

Self-employed	(1)	(2)	(3)	(4)	(5)	(6) Men	(7) Men	(8) Women	(9) Women
Social network			0.0191***	0.0192***	0.0191***	0.0218**	0.0198*	0.0162*	0.0175*
			(0.0063)	(0.0072)	(0.0072)	(0.0090)	(0.0105)	(0.0085)	(0.0103)
Personal characteristics									
Gender	-0.6298**	-0.9490***	-0.7394***	-1.0108***	-1.0031***				
	(0.2714)	(0.1542)	(0.1488)	(0.1689)	(0.1907)				
Age	-0.0066	0.0194**	0.0201**	0.0249**	0.0249**	0.0354***	0.0355**	0.0039	0.0097
	(0.0228)	(0.0094)	(0.0095)	(0.0100)	(0.0120)	(0.0118)	(0.0156)	(0.0147)	(0.0200)
Years of education	-0.1011*	-0.1069***	-0.1014***	-0.0992***	-0.1014***	-0.1287***	-0.1631***	-0.1016*	-0.0488
	(0.0577)	(0.0337)	(0.0350)	(0.0369)	(0.0361)	(0.0420)	(0.0478)	(0.0578)	(0.0633)
Years of wage employment experience	-0.1459***	-0.1524***	-0.1383***	-0.1511***	-0.1527***	-0.1197***	-0.1319***	-0.1931***	-0.2125***
	(0.0268)	(0.0147)	(0.0135)	(0.0159)	(0.0152)	(0.0181)	(0.0206)	(0.0216)	(0.0266)
Communist Party member	-0.3669	-1.2939***	-1.2486***	-1.1777***	-1.2054***	-1.3351***	-1.2966***	-0.9060	-0.6736
	(0.4969)	(0.3690)	(0.3716)	(0.3805)	(0.3658)	(0.4268)	(0.4315)	(0.7984)	(0.7585)
Experienced unemployment	0.5052	0.2993	0.3876*	0.4857**	0.4837**	0.5303**	0.6068**	0.2548	0.2581
	(0.3507)	(0.2080)	(0.1991)	(0.2195)	(0.2070)	(0.2519)	(0.2775)	(0.2935)	(0.3350)
Spouse characteristics									
Married		0.4480		0.4316	0.4643		0.2663	0.8046	
		(0.2807)		(0.3225)	(0.2953)		(0.3673)	(0.5374)	
Spouse in wage-employment		0.2681		0.2995	0.2754		0.0918	0.2059	
		(0.2032)		(0.2271)	(0.2246)		(0.3437)	(0.3439)	
Spouse in self-employment		5.1171***		5.1220***	5.0946***		6.6538***	4.8282***	
		(0.5117)		(0.4896)	(0.5150)		(1.0703)	(0.6849)	

Table 5.3   (continued)

Self-employed	(1)	(2)	(3)	(4)	(5)	(6) Men	(7) Men	(8) Women	(9) Women
Socio-economic background									
Father's educational attainment:									
College and above	0.5558	0.7248	0.4856	0.6689	0.6262	0.7501	0.9186	-0.0453	0.2452
	(0.7670)	(0.4423)	(0.4563)	(0.4593)	(0.4810)	(0.5359)	(0.5915)	(0.9539)	(0.9165)
Professional school	0.2305	0.1082	-0.2635	-0.1160	-0.0977	-0.3138	-0.0420	-0.3919	-0.2661
	(0.5713)	(0.3419)	(0.3401)	(0.3569)	(0.4004)	(0.4525)	(0.5175)	(0.6297)	(0.6581)
Secondary school	-0.2833	0.1099	-0.1172	-0.0558	-0.0383	-0.1759	0.0085	-0.0622	-0.1469
	(0.4418)	(0.2752)	(0.2759)	(0.2964)	(0.2972)	(0.3495)	(0.3966)	(0.4504)	(0.4728)
Primary school	-0.1797	0.0612	-0.1423	-0.0879	-0.0686	-0.3553	-0.2169	0.1451	0.0863
	(0.4396)	(0.2463)	(0.2494)	(0.2605)	(0.2683)	(0.3266)	(0.3565)	(0.3861)	(0.4375)
Mother's educational attainment:									
College and above	-0.1707	-0.6176	-0.8978	-0.8618	-0.8192	-0.4624	-0.4860	–	–
	(1.1786)	(0.7255)	(0.8503)	(0.8576)	(0.8584)	(0.9163)	(0.9358)		
Professional school	-1.2328	-0.9848**	-0.7996	-0.7766	-0.7646	-0.9135	-0.9594	-0.4624	-0.3435
	(0.8394)	(0.4613)	(0.5258)	(0.5006)	(0.5015)	(0.6445)	(0.6582)	(0.8472)	(0.8300)
Secondary school	-0.0723	-0.5121*	-0.3888	-0.2532	-0.2710	-0.1268	-0.2546	-0.7264	-0.4992
	(0.4443)	(0.2874)	(0.3064)	(0.3135)	(0.2998)	(0.3615)	(0.3940)	(0.5444)	(0.4925)
Primary school	0.1980	-0.5818**	-0.3269	-0.4039	-0.4018	-0.6496*	-0.7987**	0.0039	-0.0221
	(0.4366)	(0.2525)	(0.2725)	(0.2808)	(0.2662)	(0.3828)	(0.3841)	(0.3824)	(0.3960)
Father is/was a Communist Party member	-0.3159	-0.2388	-0.0692	-0.0884	-0.1111	0.0693	-0.0086	-0.2076	-0.2746
	(0.3396)	(0.2051)	(0.2069)	(0.2091)	(0.2137)	(0.2438)	(0.2805)	(0.3413)	(0.3598)
Mother is/was a Communist Party member	0.0930	0.3249	0.2880	0.2505	0.2770	0.4170	0.5823	-0.0454	-0.3819
	(0.4639)	(0.2973)	(0.2982)	(0.3012)	(0.3165)	(0.3745)	(0.3723)	(0.5198)	(0.6420)
Father's occupation	0.0433	0.0127	0.0070	0.0007	-0.0007	-0.0145	-0.0329	0.0214	0.0228
	(0.0569)	(0.0325)	(0.0325)	(0.0339)	(0.0353)	(0.0380)	(0.0466)	(0.0610)	(0.0575)

Mother's occupation	0.0638	0.0688*	0.0672*	0.0670*	0.0690*	0.0949**	0.0980*	0.0217	0.0265
	(0.0572)	(0.0370)	(0.0380)	(0.0399)	(0.0384)	(0.0476)	(0.0503)	(0.0685)	(0.0636)
Father's employment sector	−0.0405	0.0040	−0.0054	−0.0000	0.0001	0.0114	0.0146	−0.0325	−0.0265
	(0.0340)	(0.0190)	(0.0188)	(0.0201)	(0.0206)	(0.0258)	(0.0268)	(0.0313)	(0.0332)
Mother's employment sector	0.0110	−0.0021	−0.0032	0.0054	0.0049	−0.0267	−0.0225	0.0244	0.0399
	(0.0289)	(0.0173)	(0.0171)	(0.0184)	(0.0186)	(0.0240)	(0.0250)	(0.0263)	(0.0290)
Variance of income					9.02e-10***		9.01e-10***		−4.49e-09
					(2.60e-10)		(2.70e-10)		(7.41e-09)
City dummies	Yes	Yes	Yes	Yes	Yes	Yes	Yes	Yes	Yes
Constant	−1.4020	−1.0476	−0.8239	−1.4069*	−1.3950*	−1.4760*	−1.2446	−0.2612	−1.8209
	(1.2475)	(0.7202)	(0.7522)	(0.7476)	(0.8210)	(0.8652)	(1.0285)	(1.2674)	(1.4600)
Wald χ^2 (64)	489.48***								
Wald χ^2 (66)		19880.40***				23359.13***		36961.48***	
LR χ^2 (72)			24171.06***	495.88***					
LR χ^2 (74)					532.16***		294.41***		336.31***
Pseudo R^2	0.1821	0.2329	0.2276	0.1811	0.2410	0.1904	0.2431	0.2675	0.3379
Number of observations	8382	8382	7405	7405	7405	3769	3769	3636	3636

Notes:
1. Dependent variable: 2 if wholly self-employed, 1 if self-employed in a second job, and 0 if wage employed. The results for dependent variable = 2 are reported here.
2. Robust standard errors adjusted for clustering at the household level are computed.
3. *** indicates significance at the 1% level, ** at the 5% level, and * at the 10% level.
4. Instead of a Wald test, the attitude toward risk equations uses the variance of five years of income in the specification, so the likelihood used for the estimation is a true distribution of the sample and a likelihood ratio test is employed.
5. The coefficients on variables measuring parental education have been omitted where the estimates are subject to multicollinearity due to the small number of observations within the sub-sample.

also measured, as both positively increase the prospects of starting one's business and are correlated.

Amongst the spousal traits, the only significant factor for self-employment is having a spouse in self-employment and not marital status or whether a spouse is in wage employment. This variable is significant across estimations and suggests that having a spouse who is also self-employed is a strong predictor of one's own self-employment. It leads to a supposition that these are family-run businesses and strengthens the view that joining with relatives can be a strong motivator for self-employment, consistent with the responses to the questionnaire.

Among the socio-economic background factors, only mothers in more skilled occupations increase the probability of self-employment. Mothers in higher-skilled occupations could provide the aspiration for their children to seek higher incomes via self-employment and step out of the lifetime job system. Father's background has no significant impact.

The attitude toward risk variable is also positive and highly significant. The variance of income positively increases the likelihood of self-employment. As a proxy for risk, this suggests that the self-employed are more risk-loving than employed workers and that the variability in income increases the prospect of self-employment. The rest of the explanatory variables are virtually unchanged, implying a robustness of the results.

For both men and women, social networks increase the probability of becoming self-employed; the effect for men is slightly larger than that for women. There are other gender differences, though. Whereas having more education and work experience as well as being a Party member will reduce the probability, being older and having been unemployed increases it for men, whereas only employment experience reduces the probability for women. For both, having a spouse who is self-employed is important. For men, having a father who had only a primary school level of education attainment reduces the likelihood of self-employment, while a mother being in a skilled profession increases it. For women, socio-economic background does not matter. Men who are self-employed are also more risk-loving, while this is not the case for women.

Therefore, in urban China, the probability of becoming solely self-employed is driven by social networks as well as personal and household traits, more so than socio-economic background. There are gender differences in that attitudes toward risk do not affect women nor do most personal characteristics, but social networks are significant determinants for both men and women.

The overall findings support the basic hypothesis that those with networks are more likely to overcome the institutional constraints in China to start a business. Those who have social networks could be more likely to attain credit, have access to suppliers and distributors, and obtain the requisite licences to operate. The social network variable in the occupational choice regression could also pick up the economic effects of personality traits that are associated with the drive for success. Indeed, the self-employed have larger networks than the wage-employed.

Examining the sample of individuals who started their own businesses as a second job, Table 5.4 reveals that their determinants are rather different from the solely self-employed group. Social networks do not matter for the entire sample or the sub-samples of men and women. There are none who have a self-employed spouse, but marriage and whether one's spouse was in wage employment are both significant, unlike those who are solely self-employed. Being married reduces the probability of self-employment, while having a spouse in wage employment increases the likelihood of undertaking self-employment as a second job. Being married could provide more security so that taking a second job is less necessary, while having an employed spouse could provide the resources needed to start a business. Socio-economic background influences were similar to those in sole self-employment. Attitudes toward risk, however, did not matter for this group, including when men and women are estimated separately. This is presumably because they are self-employed as a second job, so there is less risk as they are still earning regular income. For men who are self-employed as a second job, more years of education and employment as well as being married reduce the likelihood, while having experienced unemployment induces taking on a second job in the form of working for oneself. For women, as with those who are solely self-employed, only more employment experience deters self-employment as a second job.

The profile of this group reveals that social networks do not play a role. This may mean that this group earns some additional income through some side work, but the demands are less than those who are solely self-employed.

Table 5.5 shows the findings for the sub-sample of the two groups of self-employed with experience of unemployment. This sub-sample was given an additional module with questions about motivation and attitudes. It is thus possible to investigate the robustness of the importance of social networks and the other identified traits related to self-employment, while also adding considerations of drive and motivation. However, the additional motivation measures are not found to be significant, while social networks continue to be significant for the wholly self-employed and not significant for the secondarily self-employed. In column (1), the coefficient on the variable indicating a motivation to improve one's own skills was -0.7583, with a z-statistic of -0.93, while the coefficient on the other

Table 5.4 Determinants of self-employment as a second job, urban sample, multinomial logit regression (robust standard errors in parentheses)

Self-employed as second job	(1)	(2)	(3)	(4)	(5)	(6) Men	(7) Men	(8) Women	(9) Women
Social network			−0.0151 (0.0269)	−0.0134 (0.0273)	−0.0134 (0.0310)	−0.0088 (0.0272)	−0.0045 (0.0360)	−0.0197 (0.0418)	−0.0237 (0.0514)
Personal characteristics									
Gender	−0.6298** (0.2714)	−0.6617** (0.2835)	−0.5610* (0.3136)	−0.5731* (0.3252)	−1.0108*** (0.1689)				
Age	−0.0066 (0.0228)	0.0004 (0.0215)	−0.0161 (0.0250)	−0.0080 (0.0245)	0.0249** (0.0100)	−0.0043 (0.0306)	0.0070 (0.0377)	−0.0317 (0.0346)	−0.0342 (0.0347)
Years of education	−0.1011* (0.0577)	−0.1045* (0.0585)	−0.1326* (0.0687)	−0.1373* (0.0702)	−0.0992*** (0.0369)	−0.1672* (0.0862)	−0.1639* (0.0870)	−0.1284 (0.0989)	−0.1324 (0.0984)
Years of wage employment experience	−0.1459*** (0.0268)	−0.1389*** (0.0269)	−0.1396*** (0.0295)	−0.1332*** (0.0298)	−0.1511*** (0.0159)	−0.1286*** (0.0352)	−0.1157*** (0.0446)	−0.1765*** (0.0478)	−0.1837*** (0.0442)
Communist Party member	−0.3669 (0.4969)	−0.3094 (0.4980)	−0.1052 (0.5233)	−0.0449 (0.5259)	−1.1777*** (0.3805)	0.0981 (0.6470)	0.1627 (0.5780)	−0.2988 (1.0364)	−0.2128 (1.0840)
Experienced unemployment in previous 5 years	0.5052 (0.3507)	0.7291* (0.4064)	0.5972 (0.4070)	0.8163* (0.4720)	0.4857** (0.2195)	1.7459*** (0.5106)	1.9255*** (0.4538)	−0.9813 (0.7081)	−0.8739 (0.7019)
Spouse characteristics									
Married		−0.7787* (0.4589)		−0.8117* (0.5258)	−0.8084* (0.4280)		−1.2794** (0.5769)		0.0469 (0.7159)
Spouse in wage employment		0.7835* (0.4158)		0.7158* (0.4692)	0.7141* (0.3746)		0.5081 (0.6267)		0.6082 (0.5608)

Socio-economic background

Father's educational attainment:

	(1)	(2)	(3)	(4)	(5)	(6)	(7)	(8)	(9)
College and above	0.5558 (0.7670)	0.5351 (0.7603)	0.3572 (0.7452)	0.3238 (0.7233)	0.6689 (0.4593)	1.0031 (0.8767)	0.8950 (1.0032)	−1.0285 (0.9956)	−1.0542 (1.5746)
Professional school	0.2305 (0.5713)	0.2065 (0.5828)	−0.3068 (0.6383)	−0.3502 (0.6580)	−0.1160 (0.3569)	−0.5970 (1.0204)	−0.7370 (1.0284)	−0.0451 (0.9872)	−0.0129 (0.9918)
Secondary school	−0.2833 (0.4418)	−0.3263 (0.4485)	−0.4985 (0.4609)	−0.5626 (0.4655)	−0.0558 (0.2964)	−0.3238 (0.7057)	−0.4086 (0.6884)	−0.5689 (0.5918)	−0.5857 (0.7914)
Primary school	−0.1797 (0.4396)	−0.1964 (0.4428)	−0.8190 (0.5042)	−0.8644* (0.5095)	−0.0879 (0.2605)	−0.7760 (0.6449)	−0.8035 (0.6533)	−1.1587 (0.8366)	−1.1661 (0.8318)

Mother's educational attainment:

	(1)	(2)	(3)	(4)	(5)	(6)	(7)	(8)	(9)
College and above	−0.1707 (1.1786)	−0.1099 (1.1845)	0.0157 (1.2235)	0.0550 (1.2159)	−0.8618 (0.8576)	−	−	1.6330 (1.3322)	1.8371 (1.6551)
Professional school	−1.2328 (0.8394)	−1.2427 (0.8593)	−0.9126 (0.8911)	−0.9471 (0.9148)	−0.7766 (0.5006)	−	−	−0.5409 (1.2988)	−0.4802 (1.2601)
Secondary school	−0.0723 (0.4443)	−0.0867 (0.4542)	−0.0168 (0.4946)	−0.0364 (0.5062)	−0.2532 (0.3135)	0.1892 (0.5952)	0.0023 (0.7160)	−0.2987 (0.7713)	−0.1605 (0.8935)
Primary school	0.1980 (0.4366)	0.2140 (0.4414)	0.5346 (0.4728)	0.5703 (0.4760)	−0.4039 (0.2808)	0.1755 (0.6844)	0.1842 (0.6349)	1.1182* (0.6590)	1.1568 (0.7419)
Father is/was a Communist Party member	−0.3159 (0.3396)	−0.3256 (0.3404)	−0.1819 (0.3614)	−0.2054 (0.3611)	−0.0884 (0.2091)	0.1417 (0.4909)	0.0518 (0.5019)	−0.4384 (0.6181)	−0.4435 (0.5753)
Mother is/was a Communist Party member	0.0930 (0.4639)	0.0825 (0.4708)	0.3823 (0.4929)	0.3812 (0.5015)	0.2505 (0.3012)	0.6707 (0.6461)	0.6600 (0.7177)	0.1262 (0.8131)	0.1407 (0.7925)
Father's occupation	0.0433 (0.0569)	0.0510 (0.0591)	0.0703 (0.0616)	0.0768 (0.0637)	0.0007 (0.0339)	0.0529 (0.0818)	0.0559 (0.0890)	0.1088 (0.0937)	0.1204 (0.0975)
Mother's occupation	0.0638 (0.0572)	0.0674 (0.0587)	0.0588 (0.0660)	0.0626 (0.0677)	0.0670* (0.0399)	0.1634* (0.0957)	0.1700* (0.0997)	−0.0518 (0.0873)	−0.0646 (0.0982)
Father's employment sector	−0.0405 (0.0340)	−0.0405 (0.0348)	−0.0413 (0.0376)	−0.0403 (0.0383)	−0.0000 (0.0201)	−0.0127 (0.0445)	−0.0093 (0.0491)	−0.0399 (0.0645)	−0.0368 (0.0572)

Table 5.4 (continued)

Self-employed as second job	(1)	(2)	(3)	(4)	(5)	(6) Men	(7) Men	(8) Women	(9) Women
Mother's employment sector	0.0110	0.0129	0.0194	0.0201	0.0054	0.0344	0.0315	-0.0335	-0.0306
	(0.0289)	(0.0295)	(0.0321)	(0.0329)	(0.0184)	(0.0412)	(0.0431)	(0.0572)	(0.0497)
Variance of income					-1.96e-09		-3.18e-10		-1.78e-08
					(7.15e-09)		(3.31e-09)		(2.65e-08)
City dummies	Yes	Yes	Yes	Yes	Yes	Yes	Yes	Yes	Yes
Constant	-1.4020	-1.4334	-0.7517	-0.7213	-1.4069*	-3.2704	-2.9285	1.6461	1.4788
	(1.2475)	(1.2428)	(1.3965)	(1.4025)	(0.7476)	(2.1261)	(2.0013)	(1.7072)	(2.2082)
Wald χ^2 (64)	489.48***					23359.13***		36961.48***	
Wald χ^2 (66)		19880.40***	24171.06***						
LR χ^2 (72)				495.88***			294.41***		336.31***
LR χ^2 (74)					532.16***				
Pseudo R^2	0.1821	0.2329	0.2276	0.1811	0.2410	0.1904	0.2431	0.2675	0.3379
Number of observations	8382	8382	7405	7405	7405	3769	3769	3636	3636

Notes:
1. Dependent variable: 2 if wholly self-employed, 1 if self-employed in second job, and 0 if wage-employed. The results for dependent variable = 1 are reported here.
2. Robust standard errors adjusted for clustering at the household level are computed.
3. *** indicates significance at the 1% level, ** at the 5% level, and * at the 10% level.
4. Instead of a Wald test, the attitude toward risk equations uses the variance of five years of income in the specification, so the likelihood used for the estimation is a true distribution of the sample and a likelihood ratio test is employed.
5. There were no spouses in self-employment among those who are self-employed as a second job.
6. The coefficients on variables measuring parental education have been omitted where the estimates are subject to multicollinearity due to the small number of observations within the sub-sample.

128

measure of seeking to earn more income was 1.5095, with a z-statistic of 1.17. The results are unchanged from their inclusion, so are not reported. In any case, the determinants of self-employment for this group are indeed different from the main sample, as seen in Table 5.5.

Table 5.5 is divided into findings for the wholly self-employed and the self-employed as a second job. Columns (1)–(3) report the findings for the first group, divided into the whole sample and then men and women for the former, while columns (4)–(5) do the same for the whole sample and men. There are only six women who are self-employed as a second job after experiencing unemployment, so the extent of multicollinearity among the explanatory variables precludes estimating the determinants of their occupational choice.

Column (1) for the solely self-employed shows that age and Party membership do not matter for self-employment in contrast to the main sample and suggests that when forced to seek work, age is not a significant factor. Party members could also be less likely to become laid-off and therefore membership would be insignificant in this estimation. Spousal characteristics, such as having a spouse who is also self-employed, continue to matter and having a spouse in wage employment is also significant, suggesting that a spouse with a steady income makes undertaking self-employment more probable for those who have been unemployed. Socio-economic background and attitudes toward risk do not matter for this group either.

For men who have experienced unemployment, social networks have a larger effect on self-employment than for any other group or sub-group examined in Tables 5.3–5.5. Only education reduces that probability, while mothers in skilled professions and a risk-loving attitude increase the possibility of starting a business. Spousal characteristics do not matter. As the expected breadwinner, men who have experienced unemployment appear to be willing to embrace risk and use their social networks to become self-employed. For women in the same position, social networks interestingly have a negative effect on their occupational choice. This suggests that women who have networks may be better protected in their jobs and do not need to choose the more uncertain profession of starting a business. More years of employment experience continue to deter self-employment, while having a spouse in either wage or self-employment increases the probability. Having a father in a more marketised sector of employment reduces the prospect of self-employment, suggesting that fathers would deter their daughters from entering the less certain private sphere. A further difference from men is that attitudes toward risk do not matter for women.

For those who have been unemployed in the previous five years and choose self-employment as a second job, social networks continue to be

Table 5.5 *Determinants of self-employment, unemployed sub-sample, multinomial logit regression (robust standard errors in parentheses)*

	Wholly self-employed			Self-employed as second job	
	Whole sample (1)	Men (2)	Women (3)	Whole sample (4)	Men (5)
Social network	0.0179*	0.0233*	−0.1588*	−0.0038	0.0081
	(0.0099)	(0.0137)	(0.0873)	(0.0373)	(0.0269)
Personal characteristics					
Gender	−0.9377***			−2.8419***	
	(0.3603)			(0.8282)	
Age	0.0392	0.0261	0.0751	0.0508	0.0717
	(0.0336)	(0.0563)	(0.0526)	(0.0607)	(0.0710)
Years of education	−0.1638**	−0.2197**	−0.1859	−0.0558	−0.0832
	(0.0793)	(0.1103)	(0.1504)	(0.1308)	(0.1504)
Years of wage employment experience	−0.0880***	−0.0542	−0.1817***	−0.1329**	−0.1486**
	(0.0329)	(0.0570)	(0.0558)	(0.0603)	(0.0742)
Communist Party member	−0.2375	−0.7539	1.5344	1.5710*	1.5154*
	(0.6746)	(0.8825)	(1.3475)	(0.8138)	(0.9147)
Spouse characteristics					
Married	−0.0609	−0.4851	−0.1716	−1.7071*	−2.0185*
	(0.7018)	(0.9323)	(1.4253)	(0.9539)	(1.1407)
Spouse in wage employment	1.3556***	0.8688	1.6656**	2.3487***	1.3494
	(0.4257)	(0.8674)	(0.6514)	(0.7581)	(1.1219)
Spouse in self-employment	5.6808***	40.2093	7.9511**		
	(1.3501)	(0.0000)	(3.3132)		

Socio-economic background

Father's educational attainment:				
College and above	1.0503	0.8954	1.9515	1.4346	0.7681
	(0.9250)	(1.2408)	(1.5636)	(1.6031)	(2.4649)
Professional school	−0.7793	−0.1941	−43.2747	−0.0593	—
	(0.9197)	(1.1380)	(1.8276e+09)	(1.5818)	
Secondary school	0.3338	−0.3956	0.6261	0.7340	1.0954
	(0.5287)	(0.8045)	(0.9494)	(0.9467)	(1.0153)
Primary school	−0.2818	−0.4007	−0.4548	−0.7481	−0.4909
	(0.5067)	(0.6717)	(0.9701)	(0.8932)	(0.9907)
Mother's educational attainment:				
College and above	0.6339	2.1235	−44.2673	0.1650	—
	(1.4335)	(2.0198)	(0.0000)	(1.9278)	
Professional school	0.2311	−0.1238	0.2939	−1.9755	—
	(0.9375)	(1.3595)	(1.8710)	(1.7094)	
Secondary school	0.0512	−0.8105	0.6659	−2.0354*	−1.9240
	(0.5718)	(0.9498)	(0.9101)	(1.1209)	(1.2043)
Primary school	0.3876	0.2744	0.7728	−1.8591*	−1.7768*
	(0.4650)	(0.7030)	(0.7735)	(0.9793)	(1.0525)
Father is/was a Communist Party member	0.0768	0.3750	0.0128	0.5600	0.5131
	(0.4017)	(0.6006)	(0.7150)	(0.7193)	(0.8938)
Mother is/was a Communist Party member	0.6208	0.8313	0.0345	0.4922	2.0012
	(0.6419)	(0.8513)	(1.4508)	(1.0763)	(1.4951)
Father's occupation	0.0399	−0.0262	0.0761	−0.0321	−0.0900
	(0.0678)	(0.0976)	(0.1110)	(0.1400)	(0.1816)

Table 5.5   (continued)

Wholly self-employed	Whole sample (1)	Men (2)	Women (3)	Self-employed as second job	Whole sample (4)	Men (5)
Mother's occupation	0.0944	0.2687**	−0.0641		−0.0193	0.1808
	(0.0743)	(0.1198)	(0.1297)		(0.1401)	(0.1893)
Father's employment sector	−0.0339	0.0497	−0.1363**		−0.1237	−0.0740
	(0.0385)	(0.0571)	(0.0682)		(0.0800)	(0.0981)
Mother's employment sector	0.0351	−0.0419	0.0872		0.0852	0.0447
	(0.0339)	(0.0556)	(0.0533)		(0.0658)	(0.0784)
Variance of income	−1.09e-09	1.26e-08	−8.17e-09		7.78e-10	9.82e-09
	(4.40e-09)	(7.40e-09)*	(1.29e-08)		(5.03e-09)	(1.47e-08)
City dummies	Yes	Yes	Yes		Yes	Yes
Constant	−2.4213	−2.4551	−1.1177		−21.3405	−23.7944
	(1.7155)	(2.3883)	(3.0665)		(0.0000)	(0.0000)
LR χ^2 (70)		94.03**	123.08***			94.03**
LR χ^2 (72)	148.61***				148.61***	
Pseudo R^2	0.2525	0.2860	0.4981		0.2525	0.2860
Number of observations	1219	525	694		1219	525

Notes:
1. Dependent variable: 2 if wholly self-employed, 1 if self-employed in second job, and 0 if wage-employed.
2. As there are only six women who entered self-employment as a second job after experiencing unemployment, there was an issue of multicollinearity and the determinants of that group are not reported. The coefficients on variables measuring parental education have also been omitted where the estimates are subject to multicollinearity due to the small number of observations within the sub-sample.
3. Robust standard errors adjusted for clustering at the household level are computed.
4. *** indicates significance at the 1% level, ** at the 5% level, and * at the 10% level.

insignificant as is the case for those who do so without having experienced unemployment. Gender and employment experience continue to reduce the probability, but other personal traits do not matter. Marital status affects this group, as does having a spouse in wage employment, unlike for the main sample of the secondarily self-employed. A spouse in wage employment raises the probability of self-employment but few other variables matter, nor do attitudes toward risk, similar to the findings in Table 5.4. Men are not influenced by having a larger social network, though self-employment is negatively affected by employment experience and being married, and positively affected by Party membership. Attitudes toward risk remain insignificant for starting a business on the side.

Social networks continue to influence the choice of self-employment, but they do not influence self-employment as a second job for the sample of those with experience of unemployment unlike the main sample. Gender differences abound in this sample and are more striking in many ways than for the larger population of respondents. Social networks matter, but differently for men and women.

The importance of networks is not limited to entrepreneurship. Social capital – *guanxi* or interpersonal relationships – affects the wider labour market in China. This chapter has attempted to shed some light on the importance of networking, as well as the various factors that influence the probability of entrepreneurship. Self-started firms are essential for driving the development of the private sector; nowhere more so than in China, where successful transition will depend on the growth of the non-state sector, giving space for the state-owned sector gradually to be reformed.

4. CONCLUSION

This chapter investigated self-employment and the role of social networks amongst two groups of the self-employed (wholly and secondarily self-employed) in urban China, and also men and women separately in each of the groupings. A sub-sample of those who had experienced unemployment was also investigated. First, the socio-economic background and attitudes of the self-employed were similar to those of the wage-employed, but personal traits and incomes differed. The gender gap that has become evident in the employment market also characterises the self-employed. Women who are self-employed earn around half of that of men.

Next, multinomial logit regressions were estimated to analyse the determinants of self-employment and whether social networks were a significant factor, holding all other observable entrepreneurial traits constant. Social networks are consistently significant as a determinant of self-employment, except for these self-employed as a second job and for women who had experienced unemployment and then started a business. For that group of women, social networks reduced the probability that they would become self-employed after experiencing unemployment, suggesting that the nature of their networks is perhaps such as to generate information that could help them find another job rather than striking out on their own. For men who have experienced unemployment though, their social networks increase the probability of self-employment, possibly through helping them obtain the necessary permissions, credit, distributional or production channels. This is not dissimilar to the main sample of the wholly self-employed where social networks increase the prospects of starting a business. For women who did not experience unemployment, their social networks could have prevented them from being laid-off and served as conduits for their starting their own businesses. This is similar to men and dissimilar to women who lost their jobs. Spousal characteristics further suggest that family businesses are a strong factor in the burgeoning *de novo* private sector.

The growth of the non-state sector during China's gradual transition has undoubtedly been a driver of economic growth. Going into business for oneself plays an important role in the development of the non-state sector. The decision to become an entrepreneur could be informed by institutional and personal, as well as socio-economic factors. Institutional barriers to starting a business could include credit constraints, lack of access to supply networks, and regulatory complexity. Having a social network could help ease these constraints. Networks of relatives, friends, etc. could help with credit constraints, improve access to supply and distribution networks, and help gain the necessary licences to operate. Family businesses are not atypical. Becoming self-employed is also likely to be associated with personal traits, such as attitudes toward risk, spousal traits, and socio-economic background, such as parents' occupation, which feed into such motivations.

Therefore, the self-employed in urban China are likely to have larger social networks and there is a relationship between starting a business and having the network to do so. Those who work for themselves on the side are not affected by their networks. The evidence generally suggests that relationships are important in starting a business in China during a time when the legal and financial contexts are imperfect and uncertain, but economic development is rapid.

The finding that social networks negatively influence women's decision to become self-employed after experiencing unemployment is a surprising one. Social networks might help them gain wage-employment in that instance and deter them from entering into self-employment. Women who have not suffered unemployment may have networks that are more similar to men and therefore use them in a like fashion to start a business. It is evident that female entrepreneurs are indeed different from male ones and likely within their group, and this chapter has only shed some preliminary light on them, though their differences have been noted.

The main finding of this chapter is that social networks facilitate self-employment in urban China, but not for those who only undertake self-employment as a second job. The reasons for their influence could have to do with easing credit and institutional constraints to make up for an imperfect banking/financial system as well as opaque regulatory environment. The insecurity of property rights in a country would also cause the self-employed to rely on relational-based contracting so that disputes can be resolved via trust rather than the courts. With better protection of property as evidenced by the 2007 Property Law which granted equal protection to private and public property, the reliance on social networks as an enabler of self-employment should decline. However, China's marketising process is as yet incomplete and it will for some time have an imperfect contracting regime and credit system, which suggests the continuing use of social networks. Indeed, even as China's environment for starting a business improves with marketisation, social networks are likely to retain their importance. This can be seen in the reliance on relationships with the overseas Chinese diasporas in countries with very good legal systems such as the United States, as networks can still reduce transaction costs and help businesses avoid what is often an expensive and lengthy legal process.

NOTE

*   See further my 'China's Entrepreneurs', *World Development*, 37(4), 2009, 778–86; 'Self-employment in Urban China: Networking in a Transition Economy', *China Economic Review*, 20 (3), 2009, 471–84.

6. Banking and finance

1. INTRODUCTION

The health of China's banking and financial sectors is critical to the growth prospects of the economy. These sectors, though, require a number of significant reforms, not limited to the legacy of issues from a centrally planned economy such as the problem of non-performing loans (NPLs), but also the challenges raised by foreign competition after China's accession to the World Trade Organization (WTO) in 2001.

Despite having an underdeveloped banking and financial system, China agreed to liberalise these sectors as part of its WTO commitments. Financial liberalisation after WTO accession will be one of the major sources of opportunities to stimulate growth, but will also pose risks for China in the near future. The reform of these sectors will also affect the reform of the currency, the future of savings and investment, and the risk of macroeconomic instability, among other things, all of which will have implications for China's ability to sustain its economic growth.

2. BANKING IN CHINA

2.1 Background

Under central planning, China's banking and financial system was essentially an arm of the state. The People's Bank of China (PBOC) was the sole bank from 1949 until the 1980s reforms with responsibilities for both central and commercial banking operations. Cooperative banks existed to serve rural areas, but there was little else in terms of a financial system.

Since market-oriented reforms began in 1979, the banking sector has gradually been reformed. In the mid 1980s, the commercial banking functions of the PBOC were split off into four state-owned banks (Bank of China, Industrial and Commercial Bank of China (ICBC), Agricultural Bank of China, and China Construction Bank) and the PBOC was directed to serve as a central bank. These state-owned commercial banks (SCBs), though wholly stated-owned, were to be independent and to operate on the basis of profitability and 'hard' budget constraints. The People's Bank of China Law, adopted in 1995 eventually established the legal foundations of the central bank. Following on from these reforms, in 1998, the PBOC underwent a major restructuring, where all of its provincial and local branches were abolished. The PBOC instead has nine regional branches, similar to the US Federal Reserve System.

After WTO accession in 2001, when China realised that it would be competing with foreign banks at the end of 2006, a decision was taken to transform the SCBs into joint stock companies, with the state as the dominant shareholder. At the end of 2003, the Bank of China and the China Construction Bank were selected to be the first of the big four SCBs to undertake this transformation. All except for the Agricultural Bank of China have had initial public offerings (IPOs) on stock markets, domestically and internationally, as of 2009.

Also in 2003, reforms speeded up, with the creation of the China Banking Regulatory Commission (CBRC), which removed the role of regulatory overseer from the PBOC. Two other major regulatory agencies, China Securities Regulatory Commission (CSRC) and the China Insurance Regulatory Commission (CIRC), had been established to supervise the securities and insurance sectors respectively, functions also previously performed by the PBOC.

In addition to the SCBs, three policy banks, the China Development Bank (CDB), the Export-Import Bank of China, and the Agricultural Development Bank of China, were also established to perform the developmental role previously undertaken by the PBOC. They are charged with financing infrastructure projects and other state-supported or non-profit-making projects.

There is also a second tier of state-owned banks. They are effectively joint stock banks, which have shares owned by the government and private entities. There are approximately 14 joint stock commercial banks, most of which were set up in the 1990s. They include the Bank of Communications, China Everbright Bank, CITIC Industrial Bank, Shenzhen Development Bank, Shanghai Pudong Development Bank, China Merchant Bank, Fujian Industrial Bank, and Guangdong Development Bank. Several are listed on the domestic stock market, including the Shanghai Pudong Development Bank, the Shenzhen Development Bank, and the China Merchants Bank. In the 2000s, China gave permission for the establishment of private banks, the first being China Minsheng Bank. At the time, China Minsheng Bank was certainly unique in having mostly private owners and being publicly listed on the domestic stock market.

At the local level, there were originally some 3000 urban and 50 000 rural credit cooperatives, which have gradually merged into banks. For example, the Shenzhen Cooperative Bank was created from 16 urban cooperatives and the Shanghai City United Bank from 99 urban cooperatives.

In terms of foreign banks, there are nearly 200 operating in China, of which just under half had approval to conduct RMB business prior to the opening of the sector in December 2006, five years after WTO accession. Since then, restrictions still remain, but foreign banks, particularly those which are also locally incorporated, are able increasingly to undertake RMB business. Also, prior to the IPO of three of the four SCBs, minority equity stakes in the SCBs were sold to foreign banks to improve governance and help the SCBs to operate commercially. The stakes were bought by a wide range of international banks, who viewed China's high savings economy as an attractive market for developing financial services and equity holding in SCBs gave them a foothold. In the aftermath of the 2008 global financial crisis, though, a number of these foreign banks withdrew in order to re-build their balance sheets, shattered by their exposure to sub-prime mortgages and the securitisation of such, which led to part or whole nationalisation and failure of previously blue chip banks. As a further consequence, China's SCBs are now among the largest banks in the world.

For most of the reform period, there had been only one investment bank in China, the China International Capital Corporation (CICC). CICC was established in 1995 as a joint venture between China Construction Bank, Morgan Stanley Dean Witter, and several other smaller shareholders. Its remit includes underwriting domestic equities, taking equity stakes in foreign investments in China, undertaking mergers and acquisitions, organising project finance, and handling foreign exchange transactions. Bank of China was the only other bank which has provided investment banking services, although the other SCBs and one of the policy banks (China Development Bank) eventually set up investment banking services of their own. Foreign competition after WTO accession provided a further impetus for China's banks to develop in this area. However, the relative underdevelopment of its investment banking functions meant that China was not badly affected by the 2008 global financial crisis. Its SCBs had some exposure as creditors of Lehman Brothers, but its banking system was not brought to the brink of collapse, nor do its banks hold the troubled assets linked to sub-prime mortgages in America that have led to the collapse or nationalisation of numerous Western banks.

2.2 Banking Sector Reforms

Chinese reforms of the banking sector have taken place in stages. The main focus of the first stage was to improve asset quality by reducing the amount of non-performing loans and increasing the responsiveness of lending to commercial signals. For instance, in 1998, the government issued special bonds to recapitalise the big four state-owned banks in order to improve their capital adequacy ratios. Further recapitalisation also took place later on, using funds from China's vast foreign exchange reserves. In 1999, the most significant reform was undertaken: 1.4 trillion RMB worth of NPLs were offloaded onto four newly established asset management companies (AMCs), each attached to a SCB. The Chinese government also abolished the credit quota policy, so that banks could lend on the basis of returns rather than by political diktat.

The next two stages are to improve corporate governance and convert the SCBs into joint stock companies. The Bank of China and the China Construction Bank were the two SCBs selected to undertake the pilot programme, and they have worked on improving accountancy standards and corporate governance. This was with an eye toward listing on domestic and foreign stock markets. For instance, the Bank of China's IPO to transform itself into a joint stock company was preceded by selling minority equity stakes to a consortium led by the Royal Bank of Scotland. The sale of minority equity stakes in the smaller banks had also been happening quietly for a number of years. And, since it was viewed as relatively successful, it is now permitted with the requirement that foreign equity shareholding in a SCB must not exceed 25% of the total.

2.3 Assessment of Reforms

Excess cash holdings estimated at over two trillion RMB and a savings rate of 45–50% of GDP make China an attractive market with vast potential, but numerous reforms of the banking sector are needed. The core problems in the banking sector stem from the close relationship among the three main state sector players from the command period that continues through the reform period: state-owned enterprises, the government, and state-owned commercial banks. These problems are also a result of China's gradualist transition path. By gradually introducing market forces into the economy, the most difficult problems in the reform path have remained unresolved. China's remaining difficulties are further highlighted by its accession to the World Trade Organization, which requires significant liberalisation in trade and financial services. Although there have been many benefits from WTO membership, accession has also contributed to a reduction in competitiveness of SOEs and exposed the lack of market forces governing lending by SCBs. The decline of SOEs had further drained the government of its traditional source of revenue and had instead increased the amount of subsidies, including loans from SCBs. The transfers from SCBs to loss-making SOEs and the lack of credit assessments in lending generated significant amounts of non-performing loans. The culmination of policy loans, 'soft' budget constraints for state-owned enterprises, and the decentralisation of local state-owned commercial banks have resulted in a significant stock of NPLs that was estimated at RMB 2 trillion (in the early 2000s). As a proportion of GDP, NPLs were in the region of 20% of total national income. Other estimates put the figure higher (see, for example, Woo 2007). The root of the NPL problem, however, cannot be solved without addressing the inefficiency of SOEs, which has accordingly generated substantial urban unemployment for the first time in the reform period. However, even after restructuring in the late 1990s, the SOEs are still burdened with social security provision and find it difficult to shed workers. The key to resolving the NPL problem must therefore be focused on the flow, as well as reducing the stock, of loans that are granted on the basis of policy and not profit.

The major risk in China's banking sector will be the inability of the banks to stem the flow of NPLs and to rid themselves of them. There is also a danger of excess lending in certain sectors, such as construction and real estate, due to the capital controls which trap savings in the country, fuelling too fast rises in housing and the stock market at times. These developments reinforce the need for legal measures and institutions to facilitate credit assessment and underpin the financial system, echoing the theme throughout this book.

However, there are signs that the amount of NPLs has been falling throughout the 2000s, and the CBRC has made strides in improving the governance, capitalisation and transparency of the banking sector. Though the reforms led by the CBRC look promising, success will hinge on the resolution of China's structural problems. If privatisation successfully takes place with sufficient institutional underpinnings, it has the potential to transform China's banking sector and potentially rid it of one of the lingering legacies of central planning. In 2009, however, the failure to launch an IPO for the last of the four SCBs, the Agricultural Bank of China, suggests the persistence of the NPL problem. Instead, China's sovereign wealth fund bought 50% of the stake in the Agricultural Bank of China in a sizeable recapitalisation effort. Moreover, the 2008 global financial crisis and resultant credit crunch led the government to prompt the banks to lend, reportedly without regard to the NPL issue. Although China escaped the worst of the crisis, the legacy of sustaining more NPLs is not a positive development. There will be more on the crisis in the final section of this chapter.

Another key remaining issue is the appropriate future role of the three development banks. Essentially, these banks embody the relationships which are left over from the centrally planned period and which may be useful for a time, so long as the banking and financial sectors are yet to be well-established. They are seemingly acting as a bridge to provide some of the transfers and support granted to enterprises that was previously given by the four major state-owned banks. For instance, the China Development Bank (CDB) plays a role during transition when state-owned enterprises require capital that used to come from the state and state-owned banks, but now increasingly must be obtained from imperfectly working capital markets. This would similarly be the case for the other two policy banks relating to the external sector and agriculture. In a well-functioning system, however, the finance ministry and the government's fiscal policy should be separate from banking operations and the central bank which controls monetary policy. The policy banks may be usefully thought of as arms of the state/finance ministry rather than banks, and would probably function most effectively as sources of credit in areas where the market does not yet operate well. They could, for instance, provide loans directly or offer subsidised interest rates or securitise the operations of commercial banks in areas where banks find it difficult to establish operations, such as rural areas and interior provinces. Some type of incentive structure to provide a profit motive would help with the lack of efficiency inherent in such banks. However, there is an issue about policy banks that actively promote industrial policy in the often controversial area of export credits under the current WTO regime, among others. As an example, the China Development Bank, along with SAFE (State Administration of Foreign Exchange) and the sovereign wealth fund (SWF) known as CIC (China Investment Corporation), act to invest China's foreign exchange reserves even though the CIC is officially the SWF set up in 2007 and charged with undertaking this task. The CDB, moreover, has invested in Barclays Bank among others to jointly develop banking projects in Africa, which transforms its remit from being domestically oriented to being an international one.

China's banks have benefited from the thriftiness of its people, which has seen savings swell over the past three decades under transition. Capital controls and credit constraints for non-state firms together fuel high corporate savings as well, since savings are constrained to stay in China and firms save to grow organically due to tight credit conditions. As seen in Chapter 2, China's savings rate has increased significantly over the reform period, rising to some 50%, at the cost of consumption, which has fallen dramatically since its peak of 50% in the late 1980s/early 1990s. Further, underdeveloped capital markets limit the investment possibilities for Chinese savers. Taken together, the banking system holds large amounts of deposits, but at the same time, these are predominately state-owned despite the decades of reform and still run the risk of a banking crisis due to the lingering problem of non-performing loans. Nevertheless, the institutional reforms have begun to corporatise all but a few of the state-owned banks and the policy direction is positive. Regression as a result of the worst economic downturn in the post-World War II period, however, posts a risk going forward and could be a worrisome harbinger of the future contour of the banking sector.

3. CAPITAL MARKETS

3.1 Background

The financial sector in China is still in its nascent stages. This was one of the reasons why China was shielded from the worst of the 2008 financial crisis, as its underdeveloped financial market did not trade in the complex securities which brought down large segments of the Western banking system. However, it is a quickly developing sector, particularly after WTO accession which saw China agree to open vast swathes of its services industries, including banking and finance. The final section of this chapter will return to the 2007/08 global crisis.

China's two stock exchanges were opened in Shanghai in 1990 and Shenzhen in 1991, with trades permitted in 1993. In late 2009, Shenzhen launched a NASDAQ-style bourse called the Growth Enterprise Board, aimed at listing smaller companies, after a trial period since 2004. In a decade, China had one of the largest stock markets in Asia in terms of market capitalisation (over $500 billion in the mid 2000s). However, this measurement is plagued with problems, as 69% of all shares in the 1400 listed companies on these exchanges are non-tradable, so their value is prescribed rather than market-determined. The stock markets are also estimated to provide only 5% of corporate financing in China, so their reach is limited despite the market cap (Riedel et al. 2007). The numerous designations of shares as individual, government, legal persons, 'A' (RMB denominated shares), 'B' (foreign currency denominated shares) and 'H' (shares traded on the Hong Kong Stock Exchange), each with its own restrictions with respect to trading are problematic. These restrictions further insulate listed firms from feeling the discipline of the market. Corporate governance has thus not been improved significantly by the corporatisation of Chinese enterprises (see, for example, Sun and Tong 2003). Not surprisingly, returns to Chinese equities are volatile, rising during the 1990s and then losing an estimated 50% of their value in the early 2000s, before growing quickly and then falling with the global financial crisis. In the first half of 2009, the

Shanghai market was up over by 80% in about seven months, further displaying the roller-coaster trajectory evident throughout its short history.

The underdevelopment of the stock market is symptomatic of the state of the financial system. Chinese financial markets are 'thin' (Allen et al. 2005) This is not atypical of emerging economies; however, for China, it is exacerbated by a stock market with a significant portion of non-tradable shares, belying the large capitalisation of the Shanghai and Shenzhen stock exchanges. On the whole, Chinese firms do not meet many of the accounting practices or reporting requirements that permit assessment of riskiness. One danger is the transfer of risk from the capital market to the banking sector, among others.

China's WTO obligations have hastened the development of the financial sector. The expectations of international financial markets in terms of corporate governance and reporting requirements are fuelling reforms in China, particularly as its 'going out' strategy suggests that more firms will be seeking to establish themselves internationally. Reforms, such as permitting the creation of fund management companies, developing investment banks, and liberalising some aspects of the currency, are all aimed at strengthening financial markets in China.

3.2 Assessing the Reforms

In some ways, the development of the financial sector has been less burdened by the legacy of central planning in the way that the banking sector has been forced to cope with the complicated relationships that drive lending in a partially marketised economy. China, moreover, is not typical of a developing country because it has infrastructure for financial services in place, for example, rural cooperative banks, due to its period of central planning. However, it still suffers from many of the informational asymmetries and imperfections that plague financial markets in a developing country. The mind-set from the centrally planned period also means that commercial credit culture is lacking, and this needs to be developed. For instance, though interest rates were partially liberalised in October 2004, Chinese banks and financial institutions found it difficult to use interest rates to price for risk, as they had not needed to do so under central planning.

Gradual reforms along these lines, including regional currency swap agreements, are positive developments. But there are still a number of much-needed reforms, and the lack of capital convertibility, which also applies to the still restricted currency, needs to be addressed. The inability to repatriate profits and move capital out of China will eventually become an ever-growing problem.

China's focus on attracting foreign direct investment (FDI) or long-term investment has been accompanied by restrictions on short-term portfolio flows. Despite its efforts, however, an estimated $100 billion in capital has moved across its borders in each of the past few years. Nevertheless, the lack of convertibility of the capital account will stymie the development of a liquid capital market.

The Chinese authorities view this issue in tandem with currency reform. The Asian financial crisis highlighted the risk of macroeconomic instability arising from a currency and financial crisis. 'Hot money' flows, coupled with 'thin' financial markets are ingredients in the third generation financial crisis models. With a fixed exchange rate and increasingly liberalised lending, China may be at risk in the future. This raises the issue of the lack of established credit or risk assessment in financial markets as well as the banking sector. Developing the capability to undertake these assessments will be essential.

Finally, the main issue with capital markets in China is undoubtedly the continued existence of non-tradable shares in its volatile stock exchanges. In recognition of this, the Chinese authorities announced in August 2005 that it would allow SOEs to sell shares of stock controlled by the Communist Party, amounting to nearly $270 billion worth of state assets. Most of the listed companies on the two stock exchanges are subsidiaries of large SOEs controlled by the state or small firms that are in inconsequential industries. The large SOEs are still in the hands of the state, so the knock-on effects of this reform in terms of corporate governance could be large.

These reforms are to be implemented in three stages. Four companies were selected for the first stage, in which they were to negotiate a compensation plan for shareholders of the tradable shares. Then, the split-share reform plans were to be approved by a majority of holders of tradable shares, accounting for at least two-thirds of voting rights. The second stage of the programme involved 42 companies, including some large SOEs (Baosteel, Yangtze Electric Power and CITIC Securities). The compensation plans were typically two to three bonus shares for every 10 tradable shares held, although some firms have adopted more complex proposals involving instruments, such as warrants. If the first two stages are successful, then the government will release state-owned shares in the remaining companies on the stock exchanges. Progress has been halting and the final stage had not yet been reached as of 2010.

Even though existing owners of tradable shares will be given compensation in the form of stock or cash, the payout has been viewed as insufficient to offset the dilution in value from the flotation of state-owned shares. To counter the negative market reaction to these reforms, the Chinese government in August 2005 implemented a series of measures to bolster the market, including halving individual capital gains taxes on dividends from publicly traded companies, allowing insurance companies and social security funds to invest in the stock market, increasing the QFII (Qualified Foreign Institutional Investors) quota from $4 billion to $10 billion, allowing fund management companies to use their shareholdings as collateral for raising capital, and allowing listed companies to buy back tradable shares to boost their share prices, among other things. Although these reforms are moves in the right direction, the Chinese government must instil confidence in its listed companies by improving corporate governance and imposing better regulation to make Chinese equities attractive. If they succeed in doing so, the impressive growth of China's economy may yet be reflected in its capital markets.

4. CHINA AND THE GLOBAL FINANCIAL CRISIS

No assessment of banking and finance can avoid analysing the impact of the worst financial crisis in nearly a century. This section will attempt to provide the context for how China fared in the crisis and the indirect role it played in contributing to the larger global macroeconomic environment. Although it is certainly true that excessive risk-taking by financiers and inadequate regulatory supervision are to blame for the global financial crisis, international macroeconomic forces should not be overlooked as a contributing factor. This is particularly the case as any lasting resolution must address the causes of the most significant global economic crisis in recent memory.

The economic crisis of 2008 has its roots in the last US recession. Ever since the US central bank used loose monetary policy to stave off a technical recession in 2001 after the dot.com bubble burst, low interest rates were the norm for the subsequent seven years in developed economies, even as growth was strong. That is how monetary policy is conventionally applied, but the fundamentally altered structure of the global economy of the 2000s changed everything.

The mis-priced risk at the heart of the US sub-prime mortgage crisis is a result of low interest rates and excess liquidity. Credit was cheap and plentiful, which is peculiar in a country with a low rate of saving and a high level of consumer debt, as well as highly leveraged firms. Normally, a savings deficit requiring borrowing to consume would increase the cost of borrowing on account of the low supply of funds. Moreover, the liquidity did not cause inflation. This is due to globalisation and the global appetite for US debt, which kept down prices and the cost of borrowing. The US

Federal Reserve then missed the signal that money was too cheap, and lenders continued to seek borrowers, even if they were sub-prime ones. Significant demand for US bonds further flattened the yield curve such that when interest rates began to rise in 2004 before the crisis hit in 2007, interest rates were not responsive.

This strong demand for US treasuries stemmed from the trade surpluses in the Middle East (due to oil exports) and in China and elsewhere in Asia (due to cheap manufactured goods). When combined with a high savings rate, particularly in Asia, large foreign exchange reserve holdings accumulated in their coffers. As a result of the fixed exchange rates operated by these countries, purchases of US treasuries were necessary even if the American interest rate, and therefore returns, were low. The fixed exchange rate regimes also forestalled a quick re-balancing of the global economy. When China, for instance, recorded trade surpluses, exceeding some 10% of GDP in 2007, the currency should have experienced irresistible pressure to appreciate. By so doing, goods purchased from China would have been more expensive for American consumers, who would then have bought less, thereby reducing the US trade deficit and concurrently causing the Chinese trade surplus to fall. This, however, did not happen, as the Chinese intervened to keep its currency in a managed band and instead took measures to raise reserve requirements in its banking sector, among other things, to manage the large increases in liquidity in its economy. This has not been entirely successful, as sterilisation of the inflows was incomplete and China experienced the prospect of overheating when investment, particularly in fixed assets and construction, grew rapidly and led to the prospect of an asset bubble. Exchange rates are not the only factor. The US dollar has the status of a reserve currency, demand for which does not fall purely on the basis of demand and supply due to trade balances and capital movements. If that had been the case, then the US's 'twin deficits' (budget and trade) should have been unsustainable long before. Indeed, the US external deficit, reflecting consumption based on borrowing from abroad, was a phenomenon in the 1980s even before China's significant opening up to the world economy after 1992.

It is not unusual for China or for other developing countries to want stability in their currencies and to maintain their competitiveness as they grow. Nevertheless, the so-called global imbalances of 2008 meant that the West, with low savings, was importing savings from the (Far and Middle) East, and the appetite for the US dollar kept liquidity high and cheap (as well as interest rates low) in America.

The financial crisis followed, as financiers created ever more sophisticated securitised instruments and sold them around the world. The global economy will need to be re-balanced. However, this should proceed gradually, as liquidity from China and emerging economies is needed to help the West in a 'credit crunch'. This would alleviate some of the necessary belt-tightening of Western consumers and also help deflate the asset bubbles building up in emerging economies with a lot of liquidity, as well as to stabilise the rich countries which provide many of the world's consumers upon whom most emerging economies depend for export growth. Also, Western governments have to borrow, as raising taxes is not feasible during a recession. These government bonds are likely to be bought by governments from emerging economies such as China. Therefore, rather counter-intuitively, though global imbalances led to this crisis, they should be maintained for some time longer. Cutting off liquidity at a time when the West is drawing upon it to fund their rescue efforts will likely lead to a long and painful period of austerity. The recovery of the West and their markets is in the global interest, particularly China's, as the world's largest trader. Re-balancing slowly may stave off the worst of what is likely to be an anaemic recovery.

Some sovereign wealth funds (SWFs) had helped to re-capitalise Wall Street and European banks, for example, Singapore's investments in Citigroup and UBS. Buying well-priced but illiquid companies is not new, as was seen in the rise of M&A activity in the aftermath of the Asian financial crisis. However, the political reaction to SWFs strongly suggests that private and commercial firms investing in the West would be more feasible. But China has only allowed commercial outward foreign direct investment since 2004 and even then, it is tightly controlled. From the perspective of developed countries, it is a small economic step to take direct capital investments from emerging economies through sovereign wealth funds, but it is a large step politically. Alternatively, commercial capital outflows from Asia would allow a re-balancing without so much of a political backlash. However, doing so would also erode capital controls in countries such as China, which would make a fixed exchange rate harder to maintain. This is not a position that China is ready to take, nor it appears is the Middle East. However, it should be in the interests of emerging economies to allow greater flexibility in their exchange rates to protect themselves against a currency-led financial crisis, since a floating currency appreciates/depreciates to absorb external shocks, while a fixed exchange rate can be attacked by speculators. Also, countries such as India and Vietnam experienced double-digit inflation in 2007 as a result of their low exchange rates, making imports more expensive and investment cheap, which can lead to overheating, asset bubbles and a crash. Moreover, with China and India leading global economic growth as the developed economies fell into recession, capital seeking returns is likely to contribute to the bubbles (particularly housing) in these countries, which could be building up for the next financial crisis. The speed of the growth of the Shanghai stock market in 2009 provided hints of this dynamic.

Therefore, China had an indirect part in the global financial crisis. Its actions, along with other major emerging economies, can also help to resolve it. Doing so is not just geared at aiding a US-led crisis, but at restoring the global economic and financial stability that has brought real prosperity to China and much of the developing world in the 2000s. To achieve this, reforming macroeconomic policies and improving the institutional underpinnings of financial markets are essential – for the global economy as well as for China itself.

5. CONCLUSION

Although solid progress has been made in a number of areas concerning the reform of the banking and financial sectors, there are hard issues that remain. Chief among these is the issue of non-performing loans, which has the potential of plunging the economy into crisis, a recurring characteristic of other transition economies in the former Soviet Union.

The core of the NPL problem continues to be the close relationship among the state, SCBs and SOEs. This question remains integral to China's reform plan, as the state's provision of a social safety net and reform of labour markets are linked to effective reform of SOEs and SCBs. If they continue to carry traditional state functions as well as their profit-maximising objectives (see Bai et al. 2000), then the NPLs and inefficiencies are likely to continue.

Despite numerous steps to transform the banking system, there are still fundamental, institutional issues that remain. Substantial reforms are required to improve the regulatory system and legal structure overseeing bank operations. Improving corporate governance can reduce corruption and improve confidence. The development of the CBRC, CSRC and CIRC are positive steps, but coordination among them is becoming increasingly important as well, particularly since bank lending can fuel asset bubbles in the financial market.

Although interest rates were partially liberalised in 2004, the proper assessment of risk is still lacking. Informational asymmetries are the classical economic causes of moral hazard and adverse selection. Fostering effective credit assessment institutions would aid the development of a banking sector to a large extent. These economic and legal reforms must proceed in tandem and in a coordinated fashion to support successful reform of the SCBs. The continuing involvement of the state should not be ruled out, but the distortion of incentives that can result from the implicit backing of the state must be acknowledged and addressed. The transfer of losses to SCBs is another source of concern as the state must itself reform its budgetary process and fiscal system, including strengthening tax collection and managing the structure of the decentralised fiscal system. This, though, must be balanced with the important role of the state in spending on investments in human capital, science and technology, and infrastructure. Finally, the entry at the end of 2006 of foreign banks into the domestic lending market gives a further impetus for corporate governance reform and improving competitiveness. The sophistication of foreign banks in providing customer products and services will be balanced against domestic banks' knowledge of the local markets for a time. As the market evolves, though, Chinese banks will increasingly need to prove that they are competitive and solvent.

As for the policy banks, there is no place for banks which engage in policy-driven transfers instead of market-determined loans in a market economy. Thus, if they are interim/transition institutions, and if there are concerns about their incurring substantial liabilities and losses, then restricting their scope to being solely financing arms of the state would be a feasible course. In this way, they would not compete with commercial banks. Instead, the state could identify poorly-served segments of the market and also areas of priority for industrial policy. If these markets are insufficiently served by commercial banks because they tend to be areas where there is market failure or social returns exceed private returns, then the state can step in to fund these activities. The state could even preempt funding of certain areas of importance to industrial policy, such as research and development, until the non-state sector steps in, such as when private capital funds innovation.

Finally, in terms of banking sector reforms, there needs to be a clear demarcation of the role of the central bank (PBOC), the state-owned banks which are aiming to become joint stock companies, and the regulatory body, the CBRC. The PBOC has not given many indications about the form of monetary policy for China and there are questions about its remit.

As for capital markets, the poor performance of Chinese equities during a period of phenomenal growth in the early 2000s had plunged the underdevelopment of the financial system into stark relief. The agreed financial liberalisation accompanying WTO accession was another focal point for the Chinese authorities, which led to the 2005 reforms that were intended to make shares tradable and improve liquidity and therefore market discipline for listed firms. Undoubtedly, the prevalence of non-tradable shares on the two stock exchanges has reduced confidence in the market's ability to act to discipline the listed firms. The recent reforms on shedding state shares have been met with a mixed response, wrought with concerns about dilution of the existing shares on the stock exchange. The pronouncements of the CSRC in the 2000s aimed at improving enforcement of reporting and accounting requirements are geared at bolstering confidence in Chinese equities and that corruption will be addressed.

Moreover, so long as the listed firms are primarily subsidiaries, then asset quality will continue to undermine fundamentals. In recognition of this, the Chinese authorities had also prompted 'blue chip' Chinese companies to list not only in Hong Kong and on international stock exchanges, but also in Shanghai and Shenzhen. Reforms, though slow, are heading in the right direction.

Finally, there has for some time been discussion about merging the two stock exchanges, and the increasingly close ties with the Hong Kong stock exchange could portend eventual reforms to unify the stock market in China, since companies which trade in both the mainland and Hong Kong often have different premiums attached due to the capital restrictions in place in China.

In terms of financial liberalisation more generally, there are numerous reforms which are needed. Although there are fewer legacy issues as compared with the banking sector, there is also much more of a market to develop since China has a fledging financial and insurance system. In some segments, such as insurance, Chinese firms have a strong foothold, as they have taken over as providers of life and health insurance from the declining SOEs. In terms of financial markets, though, there are numerous reforms that have begun to increase the sophistication of the market, and these are promising. However, a key issue is the lack of convertibility of capital in China, which hampers liquidity. This issue is tied closely to the reform of the Chinese currency and will be affected by not only domestic but also external factors.

Central to the reforms undertaken is recognition of the changes accompanying the entry of foreign firms into the banking and financial sectors. The Chinese authorities aimed to utilise foreign expertise with financial services to help develop the market and instil a commercial credit culture. But, in order to make this feasible, there must be better legal and regulatory foundations to support markets, so that corporate governance can be undertaken and corruption rooted out.

Finally, the banking and financial system of an economy is critical to its successful growth. Capital markets transform savings into investment and a sound financial system can allow people to get the balance right between present and future consumption. Confidence in the banking system can mitigate the prospects of a destabilising crisis, among numerous other benefits. For China, the legacy issues in the banking system, the uncertain role of the state in capital markets, and the nascent stage of its financial system are all difficult issues to address. However, China's gradualist approach to reforms has proved successful so far in taking a limited approach to financial liberalisation and this may well continue, particularly in light of the débâcle in the Western financial system. As China grows increasingly important in the global economy and the so-called global imbalances have come under scrutiny, how it proceeds with the future reform of its banking and financial sector will be of much wider interest than ever before.

7. Law and markets*

1. INTRODUCTION

One of the enduring paradoxes in China's remarkable economic growth experience over the three decades since 1978 is the lack of a well-established legal system supporting the increasingly decentralised marketising economy (see, for example, Allen et al., 2005; Cull and Xu 2005). It is a notable puzzle in that robust institutions are thought to be required both in theory and in practice to support markets (see, for example, Acemoglu and Johnson 2005). For instance, in a Coasian or Walrasian sense, a market economy is predicated on well-defined property rights and low transaction costs that permit efficient exchange to take place (Coase 1937). The transition experience of many other economies such as the former Soviet Union was in part predicated on the establishment of private property rights and removal of the inefficient state in the burgeoning market economy. In China's case, however, many of its reforms have been undertaken without an established rule of law and in the absence of a change in ownership from state (public) to private. This raises the questions as to how China was able to instil economic incentives in the absence of private property rights and how an imperfect legal system could protect against expropriation that would normally limit investment and other private economic activities, particularly foreign direct investment (FDI). The gradualist and evolutionary nature of both economic and legal reform provides a basis for understanding the relationship between law and growth in China.

Therefore, this chapter will propose that legal and economic reforms – extending beyond financial development – give rise to, and reinforce, each other in China. Also, institutional reform through administrative dictates, such as the Contract Responsibility System that injected market forces into state-owned enterprises (SOEs), was sufficient to instil incentives to create markets in the absence of strong legal protection. Then, once a market is created by law or institutional reform (for example, administrative dictate or absence of notable prohibition), interested constituencies and stakeholders will push for more formal and explicit legal reforms to protect their interests. Better legal protection in turn promotes market development by providing greater security of economic transactions. Informal, trust-based relationships supplant the incomplete legal system, particularly in the area of enforcement. In this way, the complementary processes of legal, institutional and economic reform in China can explain the paradox of remarkable growth within an underdeveloped system of law.

In the case of the early reforms of the late 1970s and early 1980s, the particular context of Chinese gradualist transition meant that institutional reform – through creating an expectation of property rights – was sufficient to instil the necessary incentives for the development of markets. However, as markets developed, more formal and explicit legal reforms were needed and thus China began to rapidly adopt laws during the 1990s and 2000s, particularly with the additional pressures of international economic laws due to WTO accession in 2001. With respect to enforcement, including foreign invested enterprises (FIEs), there was the reliance on informal relational contracting where official enforcement is weak. The chapter will conclude with an assessment of the relationship between law and economic growth in China, and posit that China's experience is unusual in the post-war period where the transition and development models are heavily tilted toward inclusion of formal legal rules, but is not atypical of the experience of developed countries' legal and economic development during their industrialisation at the turn of the last century. The conclusion will also assess the influence of international laws and rules, particularly in shaping the enforcement of laws in China.

2. LAW AND MARKETS

There are both theoretical and empirical perspectives on the relationship between law and markets that drives economic growth. At first glance, it may appear that some laws are less relevant to economic growth, such as the workings of the criminal law system. However, crime may well deter investment and social stability can be a determinant of location for risk-averse firms (see, for example, Brock 1998). Thus, the functioning of the legal system across its various dimensions may well be relevant for economic growth, though the primary focus would be on civil and commercial legal developments.

From the theoretical perspective, the 'invisible hand' of the market works efficiently when there exists optimising agents transacting in a framework of well-defined property rights and sufficiently low or zero transaction costs (see Coase 1937). Law establishes those conditions. A legal system defines the property rights and the costs of transacting and exchange. For instance, ownership recognised by law establishes the security of the private property to be exchanged. A well-functioning legal and regulatory system can ensure that transactions involving those properties take place, that is, it can provide contracting security. For China, one element of the paradox is the lack of legally protected private property rights (see, for example, Jefferson and Rawski 2002). It was not until the Property Law of 2007 that equal protection was granted to both private and public property. Indeed, much of China's growth and reform has taken place with the state retaining ownership of enterprises, land and housing. Privatisation of SOEs has only occurred gradually over the three decades of market-oriented reforms. The private housing market was lately established, perhaps measured by the conclusion of the housing privatisation reforms in 2001, and the creation of long-term rights of use rather than freehold ownership resulted since land remained largely in state hands (see, for example, Ho 2006).

From the empirical standpoint, these theoretical insights have been incorporated into the literature advocating the importance of laws and institutions in explaining persistent economic growth (see, for example, Rodrik et al. 2004; Acemoglu and Johnson 2005; Acemoglu et al. 2005). La Porta et al. (1997, 1998) emphasise the importance of legal origin, for example, whether a country has a common or civil law system, in influencing financial sector development and consequently economic development. China did not fit well within this framework, particularly because legal origin was based on the externally imposed legal system of the colonial powers on developing countries. But, for countries such as China which were not wholly colonised and did not adopt a legal system from a particular colonial power, the legal formalism hypothesis would seem to have minimal explanatory power. Studies of other transition economies conclude that the effectiveness of laws is more important than the completeness of the written formal law for economic growth, further reducing the force of the legal origins school. One significant conclusion is that a legal system 'transplanted' into a neophyte transition economy – whereby the wholly formed laws of developed countries which would presumably encompass the necessary elements for a 'rule of law' – did not work (Pistor et al. 2000). Glaeser et al. (2004) also emphasise the functional rule of law as relevant for growth. Therefore, the elements of a well-functioning legal system would include an independent judiciary, freedom of executive branch interference, and low risk of expropriation (Pistor and Xu 2005; Fan et al. 2009).

Institutional development was therefore considered to be important and the focus has shifted away from legal formalism and legal origin to some extent (see, for example, Rodrik et al. 2004). For instance, Acemoglu and

Johnson (2005) emphasise two types of market-supporting institutions which are important for economic growth: property rights institutions which protect against expropriation by government, and contracting institutions which ease contract enforcement. For China, these empirical measures also do not measure up well as compared with its impressive growth rate, giving rise to the 'China paradox' (see, for example, Lu and Yao 2009).

Various measures of the rule of law and institutional development in China all suggest that its formal legal system is underdeveloped (see, for example, Allen et al. 2005; Cull and Xu 2005 for a range of indicators). Using the World Bank's Worldwide Governance Indicators for 2006, Table 7.1 shows that China ranked in the bottom 25th to 50th percentile of all countries surveyed for rule of law. It is also evident from Table 7.1 that China grew more rapidly than comparably sized economies (largest ten economies in the world) in the top half of the table and outpaced the growth of other transition economies from 1990 to 2003. Its growth in per capita GDP, exceeding 7.6% over this period, was substantially higher than for Brazil, which ranked close to China in the rule of law indicator, and also Estonia, which had a rule of law indicator that was higher than that of the USA. No proxy for rule of law will be perfect, though nearly all studies conclude that China has an underdeveloped legal system (see, for example, Yao and Yueh 2009). When measured in terms of regulatory quality, a counterpart to an effective legal system, China fares even worse. Table 7.2 ranks the countries in terms of their regulatory quality, measuring the ability of the government to formulate and implement sound policies and regulations that permit and promote private sector development. Whereas it ranked better than Russia and Brazil on rule of law, it ranked better only than Russia on the composite index for regulatory quality.

Tables 7.3–7.6 provide more disaggregated measures of different dimensions of the rule of law in China, as compared with other countries, namely, investor protection, contract enforcement, security of property rights and freedom from corruption. Table 7.3 measures the extent of investor protection as measured by the World Bank Doing Business Survey from 2008, where China's rank out of 175 measured countries is 83 or in the bottom half. In particular, it obtained the poorest rating on the transparency of related-party transactions (extent of disclosure index), which reflects the lack of arm's-length dealing and opacity in its enterprises. By contrast, China ranks relatively well for contract enforcement (Table 7.4). The number of procedures and days, as well as the cost of enforcing a commercial contract, places China no worse than European countries. The composite indicator, though, may be biased by the low cost of enforcing contracts in China and the relative efficiency with which courts operate,

Table 7.1   Rule of law and GDP growth

Country	Percentile rank (0–100)	Rule of law score (−2.5 to +2.5)	Average annual growth rate of real per capita GDP, 1990–2003
China	**45.2**	**−0.40**	**7.61%**
Brazil	41.4	−0.48	0.96%
France	89.5	1.31	1.47%
Germany	94.3	1.77	1.43%
India	57.1	0.17	3.95%
Italy	60.0	0.37	1.25%
Japan	90.0	1.40	0.95%
Russia	19.0	−0.91	−1.27%
United Kingdom	93.3	1.73	2.03%
United States	91.9	1.57	1.75%
Select Eastern Europe and former Soviet bloc countries			
Albania	48.8	−0.14	2.58%
Bulgaria	66.3	0.54	1.03%
Croatia	61.5	0.35	0.25%
Czech Republic	79.5	0.95	0.92%
Estonia	92.2	1.42	2.45%
Hungary	85.9	1.10	1.72%
Poland	69.3	0.64	3.23%
Romania	62.0	0.37	0.19%
Slovakia	83.4	1.08	1.65%

Note: Rule of law measures the extent to which agents perceive that the rules of society, in particular the quality of contract enforcement, the police, and the courts, as well as the likelihood of crime and violence, are enforced. The percentile rank places the country on a scale of 0–100, where 100 indicates a country that scored the highest possible value on the rule of law indicator. The governance score is normally distributed with a mean of zero and a standard deviation of one. Governance is better as the value increases. See Kaufmann et al. (2007) for a complete definition and discussion. The growth rate of per capita GDP is in 1990 US dollars and calculated from Maddison (2001).

Source: World Bank Worldwide Governance Indicators, 2006.

which is picked up by the first two indicators. However, effectiveness of the legal system depends not only on efficiency and cost, but on the extent of the proffered protection of contracting security. Indeed, when the quality of contract enforcement as perceived by the respondent is considered, as in Table 7.1, in contrast to the measures of the number of procedures and days and costs of enforcement, China ranks rather worse. Interestingly,

Table 7.2   Regulatory quality

Country	Percentile rank (0–100)	Regulatory quality score (−2.5 to +2.5)	Standard Error
Russia	35.0	−0.44	0.17
China	**45.6**	**−0.24**	**0.17**
India	46.1	−0.22	0.17
Brazil	53.4	−0.04	0.17
Albania	55.8	0.09	0.18
Croatia	64.1	0.43	0.17
Romania	66.0	0.48	0.17
Bulgaria	69.9	0.61	0.17
Poland	72.3	0.71	0.17
Italy	74.3	0.81	0.21
Czech Republic	80.1	0.96	0.17
Slovakia	81.1	0.99	0.17
Japan	83.5	1.05	0.21
France	85.9	1.15	0.21
Hungary	86.4	1.15	0.17
United States	90.8	1.45	0.21
Estonia	92.2	1.50	0.17
Germany	92.7	1.50	0.21
United Kingdom	98.1	1.86	0.21

Note: Regulatory quality measures the ability of the government to formulate and implement sound policies and regulations that permit and promote private sector development. The percentile rank places the country on a scale of 0–100, where 100 indicates a country that scored the highest possible value on the indicator. The indicator score is normally distributed with a mean of zero and a standard deviation of one. Quality improves as the value increases. See Kaufmann et al. (2007) for a complete definition and discussion.

Source: World Bank Worldwide Governance Indicators, 2008.

India fares badly on quantitative measures of contract enforcement, ranking well below China in Table 7.4, and yet is better rated than China in Table 7.1 on the overall measure of rule of law that takes into account the quality of the legal system. Moreover, a comparable measure by the Heritage Foundation is that of enforcing property rights, and China fares among the worst of selected countries, as seen in Table 7.5.

Table 7.5 measures the security of property rights, both to obtain and to enforce. China has one of the least secure systems of property rights, likely due to its underdeveloped private property system that has only ostensibly existed since the notion was recognised in the Constitution in 2004 and

Table 7.3   Investor protection

	Rank	Investor protection index	Disclosure index	Director liability index	Shareholder suits index
Brazil	64	5.3	6	7	3
Canada	5	8.3	8	9	8
China	**83**	**5.0**	**10**	**1**	**4**
France	64	5.3	10	1	5
Germany	83	5.0	5	5	5
India	33	6.0	7	4	7
Italy	51	5.7	7	4	6
Japan	12	7.0	7	6	8
Poland	33	6.0	7	2	9
Romania	33	6.0	9	5	4
Russia	83	5.0	6	2	7
Slovakia	98	4.7	3	4	7
South Africa	9	8.0	8	8	8
Ukraine	141	3.7	1	3	7
United Kingdom	9	8.0	10	7	7
United States	5	8.3	7	9	9

Notes: The investor protection index (measured from 1–10) calibrates the strength of minority shareholder protection against directors' misuse of corporate assets for personal gain. The indicators, also out of ten, distinguish three dimensions of investor protection: transparency of related-party transactions (extent of disclosure index), liability for self-dealing (extent of director liability index) and shareholders' ability to sue officers and directors for misconduct (ease of shareholder suits index). Countries are ranked out of 175 countries in the sample.

Source: World Bank Doing Business Database, 2008 (www.doingbusiness.org).

with the passage of the Property Law in 2007, extending equal protection to private and public property. China performs better in Table 7.6, which measures the extent of corruption. China's degree of corruption is comparable to India and Brazil, while it fares better than Russia and the Ukraine. Overall, China ranked 126 out of 157 countries based on these two along with other like indicators produced by the Heritage Foundation's 2008 Index of Economic Freedoms.

In summary, although no indicators are perfect, across measures of rule of law, China ranks in the bottom half of countries despite being the fastest-growing major economy in the world. The accumulated evidence suggests that the paradox of fast growth and poor legal system remains after three decades of reform.

Table 7.4   Contract enforcement

	Rank	Procedures (number)	Time (days)	Cost (% of debt)
Brazil	106	45	616	16.5
Canada	43	36	570	16.2
China	**20**	**35**	**406**	**8.8**
France	14	30	331	17.4
Germany	15	33	394	11.8
India	177	46	1420	39.6
Italy	155	41	1210	29.9
Japan	21	30	316	22.7
Poland	68	38	830	10.0
Romania	37	32	537	19.9
Russia	19	37	281	13.4
Slovakia	50	30	565	25.7
South Africa	85	30	600	33.2
Ukraine	46	30	354	41.5
United Kingdom	24	30	404	23.4
United States	8	32	300	9.4

Notes: Contract enforcement measures the efficiency of the judicial system in resolving a commercial dispute. The data are built by following the step-by-step evolution of a commercial sale dispute before local courts. The data are collected through study of the codes of civil procedure and other court regulations, as well as surveys completed by local litigation lawyers and by judges in some instances. Countries are ranked out of 175 countries in the sample.

Source: World Bank Doing Business Database, 2008 (www.doingbusiness.org).

Table 7.5   Protection of property rights

United States	90
Canada	90
United Kingdom	90
Germany	90
Japan	70
France	70
Slovakia	50
South Africa	50
Italy	50
Poland	50
Brazil	50
India	50
Romania	30
Ukraine	30
Russia	30
China	**20**

Notes: Property rights are an assessment of the ability of individuals to accumulate private property, secured by clear laws that are fully enforced by the state. The index is from 1–100.

Source: Heritage Foundation Index of Economic Freedom, 2008.

Table 7.6   Freedom from corruption

United Kingdom	86
Canada	85
Germany	80
Japan	76
France	74
United States	73
Italy	49
Slovakia	47
South Africa	46
Poland	37
Brazil	33
India	33
China	**33**
Romania	31
Ukraine	28
Russia	25

Notes: Freedom from corruption is based on quantitative data that assess the perception of corruption in the business environment, including levels of governmental legal, judicial and administrative corruption. The index is from 1–100.

Source: Heritage Foundation Index of Economic Freedom, 2008.

3.   INSTITUTIONS AND TRANSITION IN CHINA

Legal development in China should be viewed as an evolutionary process, alongside incremental economic reforms undertaken during its transition from central planning. This is not dissimilar to the experience of rich countries at a similar stage of development when their legal systems developed alongside their markets. What makes China unusual is a confluence of factors. First, it was able to establish markets within a communal property system, which highlights the importance of administrative measures and institutional reforms. Second, its transition and therefore its marketisation were gradual, such that markets were not always established by laws at the outset but developed over time, after experimentation with various market mechanisms, such as the 'dual track' pricing system and the export-oriented Special Economic Zones (SEZs). Third, it is undertaking reform and global integration at a time of international economic laws and rules which extend beyond trade and affect financial regulation and intellectual property rights (IRPs). The external influence of laws and rules will affect expectations within and without China, particularly in emphasising regulatory transparency and the enforcement of laws.

There appears to be a complementary process between law and markets, where law neither entirely precedes market nor vice versa. Formal written law creates property rights in intellectual property, legitimises corporate forms and establishes capital markets. Informal markets can often also arise through barter and small-scale transactions. Once the markets are established, then in both common law and civil law traditions, there is a process of interpreting and revising the laws respectively through a judicial or legislative process. This process is driven by interested constituents vested in the markets, which can include holders of IPRs, owners of private firms, and shareholders (see Coffee 2001; see also, Sun and Tobin 2009), as well as governments wishing to reform their state-owned enterprises (for example, China in the 1990s) or restore confidence in markets (for example, US Securities and Exchange Commission or SEC). Countries which produce more effective laws and regulations will have better functioning markets, which in both the common and civil law traditions occur over time. For instance, better shareholder protection is associated with higher growth rates (La Porta et al. 1997). Provinces in China with better legal protection are associated with improved firm performance (Cull and Xu 2005).

Evaluating the US at the time of the adoption of its corporate laws, the indicators of effectiveness of laws are unlikely to be as strong as they are at present, since key protections are not specified in a statute at the time of adoption, but develop over time with judicial and legislative review. Looking more widely, a historical review of common and civil law countries reveals that the countries do not have strong rule of law at the inception of the laws but effectiveness, such as measured by shareholder protection, develops over time (Pistor et al. 2003).

The sequence of law and markets is not the only paradox of China's economic success. Markets were created in the absence of private property rights, as China's transition has been largely undertaken in a communal property system. Laws therefore did not play the main role in creating markets during much of China's reform period; instead, administrative dictates and institutional reform were often more crucial. For instance, the passage of the Company Law in 1993 occurred after the start of the transformation of SOEs into shareholding companies, just as private firms emerged during the mid 1990s prior to the passage of the Law on Individual Wholly-owned Enterprises in 1999. Indeed, some have argued that administrative arrangements took the place of laws in creating China's capital markets (Du and Xu 2009). In numerous respects, markets started with institutional reform in China.

Hearkening back to the agricultural reforms of the late 1970s and early 1980s, the 'institutional innovations' of the Household Responsibility

System (HRS) created property rights by allowing farmers to retain a portion of their earnings under the still communal land system, as discussed in Chapter 3. Much of China's reform of SOEs has occurred without an explicit change in ownership from state to private, as the gradual corporatisation and the share issue privatisation processes are ongoing after nearly three decades (see Chapter 4).

China's approach has been to pass laws or administrative dictates to reflect a successful experiment. The Household Responsibility System, responsible for raising agricultural productivity during the early 1980s, was initially banned, then permitted, which has been described as a 'no encouragement, no ban' approach (Naughton 1996). The same occurred with land tenure rights which led to farmers selling their leaseholds in rural areas, which was initially banned until it became widespread and also pre-dated the passage of the Property Law in 2007. Many identify this flexible approach to 'experimentation' as the source of China's success (see, for example, Qian and Xu 1993).

The notable 'institutional innovations' were the Household Responsibility System for rural residents in the late 1970s and early 1980s, the Budgetary Responsibility System (BRS) allowing decentralisation of state-owned banks and local authorities in the early 1980s, and the Contract Responsibility System (CRS) instigated in the mid 1980s for state-owned enterprises. A more formal set of legal property rights was created for foreign investors in the late 1970s/mid 1980s in the form of joint venture laws, discussed later, as this was quite separate treatment than that accorded to Chinese domestic enterprises.

China's 'dual track' transition, in which one part of the market was liberalised while the other was kept under administrative control, generated growth from the marketised part to support the gradual reform of the faltering state-owned sector and maintain overall economic stability during the transition (Lau et al. 2001). Prior to the 'institutional innovations', collectivisation meant that there was little incentive for farmers to produce output, as their work points were allocated on the basis of a day's labour irrespective of effort. Adopted by households gradually in the early 1980s alongside a move to de-collectivise agriculture, the incentives generated from receiving some returns from own labour caused agricultural output to increase substantially (Riskin 1987). A significant part of China's growth in agricultural productivity and the overall rural economy can be traced to both the HRS and de-collectivisation (Huang and Rozelle 1996).

Whereas the HRS refined the incentives facing households, the creation of township and village enterprises (TVEs) is a striking example of how China created a new institutional form whose parameters were defined by policy and not by private ownership or outright transfer of ownership to individuals. Yet, the reliance of the Chinese rural workers on this newly recognised institutional form of enterprise was sufficient to instil market-driven incentives to fuel rural industrialisation, whereby TVEs grew rapidly and accounted for an impressive one-third of China's total output in the mid 1990s. The evidence of growth stemming from these reforms is notable, as rural industrialisation helped remove surplus labour from the farms and contributed significantly to the remarkable poverty reduction witnessed in China in the early part of the reform period (see Chen and Ravallion 2007).

With respect to the urban economy, in the mid 1980s the CRS permitted state-owned enterprises to pay a fixed amount of taxes and profits to the state and retain the remainder. In principle, so long as the SOEs delivered the tax and profit remittances specified in the contracts, they were free to operate. This resulted in increased production by SOEs in the late 1980s through the reorientation of incentives for managers. However, the decline of SOEs in the 1990s illustrated the limits of relying on the so-called institutional innovations. 'Soft budget constraints', whereby the enterprises are not bound by the constraints of profit and cost due to the support of the state, continued to plague SOEs. This is in spite of the positive incentive effects of the CRS and eventually led to the transformation of many SOEs into stock-holding companies in the 1990s, with ownership changing into private hands.

Reform of the state sector was also important. Decentralisation has occurred in nearly all areas of decision-making in production, pricing, investment, trade, expenditure, income distribution, taxation and credit allocation through the BRS (Riskin 1987). Since 1980, under the BRS, the central government has shared revenues (taxes and profit remittances) with local governments. For local governments which incur budget deficits, the contract sets the subsidies to be transferred to the local governments. Fiscal decentralisation gave further scope for regional experimentation by local governments, a key element in China's gradualist path because it permitted market-oriented activity, while limiting the possibility of instability through enabling the fairly autonomous actions of different provinces to act relatively independently. This was instead of a top-down approach whereby a mistaken national policy could reverberate throughout the country (Qian and Xu 1993).

Therefore, across all sectors of the economy, marketisation, though imperfect, has gradually taken hold in assisting China's transition. Given the gradual reform over three decades whereby the market developed over time, the legal system supporting the market economy was likewise underdeveloped for most of this period. Instead, the development of the market in China can be traced to governmental administrative dictate and institutional reforms. For instance, administrative measures creating a quota system across provinces produced a reasonably successful stock market in China during the 1990s in the absence of a complete legal system (Du and Xu 2009). Not all reforms were initiated by the state; rather, the system was adaptable, including to economic experiments which often led to the passage of law and regulations by the government, such as the Property Law of 2007. Individuals and firms, moreover, responded well to the incentives generated by administrative measures. China's strong administrative law tradition is perhaps one explanation for the willingness of the populace to rely upon such administrative arrangements instead of clearly defined property rights established in law.

4.   FOREIGN FIRMS AND FORMAL LAWS

China's treatment of foreign firms, by contrast, was governed by formal laws which nevertheless suffered from imperfect enforcement. Gauging their response sheds some light on how China's imperfect enforcement of laws, which is as important as the written law itself, has not impeded its marketisation process.

Since the 'open door' policy reforms of China's external sector were adopted in the late 1970s and speeded up in the early 1990s, China has rapidly become one of the world's top destinations for foreign direct investment (FDI). The first significant commercial law passed in China was the Chinese-foreign Equity Joint Venture Law of 1979. This, and its counterpart laws establishing cooperative JVs and WOFEs passed in 1986 and 1988 respectively, pre-date laws establishing the legal forms for Chinese domestic firms which were passed a decade or so later. The better delineated rights of foreign investors have even been a source of contention amongst Chinese private firms whose rights were less clearly protected for much of the reform period (see, for example, Huang 2006).

For most of the reform period, especially prior to WTO accession in 2001 after which legal reforms were targeted for improvement, the predominant form of FDI was Chinese-foreign joint ventures (JVs), where the Chinese and foreign partners set up either equity or cooperative joint ventures. Both forms of joint ventures were vested in contracts that legally specified the rights and obligations of both parties and were subject to judicial enforcement. The same could be said of the law governing wholly-owned foreign-owned enterprises (WOFEs). The uncertainty that might have been generated by the lack of adequate protection of private property due to a weak legal system, though, did not seem to serve as a deterrent to

FDI, which is another puzzle in China's growth narrative. Indeed, China is a competitive destination for foreign direct investment, even measured against developed economies, such as the US and UK, despite its underdeveloped legal and institutional system.

Therefore, China recognised early on that foreign firms operating in a global context and from developed economies needed laws to govern their rights, even if the enforcement of those rights was imperfect. Unsurprisingly, this generated an interested constituency of private Chinese firms who sought a similar level of legal protection for their property and transactional security, and this led to the passage of laws on partnerships and sole proprietorships in the 1990s. Whereas Chinese firms can accept administrative rule in lieu of judicial enforcement or an open legislative process to effect change, the puzzle is that the lack of effectiveness of laws, particularly in the area of enforcement, did not deter foreign investors (see, for example, Fan et al. 2009). However, since WTO accession, the clamour for better protection, in particular of intellectual property rights from foreign firms and governments has increased substantially.

One potential explanation has to do with the rise in alternative dispute resolution (ADR), notably arbitration, in China, which sought to supplant an incomplete legal system. The China International Economic and Trade Arbitration Commission (CIETAC) is relied upon by international investors, for instance, as is resort to international arbitration based in Europe or elsewhere (Bosworth and Yang 2000). Alternative dispute resolution has become more popular even in countries with well-developed legal systems such as the United States, due to its lesser costs. Another reason is the well-known Chinese reliance on relational contracting, that is, transacting on the basis of trust and known relations, is in part cultural, as it is evident even in overseas Chinese diasporas. Finally, there is a degree of risk in investing in any developing country, so foreign firms have a greater appetite for uncertainty when dealing in China or other emerging markets such as Russia than in the United States. In their initial calculus, they would have measured the risks of expropriation and lesser contracting security against the rewards of efficiency, cost saving and market access.

5. ENFORCEMENT AND INFORMAL INSTITUTIONS

The issue of enforcement further points to the continued presence of informal institutions, such as reliance on relational contracting or trust-based relationships, in China. There is undoubtedly a cultural element, in that interpersonal relationships, such as *guanxi,* play a notable role in economic transactions within and without China, even among the overseas diasporas. Within China itself, this was also perhaps enabled by the reliance on administrative dictates – a legacy of China's administrative law tradition.

Due to the absence of a well-established legal system, developing countries tend to rely on informal institutional arrangements, such as utilisation of social capital or relational-based contracting whereby contracting is undertaken with people on the basis of trust. Even developed countries relied on such relationships at the start of their marketisation. For instance, a study of the development of the UK capital market has found that ownership dispersion initially relied more on informal relations of trust than on formal systems of regulation (Franks et al. 2009). Enforcement, which is often a challenge in an underdeveloped legal system, can be by means of social capital instead of courts. For instance, social sanctions and norms account for the success of micro-finance institutions, such as the Grameen Bank in Bangladesh. The high repayment rate of loans is not due to threatened legal action, but on account of social capital in the community which acts to enforce the terms of the loan. By overlooking informal institutional arrangements which support the rule of law and other formal institutions, the extent of legal and institutional reform can be misjudged and developing countries could suffer from mis-fashioned policies as a result. In other words, as countries are increasingly judged on the quality of their institutions, poor legal systems are a common area of criticism of developing countries and aid or technical assistance can hinge on legal reform, so leading to adoption of laws that may not suit the country. In the extreme, 'transplanting' legal systems into less developed countries has not been successful (see Pistor et al. 2000).

Enforcement is easier within a community, but the judicial system still requires reform, as the number of arm's-length agreements increases, which makes informal enforcement less feasible. The development of legal reforms in the West followed a similar pattern, suggesting that greater marketisation will need more legal reform to govern relationships that can no longer rely on trust alone. However, relational contracting, that is, dealing with trusted parties, is much cheaper than litigation if a relationship goes sour, which also explains the continued reliance on social capital in small businesses, even in developed economies with more complete but expensive legal systems. China is at a stage where its small businesses and entrepreneurs can still effectively utilise informal institutional arrangements for enforcement alongside the reforming formal legal ones.

Given the necessarily slow pace of creating an independent judiciary, it is likely that informal arrangements, as well as particularly arbitration when the transactions are more at arm's-length, will remain in place for some time to come. But this can also help explain how China has been able to grow and marketise with a legal system that suffers from weak enforcement and thus lacks effectiveness.

6. CHINA'S LEGAL AND ECONOMIC REFORM IN AN ERA OF GLOBAL INTEGRATION

China's experience over the past 30 years has been the envy of many developing and transition economies, as well as being an 'outlier' with its poor legal system and rapid growth. A final aspect of China's reform is the influence of the international economic system. Whilst China has gradually integrated itself into the global economy during the 1990s, the world economy also underwent a transformation with the emergence of a growing body of international economic laws and rules. Although global trade rules in particular have existed previously, the creation of the WTO in 1995 brought to prominence a number of laws, rules such as those governing intellectual property, as well as a dispute resolution mechanism (DSU) with influence on China's legal reforms upon accession in December 2001. Other rules that China accepted, such as the trade-related aspects of intellectual property rights (TRIPs) provision, led to further revisions of its intellectual property rights regime in order to comply with the harmonised global laws governing IPRs. Moreover, the DSU provides a forum for countries to bring actions against other WTO members who are thought to have violated a precept of the WTO rules. For instance, China was the major target of anti-dumping actions before the DSU in the 2000s. Threatened action alone can at times discourage the behaviour, such as the US rescinding tariffs on steel imports faced with the prospect of a WTO action. Moreover, legal protection and enforcement of IPRs as provided for under the TRIPs Agreement can also be actioned before the DSU, such as the US case brought against China.[1]

Aside from trade rules, the past decade has also witnessed the development of greater integration among financial markets, which led to the creation of financial codes such as the Basel Standards governing capital adequacy ratios of banks, among other things, as promulgated by the Financial Stability Forum (recently re-constituted as the Financial Stability Board in 2009) of the Bank for International Settlements (BIS, known as the central banks' central bank). In particular, both the Asian financial crisis of the late 1990s and the 2008 global financial crisis have highlighted the linkages among banking and financial systems, which prompted the need for coordination of financial regulation and commonly understood standards. Unlike the WTO-related rules, countries voluntarily adopt the standards to signal their management of risk and financial soundness to global capital markets. Sun and Tobin (2009) argue that Chinese firms which list overseas and operate in international financial markets do so as a signal when capital could otherwise be raised in China's high savings economy. However, the more rigorous standards of overseas listings are borne as a sign of a robust enterprise that a Chinese domestic listing could not provide. Other examples include the voluntary code of conduct adopted by sovereign wealth funds (SWF), that is, state-owned funds investing their foreign exchange surplus overseas. Although there are no rules which compel a SWF to do so, countries such as Singapore declare their activities and their intent to invest as passive, minority shareholders in the companies of other countries. By so doing, they seek to avoid political interference in their investments, but do so in a lacuna as far as international economic law is concerned. All of these factors suggest that China's legal reforms will not be advanced in a vacuum, particularly given its prominence in the global economy.

7.   CONCLUSION

This chapter has examined several aspects of the relationship between law and economic growth in China. It has assessed the theoretical and empirical relationship between laws and the development of markets across countries, spanning currently developed, developing and recently transitioned economies. The sequence of laws and markets appears asynchronous for China. However, the argument that laws and markets reinforce each other (with laws more likely to follow markets in most instances) was made. Although a law or administrative dictate (or absence of strict prohibition) may create a market, even though informal relational contracting exists in any case, this is insufficient to argue that the sequence must be laws preceding markets. Even innovation can happen without IPRs. By the yardstick of whether an effective rule of law exists, which goes beyond just the provisions that create an IPR or a corporate form, laws appear to develop in response to market demands and needs.

This perspective agrees with the views of legal scholars and others such as Chen (2003), but is at odds with the work of economists such as La Porta et al. (1997, 1998) and Acemoglu et al. (2005), who argue that the existence of market-supporting institutions is the cause of subsequent robust growth. However, it agrees with the latter insofar as once a market is established, laws are needed, which in turn enables significant market development, so legal reforms are very much needed to support a mar-ketising economy. It is difficult, if not impossible, to fit China into this paradigm given its history and context. However, China's experience suggests that there are more parallels than would at first appear between its legal and economic development with the United States, the UK and other advanced economies. Specifically, China's legal development is not dissimilar to theirs at a comparable stage in their economic development.

A further paradox in China's growth model was explored, namely, the development of a market within a state-controlled communal property system. Administrative measures and ensuing institutional reform com-plete the picture for China, whereby its several decades-long economic transition has been driven by a series of experiments, trials, and a 'no encouragement, no ban' policies. Given the context, the lack of laws establishing clearly defined property rights appears not to be as pertinent as perhaps it is in other countries.

Finally, the chapter concludes by accounting for the influence of the global rules-based system that is gradually emerging and that has gained prominence around the same time as China's integration into the international system after years of inward-focused development. There are numerous limitations upon the reach of the fledging international legal system, but certain rules such as IPR protection will influence the course of China's domestic reforms. The system, though, is two-way. Particularly in the area of voluntary adherence to rules and norms, China and its firms will seek those which advantage them, while at the same time allowing them to operate in the evolving global financial system. The picture may be more complex, but looks ever more evolu-tionary as countries gather at various international forums to negotiate and agree everything from liberalisation of trade to rules governing risk assessment of banks.

China may continue to be viewed as a paradox, but its path will be enticing for many developing countries for which it is not unusual to have a nascent legal system that will not rate well in terms of effectiveness or enforcement. Figure 7.1 shows that China has made halting but gener-ally positive progress in improving its rule of law over the past decade. The success of China, and the prospect of it strengthening laws alongside robust economic growth, offers the possibility of it being a model to emulate.

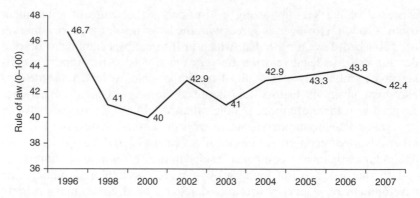

Note: Rule of law measures the extent to which agents perceive that the rules of society, in particular the quality of contract enforcement, the police, and the courts, as well as the likelihood of crime and violence, are enforced. The percentile rank places the country on a scale of 0–100 where 100 indicates a country that scored the highest possible value on the rule of law indicator. The governance score is normally distributed with a mean of zero and a standard deviation of one. Governance is better as the value increases.

Source: World Bank Worldwide Governance Indicators, 2008.

Figure 7.1   Evolution of rule of law over time, 1996–2007

NOTES

*   See further *World Development*, Special Issue on 'Law, Finance and Economic Growth in China', April 2009, especially my 'Law, Finance and Economic Growth in China: An Introduction' (with Yang Yao), *World Development*, 37(4), 2009, 753–62.
1.   WTO Dispute DS362, initiated on 17 April 2007: http://www.wto.org/English/tratop_e/dispu_e/cases_e/ds362_e.htm.

8.   Innovation*

1.   INTRODUCTION

Patent laws establish a system of intellectual property rights (IPRs) that secure returns on an innovation and provide protection against expropriation which in turn should increase the propensity to innovate. Innovation is thought to be crucial to the long-run growth potential of an economy. For a developing and transition economy such as China, there is a further prospect of obtaining advanced technology from more developed countries through foreign direct investment or FDI, which allows for 'catch up' in growth. The lack of strong productivity gains in China throughout its otherwise remarkable period of growth during the post-1979 reform period underscores the importance of assessing the determinants of innovation in its economy (Borensztein and Ostry 1996). Much of China's growth has been attributed to capital accumulation, which is not unexpected, but points to the need for innovation to stimulate technological progress and thus improve long-run growth.

China's first patent law was passed in the same year as urban reforms began in 1984. With accession to the World Trade Organization (WTO) in 2001, China adopted the associated trade-related aspects of intellectual property rights (TRIPs) agreement and has harmonised its IPR system with international standards. However, ineffective enforcement of IPRs has been an issue. Despite the imperfect legal system, patents have nevertheless increased rapidly in China in the 2000s (see, for example, Hu and Jefferson 2009).

This chapter examines the effectiveness of the patent law system in China. An assessment of the effectiveness of patent laws in producing innovation should also consider the determinants of patents. In other words, technology-oriented policies, particularly in developing countries, such as China, are likely to affect the success of patents under any system. Further, given the size and diversity of China's provinces in terms of economic development and the importance of provincial authorities in forming industrial policies, regional differences are also explored. This chapter develops a patent production function for China which is similar to the ideas function in the endogenous growth literature (Romer 1986).

An innovation function in China would include the inputs into innovation (researchers) and other factors which could increase the propensity to innovate, such as through FDI, under its IPR system.

With its incomplete legal system characterised by weak enforcement, the effectiveness of patent laws in China is an interesting question, particularly as the number of patents has grown steadily since the 1990s. As China emerges as a significant economy among the largest in the world, the scope for comparing the drivers of its innovation with OECD countries will also be of interest. With its successful record of attracting FDI, the contribution of foreign capital to innovation would be important to determine, particularly for other transition and developing economies.

The questions raised include whether China's patent laws are effective in producing innovation and on exploration of whether the contextual factors that generate innovation within such a system, for example, R&D spending, number of researchers, FDI. The chapter examines patent success rates across provinces at different levels of development; asks whether FDI matters, following the focus of developing and transition economies on seeking foreign capital and technology transfers to help them to achieve technological progress; it looks at whether China's R&D spending has generated innovation captured in patents, akin to the OECD focus on increasing expenditure on research and development to foster productivity; and whether increasing research personnel will result in technological advancement, along the lines of the studies of the US, where innovation is found not to be clearly linked to the number of researchers.

2.   CHINA'S PATENT LAWS AND POLICIES

2.1   Patent Laws

China's patent law was enacted in 1984 and promulgated in 1985. In 1992, it was revised to extend the length of patent protection from 15 to 20 years for invention patents and from five to 10 years for process patents, for example, model and design patents. In 2000, it was further revised in anticipation of accession to the World Trade Organization, which occurred in 2001. In 2001, China adopted TRIPs as part of its WTO obligations, whereby its IPR standards were harmonised with international rules. Since the passage of the patent laws, there have been dozens of regulations and guidelines adopted to promote innovation. The patent law amendments also included conditions on the granting of compulsory licences and prohibiting the unauthorised importation of products which infringe on the patents.

China's copyright law was promulgated in 1991 and has been amended several times since and limits protection to works that do not harm China's 'public interest'. Enforcement of copyright laws was further strengthened to step up criminal prosecutions in 2004. Finally, China's trademark law was promulgated in 1983 with significant revisions in 1993, which permit registration and provide protection for service marks and also criminal sanctions for trademark infringement.

Patent laws are promulgated through an IPR system that centres on a set of regulators which examine patent applications. Thus, as elsewhere, innovation is determined by the formal laws that establish IPRs, as well as the regulatory system that effectuates those laws. Imperfection in the legal and regulatory system can refer to both the formal written laws and the regulations and regulators entrusted with their enforcement. The IPR system in China is centralised around the State Intellectual Property Office (SIPO), founded in 1980 as the Patent Office and renamed in 1998, the Trademark Office started in 1982 and in 1985 the National Copyright Administration. The Ministry of Commerce has a department that deals with trade-related intellectual property issues and the Chinese People's Court system addresses enforcement in the national IPR system.

China's set of patent laws appears to largely meet the standards of international law, as do the processes of its IPR system. However, the adoption of laws does not necessarily imply effective enforcement, which will come under increasing scrutiny with the implementation of TRIPs. TRIPs should strengthen the IPR regime in China, particularly in terms of its enforcement provisions within the WTO. Approximately 10% of cases brought before the dispute settlement mechanism of the WTO relate to the TRIPs provisions, and China in 2009 lost an action to the United States over the imperfect implementation of its IPR system.

Thus, for China, TRIPs raises concerns about the development of its IPR system. It challenges China to adhere to strict standards that will place less emphasis on imitation and more on innovation by its own firms. Understanding what drives innovation under these laws will thus be important, that is, whether spending on researchers is as important as FDI policy.

2.2 Assessing Patent Laws and Industrial Policies

When considering the effectiveness of patent laws, it is not only the *de jure* law and the *de facto* enforcement that is of interest, but also the contextual factors which influence the propensity to innovate. These include industrial policies, such as China's creation of Special Economic Zones (SEZs) geared at attracting FDI, as well as domestic factors, such as R&D spending and encouraging research personnel.

Enforcement certainly matters, and the poor enforcement of laws in China is well known. However, China has managed growth from a weak institutional base, namely, the lack of well-defined property rights and an incomplete legal system with which to enforce rights, such as those granted by patents. Nevertheless, China has focused a great deal of effort on developing industrial policies to utilise the technology embodied in FDI and has increasingly spent on R&D, supporting researchers to foster innovation. Thus, the conclusions surrounding the economic impact of the patent laws are likely to be heavily linked to the determinants of patent production in China. An investigation of patent laws and innovation would need to encompass both the impact of the laws and the factors which influence their effectiveness.

Furthermore, the vast disparities in the levels of development among China's provinces and the autonomy that they have in terms of law and policy suggest that any study must also differentiate among provinces. The early opening of some coastal provinces is associated with faster growth, more FDI, and more innovation. However, the policy aimed at developing the interior in the past decade coincides with the focus on technological progress such that SEZs that are geared at high technology (the High Technology Development Zones (HTDZs) are located throughout China) and not just clustered on the coast as with the early SEZs. Assessing patent laws in China must therefore further consider the contexts of the provinces and regions.

3.   PATENTS AND GROWTH

Technological innovation, such as that which is captured in formal intellectual property rights, holds significant implications for economic growth. As innovation generates technological advancement, it is the crucial driver of long-run economic growth.

Another major area surrounds the potential for FDI to bring advanced technologies to developing countries. The relationship between foreign direct investment and economic growth is an enduring question in development, and relates to the nature of technology transmission and possible positive spillover effects from multinational investments (Rodríguez-Clare 1996). FDI is thought to allow developing countries to 'catch up' in the growth process by closing the technology gap through imitation and adoption of established technologies. The evidence, though, is limited (Rodrik 1999). The lack of convergence of the growth of rich and poor countries suggests that the process of capital and technology flows still needs to be better understood (Yueh 2007).

There are a number of studies which have examined possible spillover effects of inward FDI on host countries (see Blomström and Kokko 1998 for a survey). Of the potential spillover effects from establishing foreign direct investment, there is only limited empirical evidence as to whether FDI improves the technological capability and productivity of local firms, particularly in countries in the early stages of development (Javorcik 2004). Establishing and understanding this link would perhaps shed light on the key for developing countries to achieve longer-term growth. In particular, the means through which technology is transferred between multinational corporations and the host countries are not well understood. The possible avenues include explicit transfers, such as technology licensing contracts, and implicit transfers, including 'learning by doing' and transmission of skills from foreign skilled labour to domestic employees working in the same factory.

There is also a large literature on innovation production functions and the increasing returns which characterise endogenous growth models (see Romer 1986). Empirically, these studies attempt, among other things, to discover if increasing the number of researchers increases innovation at an increasing rate (since an invention can generate a multitude of other innovations, so there is a 'standing on shoulders' effect) or if more researchers merely duplicate research. For the United States, Jones (1995) finds evidence of the latter. As China attempts to increase innovation through spending more on R&D, this relationship is unknown, but also crucial to discover.

Despite the relatively well-defined IPR system, the attractiveness of China to FDI and the evidence of its impressive technological upgrading in manufactured goods, there are few empirical studies related to innovation in China. A main reason is due to data limitations, although there are studies emerging at the firm level (see, e.g., Hu and Jefferson 2009). Also, a positive and significant effect of FDI has been found with respect to the number of patent applications. Using data from 1995 to 2000, provinces with more FDI are found to have more patent applications (Cheung and Lin 2004). The difficulty with using filed rather than granted patent applications lies in filing not necessarily being the same thing as innovation. This chapter examines patents that have been granted, so the criteria for patents that usually include original and non-obvious innovation are more likely to have been met. A province which received substantial FDI could generate incentives to file patents, but this does not necessarily capture innovation, which is seen more readily through the number of patents that are granted than by the number of applications. This chapter will focus on patents that have been granted and a richer set of determinants in a model of patent production generated from China's patent laws. The estimation strategy will also utilise count models typically used for patents rather than ordinary least squares (OLS) with its biases.

4.   EFFECTIVENESS OF PATENT LAWS IN CHINA

4.1   China's Economic Development

China has an imperfect patent law system due to problems with enforcement, which is not uncommon among developing countries. However, the system was established fairly early in the reform process and provides for a formal system of IPRs, while many other rights in China tend to be informal, including private use of communal property, such as the Household Responsibility System. It also provides a measure of formal innovation so that a patent production function can be formulated for the economy. Moreover, China has had a successful history of attracting FDI on its own terms and is at a low level of economic development, which makes FDI more likely to embody advanced technology that could be transferred to its benefit. In addition, the government's explicit policy of targeting technology and creating science and industrial parks gives further evidence on which to judge the determinants of innovation similar to those which are found in more developed economies, notably the impact of R&D spending and researchers. The combination of law and policy within a national framework that also exhibits regional variation allows for an exploration of both the formal and the contextual factors that determine innovation.

In terms of regional variation, China's development path has been skewed toward the coastal provinces. This can be seen in the regions that have been permitted to experiment with market-oriented reforms, which were primarily urban areas in the eastern region that have contributed to rapid GDP growth. China's 'urban bias' and regional disparities are well documented (Knight and Song 1999). The resultant variation in regional and provincial growth is thus a product of government policy, which has focused on the urban areas and coastal regions.

Its FDI policy follows a similar pattern, where the 'open door' policy only applied to Guangdong and Fujian initially in 1980. Later opened areas, still primarily coastal and for the most part eastern, did not receive foreign investment until the mid 1980s, with the rest of the country opening up in the early 1990s after Deng Xiaoping's southern tour. Further, China's marketisation path is such that particularly with respect to FDI, the location of foreign investment and the clustering of economic activity would be highly conducive to agglomeration or network externalities, well-known in the new trade theory literature (Fujita et al. 1999).

In particular, since the mid 1990s, the HTDZs created 'science parks' or 'industrial parks' which aggregate economic activity in specified areas, such as the Haidian area of Beijing and the Pudong area of Shanghai. The HTDZs are geared at attracting more sophisticated technologies to China. Given the increase in FDI and the increase in the technological components of Chinese manufactured exports in recent years, the initial evidence looks supportive (Lall and Albaladejo 2004).

4.2 Patents in China

The data used in this chapter are drawn from the *China Statistical Yearbooks* and the *China Statistical Yearbooks of Science and Technology* for various years. The data cover the years from 1991–2003 and 29 provinces (not including Tibet, due to lack of data), and all figures are in 1990 prices.

There is rapid growth in patents during the reform period from just 138 patents granted in 1985 to around 20 000 two decades later, with the passage of the Patent Law. Figure 8.1 plots GDP per capita and patents awarded in China, and it is evident that patents have grown exponentially in the past few years, alongside national income.

Table 8.1 gives the number of patents filed and granted, along with GDP per capita data for each province. There is evidence of wide variation among provinces in terms of both GDP and patents. Looking at patents granted per capita, the variation remains, so it is not a result of population differences. For instance, Shanghai is nearly 50% richer than Beijing per capita, but Beijing has twice as many patents granted per capita. Comparing two of the poorest provinces, Anhui and Ningxia, with per capita incomes that are virtually identical, Ningxia has twice as many patents per capita. Although patents have grown alongside national income, provincial variations cannot be explained simply by reference to per capita GDP. Again, in terms of total patents granted in 2002, Guangdong holds 111 874. It is also the richest province, with a GDP per capita of 7482 RMB. By contrast, Ningxia, one of the poorest interior provinces of China, has a per capita GDP of 2898 RMB and 1879 patents. However, the rates of patent application to granted patents did not differ a great deal across provinces, suggesting that the reasons for the smaller number of patents in Ningxia is not necessarily the result of fewer successful applications.

Table 8.2 gives the patents granted rate for selected years and the average success rate. The average rate of patents granted to patents filed is similar across provinces, despite vastly different numbers of patents granted and levels of economic development. The lowest success rate is

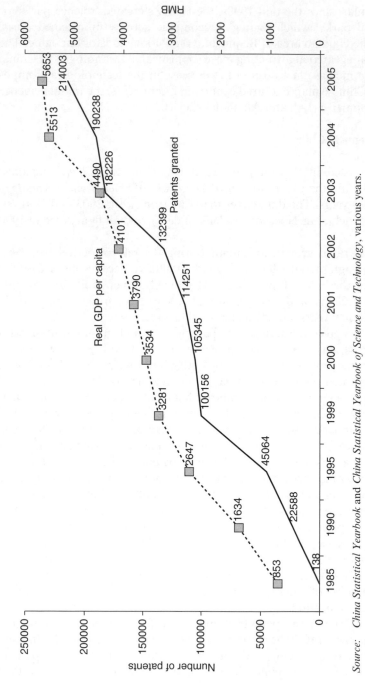

Source: China Statistical Yearbook and China Statistical Yearbook of Science and Technology, various years.

Figure 8.1   Patents and real GDP per capita (in 1990 RMB)

Table 8.1   Patents and GDP per capita by province, 2002

Province	Patents filed	Patents granted	Success rate (granted/ filed)	GDP per capita (RMB)	Patents granted per capita
Beijing	111065	60826	54.77%	14205	0.004398
Tianjin	30758	16951	55.11%	11174	0.001688
Hebei	44434	26750	60.20%	4551	0.000399
Shanxi	16012	9308	58.13%	3069	0.000284
Inner Mongolia	11031	6152	55.77%	3661	0.000259
Liaoning	80134	45965	57.36%	6484	0.001096
Jilin	27594	14672	53.17%	4161	0.000545
Heilongjiang	39194	20986	53.54%	5085	0.000551
Shanghai	76986	36474	47.38%	20295	0.002260
Jiangsu	84880	51960	61.22%	7185	0.000706
Zhejiang	91119	56119	61.59%	8407	0.001217
Anhui	18599	11229	60.37%	2891	0.000177
Fujian	36523	22150	60.65%	6739	0.000644
Jiangxi	17645	9382	53.17%	2910	0.000224
Shandong	93836	54088	57.64%	5814	0.000598
Henan	39953	22367	55.98%	3214	0.000234
Hubei	37148	19221	51.74%	4154	0.000322
Hunan	49366	26336	53.35%	3278	0.000399
Guangdong	168363	111874	66.45%	7482	0.001437
Guangxi	19183	10581	55.16%	2546	0.000221
Hainan	3860	2037	52.77%	4030	0.000256
Sichuan	62911	36918	58.68%	3586	0.000315
Guizhou	10038	5239	52.19%	1574	0.000138
Yunnan	16035	10275	64.08%	2586	0.000281
Shaanxi	27775	16397	59.04%	2847	0.000637
Gansu	8612	4724	54.85%	2243	0.000903
Qinghai	1988	1067	53.67%	3208	0.000204
Ningxia	3344	1879	56.19%	2898	0.000334
Xinjiang	10459	5917	56.57%	4185	0.000315

Note: GDP per capita has been deflated where 1990 is the base year.

Source: China Statistical Yearbook, various years; *China Statistical Yearbook for Science and Technology*, various years.

52% in Hubei while the highest is Guangdong with 67%. Hubei, is not the poorest province, while Guangdong is not the most innovative. Zhejiang is typically viewed as the province most driven by private-sector activity and technological advancement, yet its rate of patent success lags behind that of Guangdong. When considering regions, the interior has the highest

Table 8.2 Patents granted rate by province, selected years

Province	1995	1998	2001	Average grant rate, 1995–2003
Beijing	63.27%	60.12%	51.31%	57.02%
Tianjin	62.74%	70.17%	59.36%	58.82%
Hebei	58.37%	63.43%	59.45%	63.08%
Shanxi	62.05%	60.19%	71.08%	63.07%
Inner Mongolia	64.14%	66.62%	68.35%	59.29%
Liaoning	61.70%	56.03%	59.20%	58.06%
Jilin	59.32%	53.62%	54.93%	53.62%
Heilongjiang	54.61%	56.29%	50.95%	57.31%
Shanghai	58.47%	68.27%	42.04%	57.50%
Jiangsu	59.17%	64.97%	59.49%	63.39%
Zhejiang	52.72%	63.19%	64.80%	62.87%
Anhui	55.95%	62.87%	62.49%	61.49%
Fujian	47.15%	68.32%	66.30%	63.50%
Jiangxi	50.50%	60.76%	56.19%	55.69%
Shandong	61.87%	54.32%	60.21%	58.28%
Henan	47.99%	57.00%	63.08%	57.78%
Hubei	50.75%	48.12%	50.99%	52.70%
Hunan	57.65%	50.33%	55.94%	54.63%
Guangdong	59.66%	79.47%	66.17%	67.59%
Guangxi	54.02%	64.77%	59.79%	59.49%
Hainan	59.02%	51.07%	77.69%	59.67%
Sichuan	63.37%	58.15%	86.86%	63.81%
Guizhou	48.75%	52.25%	67.58%	56.22%
Yunnan	59.33%	73.24%	75.13%	67.65%
Shaanxi	63.04%	65.53%	58.21%	62.16%
Gansu	47.07%	58.36%	69.75%	59.00%
Qinghai	65.00%	45.26%	62.35%	56.45%
Ningxia	65.68%	53.63%	56.07%	59.45%
Xinjiang	51.23%	47.24%	69.52%	59.00%

Source: *China Statistical Yearbook*, various years; *China Statistical Yearbook for Science and Technology*, various years.

success rate of patent applications on average (61.04%) followed by the coast (60.51%) and the central region (57.28%) despite incomes in the coastal region being more than double that of the central and interior regions over this period (5447 RMB as compared with 2426 RMB and 2024 RMB, respectively). However, these figures are very close and given the small number of patents in the interior, they likely reflect insignificant differences in success rates.

Success rate is one measure of the economic effect of IPR rules. Applications are considered nationally and it seems that the patent grant rate is fairly uniform across provinces, despite their very different levels of development. Although not conclusive, the substantial differences in patent outcomes must be viewed within the context of underlying economic differences across provinces and not only as a result of institutional differences within the patent system. Therefore, the patent production process should be considered within the context of relevant policies and factors that affect innovation, such as R&D spending as well as the provincial environment, including its level of education and extent of openness and market development. FDI is another notable factor and China has enjoyed a rapid rate of growth of inward FDI since the 'open door' policy geared up in the mid 1980s. China had become not only the leading destination for inward FDI among developing countries, but was one of the top three destinations for global FDI, often ranking just behind the US.

Also, in the early 1990s when FDI began to pour into China primarily through the SEZs, during the early efforts to establish China's export capacity, the divergence between contracted and utilised FDI was significant. As China's technological capabilities in those areas of investment, namely, light industry and low technology products, increased, it was thought to be better able to use the agreed FDI and thus the gap between contracted and utilised FDI began to close half a decade later. A similar pattern may be emerging, corresponding to China's initiatives in the mid 1990s geared at attracting more sophisticated technologies through HTDZs. There is again a trend of divergence between the amount of contractually agreed FDI and the amount effectively utilised in the 2000s. This interpretation is consistent with the evidence of the increasingly complex technological make-up of China's exports, while China's domestic capacity lags somewhat behind.

5. DETERMINANTS OF INNOVATION

Next, the determinants of patent production will be explored. This section will present a simple model, followed by a discussion of the estimation approach, and then the empirical results nationally and by region will be presented.

5.1 Patent Production Function

The determinants of patents can be thought of as a production function that follows a Poisson process. As seen in Table 8.2, the success rate of patent applications is similar across provinces, despite vast differences in the level of development and the stock of innovation. The provincial variation allows for comparisons to be made within a national patent law system.

This patent production function would equate to the ideas/innovation production function in an endogenous growth framework (Jones 1995). This is not an attempt, however, to estimate the contribution of innovation to economic growth, but to determine the parameters of the ideas/innovation production function for China.

To address the overdispersion problem, whereby the standard errors for the Poisson estimator are too small, the Poisson Quasi Maximum Likelihood (PQML) estimator will be used. A negative binomial model will also be reported, which tests for the existence of the overdispersion issue. Thus, the negative binomial models are provided in the national estimates, though the more robust PQML estimates are interpreted in the chapter.

5.2   Estimating the Model

To estimate the patent production function, the main production input of R&D personnel is first entered in logs. Other factors that could affect the propensity to innovate, such as FDI, GDP per capita, degree of openness of the province, human capital, large and medium-sized firms (*guimo yishang*) measured in terms of sales, the extent of private sector development measured as the proportion of non-state sector firms' contribution to output in a province as well as the share of manufacturing output in a province, are also included. Year and province dummy variables are further accounted for.

From the *Science and Technology Yearbooks*, measures of the number of researchers can be obtained. R&D personnel, resulting from spending on R&D, can be a measure of a region's R&D stock. R&D expenditure has been shown to increase innovation in OECD economies (Bloom et al. 2002). The number of R&D personnel would be a relevant determinant of innovation, since individuals innovate and greater numbers of researchers could lead to more patents. However, the relationship would depend on whether having more innovators increases or duplicates existing research (Jones 1995). Researchers are, therefore, an ambiguous input in such functions and must be empirically determined.

Once the innovation input of R&D is controlled for, provincial characteristics may influence the productivity of the innovation process, via either a knowledge spillover or an incentive effect. These variables are obtained from the *China Statistical Yearbooks*. FDI is measured as the annual flow reported by the provinces. FDI is often associated with the transfer of more advanced foreign technologies to a developing country such as China, although the evidence of its effects can also be ambiguous as to innovation. FDI can either increase know-how or introduce competition that decimates domestic competition. There is mixed evidence surrounding the effects of FDI, as well as the criticism that Chinese technological upgrading in exports is not a result of innovation but of the significant contribution of foreign firms to producing exports.

Other provincial characteristics can also increase the propensity to innovate, if not the amount of resources that end up in the patent production process. Per capita GDP reflects the level of economic development of the province. The variable for per capita GDP is deflated by the consumer prices index (CPI), so that the reported figures are in 1990 prices. The degree of openness is also included because a province that exports may be more affected by pro-competitive forces derived from international trade, which can influence the propensity to innovate due to greater competition. Human capital, in the usual form of educational enrolment of school-aged children, is also entered as a measure of the level of education in the province, which can also increase the inclination to innovate by providing a skills base.

Key firm characteristics, such as the average firm size, the share of private sector and manufacturing share of output in provincial output are all included, as they can influence the propensity to innovate. Again, the relationship is determined empirically, since there is a long-standing debate as to whether larger or smaller firms innovate. Average firm size is measured by sales of industrial firms in a province. After 1998, the category used is the newly created category of large and medium-sized firms (*guimo yishang*) which refers to firms that report annual sales of five million RMB or more. Private sector development can suggest more competition that affects the propensity to innovate, while the state-owned sector could have more resources and be a direct instrument of the state in promoting innovation. Finally, manufacturing firms are the ones that often undertake innovation, so how industrialised a province is would also influence the tendency to innovate. Year dummies are entered to account for any overall trends in productivity during the period, 1991–2003, and a provincial dummy is included to control for other unobserved fixed effects. This chosen period coincides with the 'open door' policy taking off in China and accession to the WTO. This is also the period of significant economic growth in China, deriving from reform of the state sector and increased opening up to the global economy, which makes it an appropriate period of study. Finally, as FDI can be realised only with a delay, a lagged FDI variable is included. For instance, time is required between signing a contract to take over a factory in China and making it operational.

5.3   Empirical Results: National Estimates

First, there is evidence of overdispersion in the data, seen in the significance of the alpha parameter reported in Table 8.3. Therefore, the PQML estimator will be relied upon.[1] The results show that more R&D personnel significantly increases the number of patents. This is evident in column (1) and also in (2), where FDI is entered with a lag. The fixed effect negative binomial model produces the same significant result for R&D personnel. As such, the innovation input of more provincial R&D expenditure on research personnel is associated with more patents granted in a province. The marginal effect of R&D is a positive 8% improvement in the innovation process, holding other factors constant.

Among the other provincial characteristics that might increase the propensity to innovate, only per capita GDP is significantly positive. Richer provinces are associated with a greater propensity to innovate, which is consistent with higher income incentivising technological improvements to produce more sophisticated output to suit a more developed market.

Unlike the effect of R&D spending, which is a fairly straightforward input into producing patents, the estimate for FDI likely reflects the more complex relationship of foreign investment to patents. FDI can increase the propensity to innovate through knowledge spillovers, but the impact of FDI may also be to shield proprietary knowledge or to make it available through licensing, so that domestic firms either do not learn or simply imitate the more advanced technology, and thus do not patent. Foreign firms can also dominate the sector or market so that the competition they introduce relegates domestic firms to less innovative functions in the production/supply chain. It is not possible to disaggregate these effects, which attests to the conflicting evidence surrounding FDI spillovers. FDI is not a significant determinant when entered contemporaneously, but it is a negative factor when entered with a lag. It appears that when foreign investment is established rather than contracted, there is an effect. Therefore, FDI may produce exports with increasing amounts of technological improvement, but it does not increase the propensity to innovate in the province and instead reduces the tendency for Chinese firms to undertake innovation.

Turning to other control variables, the average size of above-size firms (*guimo yishang*), the ownership composition of the province in terms of share of the private sector, and the share of manufacturing output in a province are not significant. At the firm level, these are likely to be significant factors, but at a more aggregated level, these provincial traits are not significantly associated with a greater propensity to innovate.

Table 8.3   Determinants of patents in China, 1991–2003 (z-statistics in parentheses)

	Poisson (PQML) Model (1)	Poisson (PQML) Model with lagged FDI (2)	Negative Binomial Model (3)	Negative Binomial Model with lagged FDI (4)
R&D personnel	0.0814 (2.12)**	0.0690 (2.01)**	0.4511 (12.03)***	0.4588 (11.56)***
Foreign direct investment	−0.0886 (−1.30)	–	0.1970 (7.08)***	–
Foreign direct investment (one year lag)	–	−0.1742 (−2.43)***	–	0.2141 (5.81)***
Per capita GDP	1.6979 (5.91)***	1.7325 (5.70)***	0.0873 (0.84)	0.1126 (1.04)
Openness	0.0152 (1.29)	0.0158 (1.39)	0.0087 (2.89)***	0.0079 (2.47)**
Educational enrolment	0.0183 (0.85)	0.0261 (1.28)	0.0578 (2.09)**	0.0614 (2.16)**
Average firm size	−0.0139 (−1.25)	−0.0140 (−1.15)	0.0097 (0.60)	0.0140 (0.83)
Share of non-state sector in provincial output	−0.4576 (−0.74)	−0.03219 (−0.55)	0.4401 (1.47)	0.3650 (1.15)
Share of industry in provincial output	0.0107 (0.07)	−0.0290 (−0.21)	−0.1334 (−1.05)	−0.1293 (−0.95)
Overdispersion parameter	–	–	0.2190 (10.57)***	0.2294 (10.37)***
Wald $X^2(8)$	361.69***	249.76***		
LR $X^2(10)$			423.39***	386.40***
Pseudo R^2			0.1133	0.1075
N	212	203	212	203

Notes:
1. Dependent variable: patents granted. Mean is 2121.
2. Independent variables are: log of number of R&D personnel, log of foreign direct investment and with a one-year lag, log of per capita GDP, export-to-GDP ratio is the measure of openness, educational enrolment rate of school-aged children, average firm size including large and medium-sized firms (*guimo yishang*) measured by sales from 1998 onward, share of non-state (for example, not state-owned or controlled) firms in the output of the province as well as the share of industry in provincial output. Dummy variables for province and year are also included to control for time-invariant and time-varying effects.
3. Coefficients are followed by z-statistics, where *** denotes statistical significance at the 1% level, ** at the 5% level, and * at the 10% level.

Source: China Statistical Yearbook on Science and Technology, China Statistical Yearbook, various years.

5.4   Empirical Results: Regional Estimates

Given the earlier opening up of China's coastal provinces and their accounting for the bulk of GDP, there could be regional differences that are obscured by the aggregate estimations. Table 8.4 divides the provinces into the coastal region, which includes provinces early to open up, such as Guangdong; the central region, with provinces such as Hunan; and the interior region, which includes some of the least developed provinces like Qinghai, which does not have a High Technology Development Zone.

Not surprisingly, there are significant differences in the mean annual number of patents awarded in the regions. For the coast, the average number of patents during this period was 3492, while it was 1117 for the central region and 841 for the interior. However, the average success rate of patent applications is similar across regions. Indeed, the interior has a marginally higher rate of patents granted than the coast, which has a slightly higher rate than the central region. Thus, there is no correlation between the number of patents held and the grant rate. The regions exhibit rather different determinants of innovation.

Table 8.4 presents the estimates, which confirm that for every region, R&D is a significant determinant of innovation, but differently so. The findings for the coastal region are that the number of R&D personnel determines innovation with a similar magnitude (5–7% marginal effect) as the national estimates. Similar to the national estimates, FDI has a significantly negative effect on the propensity to innovate, as does FDI entered with a lag. This suggests that FDI in the coastal region, which receives the bulk of the investment, does not increase the innovation tendency of the province. It has the opposite effect, such that innovation on China's coast increases when there are R&D personnel undertaking innovation, rather than the expectation of spillovers from foreign investment.

Per capita GDP continues to promote innovation, and this effect is robustly evident across all regions. Unlike the national estimates, average firm size reduces the propensity to innovate, suggesting that smaller firms are more likely to innovate than larger ones in the more developed coast. This is found after controlling for private sector and manufacturing sector development, as well as openness and education, which are not significant factors.

The evidence for the central region is notably different from the coast. For these provinces, the number of researchers reduces innovation, while larger firms and the size of state-owned sector increase the propensity to innovate. Per capital GDP continues to show that innovation tendencies follow from greater economic development. FDI, openness and educational environment do not matter. The centre of China is poorer than the

Table 8.4 Determinants of patents in China by region, 1991–2003: Poisson (PQML) model (z-statistics in parentheses)

	Coast (1)	Coast (2)	Central (3)	Central (4)	Interior (5)	Interior (6)
R&D personnel	0.0745 (2.69)***	0.0535 (1.99)**	-0.2307 (-2.95)***	-0.1997 (-1.89)*	0.1859 (2.19)**	0.1593 (2.21)**
Foreign direct investment	-0.01739 (-1.88)*	—	0.0725 (1.33)	—	0.0314 (0.56)	—
Foreign direct investment (one year lag)	—	-0.2460 (-2.52)**	—	-0.0066 (-0.14)	—	-0.0778 (-1.49)
Per capita GDP	2.2864 (6.66)***	2.3733 (6.38)***	1.0123 (4.62)***	1.0367 (4.24)***	0.5142 (2.23)**	0.4248 (1.92)*
Openness	0.0048 (0.36)	0.0053 (0.43)	-0.0523 (-1.51)	-0.0569 (-1.41)	0.0133 (0.77)	0.0109 (0.56)
Educational enrolment	0.0250 (0.97)	0.0336 (1.65)*	0.0328 (1.48)	0.0380 (1.68)*	0.0314 (1.19)	0.0319 (1.12)
Average firm size	-0.0273 (-2.48)**	-0.0314 (-3.06)***	0.1354 (2.90)***	0.01219 (2.47)***	0.2590 (3.92)***	0.2329 (5.06)***
Share of non-state sector in provincial output	-0.6063 (-0.97)	-0.05093 (-0.94)	-0.6944 (-2.61)***	-0.6076 (-1.92)*	-1.3957 (-1.16)	-0.8622 (-0.82)
Share of industry in provincial output	0.1650 (0.88)	0.01403 (0.90)	-0.2410 (-1.75)*	-0.2355 (-1.53)	1.1552 (1.86)*	0.8021 (1.93)*
Wald X^2(8)	537.65***	917.37***	7679.66***	6048.80***	5241.29***	4649.07***
N	86	84	55	52	71	67

Table 8.4 (continued)

Notes:
1. Dependent variable: patents granted. For the coastal region, the mean is 3492. For the central region, the mean is 1173. For the interior region, the mean is 841.
2. Independent variables are: log of number of R&D personnel, log of foreign direct investment and with a one-year lag, log of per capita GDP, export-to-GDP ratio is the measure of openness, educational enrolment rate of school-aged children, average firm size including above-size firms (*guimo yishang*) measured by sales from 1998 onward, share of non-state (for example, not state-owned or controlled) firms in the output of the province as well as the share of industry in provincial output. Dummy variables for province and year are also included to control for time-invariant and time-varying effects.
3. Coastal region includes Beijing, Tianjin, Hebei, Liaoning, Heilongjiang, Shanghai, Jiangsu, Zhejiang, Fujian, Shandong, Guangdong, Guangxi and Hainan. Central region includes Shanxi, Inner Mongolia, Jilin, Anhui, Jiangxi, Henan, Hubei and Hunan. Interior region includes Sichuan, Guizhou, Yunnan, Shaanxi, Gansu, Qinghai, Ningxia and Xinjiang.
4. Coefficients are followed by z-statistics, where *** denotes statistical significance at the 1% level, ** at the 5% level, and * at the 10% level.

Source: *China Statistical Yearbook on Science and Technology, China Statistical Yearbook*, various years.

coast and it is firm characteristics that matter rather than spending on researchers. There is thus some evidence that there is 'crowding out' in that increasing the number of researchers does not increase the number of patents produced, but rather results in duplicated effort. More above-size firms also increases innovation, suggesting that larger firms have the resources and capacity to innovate. The importance of the state-owned sector, which is dominated by larger firms, offers further evidence. These findings together suggest that it is the state-owned or state-controlled enterprises that are likely to be the larger firms that innovate. The central region has retained a number of large SOEs, which have the resources to patent in a range of industries in which they still dominate, including telecommunications, while smaller, private firms that sell for export could be marketing goods that are lower in the technology spectrum and compete on price rather than innovative quality.

Finally, the evidence for the interior provinces is different again from the coastal and central provinces. There are some similarities in that, as with the national picture and the coast, R&D personnel and GDP increase the number of patents for these provinces. Larger firms are associated with a greater propensity to innovate, probably due to their having more resources. As many of the western provinces are among the poorest and most underdeveloped in China, those with a greater share of industry in their economy are also more likely to innovate. This increased propensity can be traced to most innovation being conducted by manufacturing firms.

The regional differences are notable, but R&D personnel are a consistently significant factor. Also robust is per capita GDP, which shows across all provinces that more developed markets have a greater tendency to innovate. This is similar to the observation that rich countries around the world are the most innovative, for example, the United States. FDI also has the same negative effect on the coast as for the national estimates, though with no effect in the poorer central and interior parts of China which receive less FDI and may also be less able to absorb the more advanced technology associated with it. Regional differences therefore abound and show that the determinants of patents are associated with varying factors across China.

6. CONCLUSION

Innovation as captured by patents has been increasing in China. The expectation of the implementation of TRIPs is likely to increase this incentive to patent, though the rate of successfully innovating is roughly the

same as before WTO accession. Nevertheless, the amount of formally captured innovation in the form of patents is indeed growing in China, despite
a much criticised imperfect legal system. Moreover, in spite of vastly different levels of regional economic development, the patent laws in China
have produced a steady rate of growth of patents across the country.

Despite similar grant rates, there remain vast differences among provinces in terms of their levels of innovation. Contextual factors and industrial and R&D policies are likely to play a role in explaining innovation.
Innovation in China is posited to be determined not only by the legal
system but also by factors that affect the production of patents, such as
R&D personnel, and provincial traits that could influence the propensity
to innovate.

R&D personnel are indeed found to be a significant determinant of
innovation, though the effects vary notably across China's regions. The
number of researchers matters in the coast and the interior, while increasing R&D stock depresses innovation in the central region, which relies
instead on SOEs and larger firms. Per capita income in a province is positively associated with a greater tendency to innovate across all regions,
while smaller firms on the coast are more likely to innovate, in contrast to
larger firms, which have an increased propensity to innovate in the poorer
central and interior regions. Interestingly, openness and educational enrolment do not matter, nor does FDI, except on the coast where it reduces
the propensity of a province to innovate, leaving no evidence of positive
spillovers, measured in terms of patents.

Therefore, the key drivers of innovation are found to be closely related
to China's R&D expenditure on researchers. Regional differences do exist,
reflecting the complexity of promoting technological advancement across
a nation as large as China.

The determinants of innovation are difficult to assess for any country
and patents are an under-measurement. China's patent laws have created
these formal measures of innovation despite a much-criticised IPR system.
Moreover, it has a growing stock of patents which has accompanied its
economic growth. The very different determinants for the coastal, central
and interior regions of China confirm that an economic analysis of the
impact of patent laws on innovation must also consider that the relevant
factors will probably depend on the context of the region. China's patent
laws have produced innovation despite their imperfections and innovation
is found to be largely affected by R&D personnel and not by FDI or other
policies such as openness to trade. As China contends with TRIPs and its
policies are scrutinised by developed and developing countries – the latter
coping with adjusting to an increasingly harmonised international IPR
regime – there is evidence of the importance of domestic spending on R&D

in generating innovation that will ultimately influence long-run economic growth.

NOTES

*   See further my papers 'Patent Laws and Innovation in China', *International Review of Law and Economics*, 29(4), 2009, 304–13; 'Global Intellectual Properly Rights and Economic Growth', *Northwestern Journal of Technology and Intellectual Property*, 5(3), 2007, 436–48.
1.   The coefficients are expected to differ due to the different underlying models, for example, the negative binomial model allows for between-subject heterogeneity, though its assumptions are stronger and may be violated, and thus the PQML estimates are interpreted.

9. Social coverage: education, pensions, health system and poverty*

1. INTRODUCTION

One of the key challenges confronting China as it proceeds with market-oriented reform is how it addresses the issues surrounding social coverage. Central to this is the high savings rate as insecurity over health, pensions and education has stymied consumption, which has fallen from 50% of GDP in the late 1980s – close to the share found in market economies – to around 35% in the late 2000s. Social securities were provided as part of the employment package in state-owned enterprises (SOEs) and these have proved problematic to reform. With the dismantling of the previous system, social securities will need to be shifted from SOEs, which had the task of providing welfare on behalf of the state, to a direct system run by the state. By so doing, China will begin to remove the 'multi-tasking' role of SOEs that has impeded their reforms, as discussed in Chapter 3, as they have had not only to maximise profits but also to achieve other aims such as maintaining social security and employment (Bai et al. 2000).

The maintenance of lifetime employment with such in-kind benefits generated the term 'iron rice bowl', to describe employment in urban China. The dismantling of this system, sometimes referred to as the cracking of the 'iron rice bowl', is essential to improving the competitiveness of enterprises, as China enters a more marketised era. The challenges in the labour market were discussed in Chapter 4.

Finally, no assessment of China can overlook the remarkable reduction in poverty over the past three decades. Thus, social coverage affects several aspects of China's transition and growth, and this chapter will discuss the background and reforms undertaken in the key areas of education, pensions and health insurance, during the reform period starting in 1979. Each of the areas will be assessed in turn and further much-needed reforms will be discussed where relevant. This will be followed by a discussion of poverty in China. The chapter will conclude with an assessment of the prospective impact of these social issues on the sustainability of China's economic growth.

2. EDUCATION

China's several million skilled graduates per year have been the source of envy for other economies. Tertiary education has doubled in enrolment since the 1990s and China produces over six million graduates per year. The record looks even better for secondary and primary schools. As such, in terms of educational attainment, China has indeed done comparatively well, producing the reasonably skilled labour that has manned its factories to become one of the largest industrial powers in the world.

2.1 Chinese School System

The Chinese educational system is generally comprised of primary (six years), secondary (six years, three years of lower- and three years of upper-middle school), and tertiary or higher education (varying between two and five years). Education is officially compulsory for nine years to the completion of lower-middle school, though not always in practice.

In the Chinese school system, students attend lower-middle school after completing primary school. They then go on to upper-middle school or middle-level professional school, depending on test results. Middle-level professional school generally takes one more year to complete than upper-middle school and is typically the last level attained. Those who complete upper-middle school are likely to apply and be tested for college. The examinations are very competitive and going to university could mean gaining an urban *hukou* to settle after graduation in the faster growing cities. Professional school is an alternative to college. Those who are selected for professional schools are likely to take on administrative or clerical work, and those who do not continue are likely to enter the labour force as factory or manufacturing workers.

Overall, school enrolment in China is high and there are no large gender differences in educational enrolment in urban China. UNESCO estimates the gross enrolment ratio of all school-aged children is around 94%; 91% for girls and 96% for boys.

In terms of higher education, China has graduated more engineers than the US, Japan and Germany combined every year since 1997, and some 60% of all students are enrolled in science and engineering degrees, according to China's National Bureau of Statistics. The relative equality in educational attainment and the focus on technical training in China's universities underpin a solid educational system.

2.2   Labour Market Reforms

Regardless of how good a basic educational system is, the decision of an individual to invest in accumulating human capital depends at least in part on the expected returns in the labour market. The lack of return to education and experience underscores the low stock of human capital in a number of developing countries. China's challenges in this area, in contrast, are more closely related to its status as a transition economy. In particular, China had a wage structure which was not based on productivity, but was administratively determined and governed by age and seniority.

When reforms started in the 1980s in urban areas, the state monopoly of labour allocation was replaced by a somewhat more decentralised system. Central and local labour authorities continued to plan the labour requirements of state and large collectively owned enterprises and remained responsible for the placement of college graduates. However, labour exchanges began to be established for the registration of job vacancies, job placements and training. By the 1990s, recruitment quotas for state enterprises were abolished and firms were largely allowed to choose their employees.

The reforms have appeared to be largely successful in that returns to productive characteristics, such as education, appear to be rising during the reform period (see Chapter 3), though the estimated returns to schooling are comparatively low for China. And returns to non-productive characteristics, such as Communist Party membership, also appear to be on the rise. Nevertheless, the move toward increasing rewards to human capital in China has transformed a labour market characterised by administered wages without incentives to one which encourages investment in human capital. This, in turn, fuels acquisition of education and training. Given the growing technological focus of China's economy, it has also helped foster attainment of education in science and technology. It is the creation of future innovators equipped for the knowledge economy which has the potential to stimulate the rate of economic growth in China. The worrying areas, though, include the growing importance of Party membership and the increasing gender wage gap.

3.   PENSIONS

Under the centrally planned economy, pensions were one of the in-kind benefits that accompanied the 'iron rice bowl' in urban enterprises and they were entirely the responsibility of the employer or work unit, as SOEs in particular are called. Each SOE paid pensions out of its own revenues, and likewise, state employees were paid out of governmental budgets. There was no accumulation or pooling across work units. As the payment of pensions depended on the work unit, only large SOEs and urban collectives could afford to make regular payments.

In 1984, some local governments initiated a system of pooling for the pensions of SOE employees. Then, in 1986, the State Council required both enterprises and individuals to contribute to the pooling funds. SOEs were required to pay an amount equal to 15% of the employee's wage, while individuals were required to contribute up to 3% of their wages.

Starting in 1995, a two-tier pension system was established. It included a pay-as-you-go system, with defined benefits equal to 20% of the average local wage and an individual account, into which employers and employees both contributed. There was also a move to include all urban workers regardless of the sector of employment. And local governments received permission to design their own pension systems.

In 1997, there were further reforms of the pension system. This system had three components: a small basic pension (pay-as-you-go), an individual account pension which could be fully funded, and a voluntary individual supplemental account, which could also be fully funded and would be tax exempt. The first component was to be funded by a payroll tax of 13% from pre-tax enterprise revenues, which would guarantee a replacement rate of 20% of the prevailing average wages at retirement, with a minimum of 15 years of contribution. The second would be funded by a payroll tax of 11%, contributed by both the enterprise and individual workers. At retirement, the worker would receive a monthly pension equal to the account balance at retirement, divided by 120.

These reforms were fuelled by a number of factors, including the rising dependency ratio due to an aging population and the restructuring of SOEs. Between 1993 and 1998, while participants in the pensions system grew by 15.5%, retirees increased by 67.5%. This was accompanied by a shrinking pension surplus and the emergence of a deficit in 1998. In addition to a rising dependency ratio, there was also rising non-compliance in payment which contributed to the deficit. Finally, many SOEs were simply loss-making and could not make regular pension payments.

Pension reforms since 1997 have attempted to address these issues by making pension benefits mobile and improving the financial balance of pension programmes. In the set of reforms implemented in 2000, enterprise contributions were used to finance the social pooling funds, while individual accounts were separated from the pooled funds. In 2001, further reforms were undertaken, including the government making more fiscal commitments to address the pension deficit in order to remove disincentives to making contributions into an indebted system. In 2003, the government transferred some of its shares in SOEs, including listed companies, into a National Social Security Fund (NSSF). The potential returns from the stock market make this reform a guardedly positive development, but progress has been slow and few shares have been transferred. Coverage is also incomplete. Some 46% of urban workers are covered but only 11% of rural workers, who suffer from never having had SOEs that provided coverage during the planned period.

The central government also initiated an experiment in Liaoning province that would transfer the responsibility of pension and other social security responsibilities from enterprises to social security agencies. This is intended to detach pension programmes from enterprises and guarantee the portability of pension accounts across firms and ownership types. The creation of a *dibao*, or minimum income guarantee system for the poor, as one component has been rolled out across China.

Government employees, however, are not governed by this system and they have continued to enjoy state-financed benefits. Without any individual contributions, these employees receive more than 90% of final year salaries as pensions, which are guaranteed by the state. In 2001, the average pension of government employees was more than 60% greater than the average pension for a SOE employee, for instance.

On account of China's rapidly aging population and its one-child policy, the pension system is on the brink of bankruptcy. The deficit is projected to grow and by 2010, there will be a financial gap of $110 billion. The support ratio in China, which is calculated as the proportion of individuals aged 20–64 to those aged 65 and over, was 8.8 in 2000. By UN estimates, it will be 2.4 in 2050, placing China on comparable terms with other aging OECD countries, but with an estimated 400 million pensioners to support.

With declining support ratios, there are three alternatives (see also West 1999). The retirement age could be raised, pensioners could be left poorer, or worker contributions could increase. These are issues that many countries are struggling with, and China is no exception. The declining support ratio does raise fundamental questions about the future of demographic changes in China and the one-child policy.

As for the reforms undertaken to make pensions portable and reduce the dependency on payments from the work unit, these are useful measures. China must first, however, address the implicit legacy of inheriting pension liabilities from the centrally planned period. The gap between governmental and SOE employees is another issue. The creation of the NSSF and moves to increase fiscal commitments are moves in the right direction, but China's fledgling and rather volatile capital market is not yet in a position to generate sufficient returns to adequately address the problem. Recent pension reforms announced in 2009 to reform the rural pension system are welcome but seem woefully inadequate, since only $400 million will be spent on around 500 million people in the rural labour force.

The reforms which have been undertaken to make pensions portable and the transfer of social security provision to state agencies are critical steps in relieving SOEs from their multi-tasking obligations and granting them greater scope to be competitive. This also helps China move toward a pension system that includes non-state enterprises and reduces regional inequities in pensions. These reforms could improve enterprise profitability with positive knock-on effects for capital markets, investment returns, and a better functioning labour market, which could sustain economic growth. But the question of demography remains.

4. HEALTH INSURANCE

As with pensions, health insurance was one of the in-kind benefits traditionally provided by the work unit. In rural areas, funding for health care was arranged through the collective known as the Rural Cooperative Medical Schemes (RCMS). But these declined when collectives were dismantled with the introduction of the Household Responsibility System in 1979 which allowed individual households to sell their own produce. The coverage of the rural medical insurance schemes fell from 85% to less than 10% during the reform period.

In urban areas, the work unit provided medical insurance and often also direct health services, which continued into retirement. However, this picture changed with the restructuring of SOEs and the growth of the non-state sector in the mid 1990s. In short, if the enterprise is loss-making, then it cannot afford to pay for medical costs, while the non-state sector was not subject to the provision of insurance required of SOEs. As a result of these shifts, fewer are now insured in urban areas than before, according to China's National Household Health Survey. In 1993, only 27% of households were uninsured. By the end of the decade, 44% of the population did not have insurance. The picture was worse in rural areas. In 1993, only 13% of the rural populace was covered, following the collapse of the RCMS in the 1980s. By the end of the decade, less than 10% were uninsured (Liu 2004).

These problems are further exacerbated by the rapidly increasing cost of health care in China. The cost of medical treatment has increased at a rate which is faster than income growth (Liu and Hsiao 1995). The combination of lack of coverage with rising health care costs has resulted in health care becoming a catastrophic event for households and a cause of precautionary savings, driving down consumption since the 1990s despite the economy growing at 9–10% per annum. Furthermore, rural-urban migrants, who are not entitled to in-kind benefits due to the nature of their casual employment contracts, are often uninsured in urban areas.

Moreover, there is a complicated system of health services provision, including each level of government running their own hospitals and clinics run by SOEs. Quality varies considerably. Governmental funding of public hospitals has also declined, with a majority of funding now coming from fees and insurance, including private insurers. There are, though, two public health programmes – the Epidemic Prevention Service (EPS) and the Maternal and Child Health (MCH) Service. The EPS provides preventive care, such as immunisation, while the MCH offers ante-natal and post-natal care. These are publicly funded, but charge for services.

The Chinese authorities recognise the importance of creating a functioning health care system and have undertaken a number of reforms to improve insurance provision and increase access to health care. In rural areas, the government is encouraging the development of local cooperative medical schemes, which will provide insurance for members, and is not dissimilar to the previous system of insurance provision by collectives. Beginning in 2003, the central government allocated a subsidy of 10 RMB per year for each rural resident signed up to the cooperative health care system in those areas. Local governments are required to match this subsidy and must also provide at least 10 RMB per person per year. The Chinese authorities are particularly concerned about the underdeveloped state of the rural health care system, which can lead to challenges when dealing with epidemics such as bird flu. Unlike in urban areas, where diseases such as AIDS and cardiovascular diseases are of concern, rural areas still suffer from diseases associated with unhygienic health conditions. This has caused many to describe the state of health care in China as also suffering from a rural-urban gap.

In urban areas, the government has rolled out a range of policies, including reform of medical insurance and rationalisation of hospitals. A unified medical insurance scheme at the municipal level is being promoted to which employers must contribute. This would increase coverage and spread risk. An estimated 86 million people are covered by the new system, the Basic Medical Insurance System for Urban Employees. The government is also asking cities to prepare plans regarding their hospital facilities, while developing community health services, which can offer a cheaper source of care. However, the lack of comprehensive coverage and the rising cost of health care have left urban residents feeling insecure about the potential financial exposure from illness.

The withdrawal of the state and the delinking of health care provision from enterprises have contributed to a dysfunctional health care system in

China. The government's share of national health spending has decreased from nearly 100% to 16% by the 2000s. This is compared with the US at 44% and more than 70% for other industrialised economies. The inadequate state of the health insurance system has come under increasing criticism, as it is increasingly the case that those who can obtain health care in China are the ones who can afford it (see, for example, Akin et al. 2004).

The increase in life expectancy for the Chinese has been 3.5 years since 1979, which is a small increase compared with other Asian countries during their periods of rapid economic growth. The prerequisite of a healthy population for sustained economic growth further highlights the importance of a functioning health care system. Moreover, the lack of effective coverage has contributed to the motive for precautionary saving in China. The high rate of savings of over 45% of GDP has been a boon to fuelling investment-led economic growth, but at the expense of consumption. Shifting away from investment toward consumption is essential, as China should aim for an optimal saving rate that better trades off current and future consumption. The risk of health-related expenses contributes to low rates of consumption and possibly excessive savings. The decision to spend $125 billion on health in the aftermath of the 2008 global financial crisis, which underscored the detrimental effects of low rates of consumption, was intended to try and address the motives for precautionary savings. The intent is to introduce universal health coverage over the next decade.

The recent reforms are moves in the right direction, but the state should aim for a larger role in the provision of health insurance. Private provision and the decentralised nature of the governmental structure in China could lead to a fragmented system in which some localities may sufficiently spread risk, while other areas could have incomplete coverage. Central government spending on public insurance for the poor, supporting health care provision through investment in hospitals and medical personnel, and regulating health care costs are all steps that still need to be taken. The resolution of this issue will be critical for China's growth prospects.

5. POVERTY

Despite achieving a rapid ascendancy in the size of the economy, per capita GDP in China only recently passed the $1000 level, which demarcates the world's poorest economies. GDP per capita reached $3000 in 2008, which classifies China as a middle income country; but compared with economies such as the UK, France and other OECD countries which it outranks in aggregate size, the average expected standard of living in China is but a fraction of that of these countries.

International comparisons, though, should be used sparing in this context. It does highlight the potential for economic growth that is still inherent in China, given its low level of per capita income in a massive $3 trillion economy. By comparison, the other large emerging economy with over one billion people is India, which still has only recently become a $1 trillion economy and its per capita GDP is significantly less than that of China.

A notable feature of China's economic growth during these past three decades is its remarkable track record in poverty reduction. Since 1980, around 400 million people have been lifted out of poverty, defined by the international poverty line of living on $1 per day. Remarkably, China's poverty reduction accounted for three-quarters of the total fall in poverty in all developing countries during this period. Within China itself, in the two decades since 1981, the proportion of people living in poverty fell substantially from over half of the population to under 10% (from 53% to 8%), according to World Bank estimates. The impressive progress of China has undoubtedly contributed to the prediction that poverty could be history in Asia in the next few decades.

This section will cover how China was able to achieve this dramatic and significant reduction in poverty, while maintaining a high rate of growth. The argument put forth is one that is often heard, though no consensus has been reached for China or more broadly for other countries. It centres on poverty, its relationship to inequality, and to growth. Unlike the experience of the newly industrialising countries in East Asia which have grown largely equitably, growth in China has been accompanied by rising income inequality, even as the absolute numbers of those living in poverty have fallen. The consequence of China's growth, therefore, is a dramatic fall in poverty, but an accompanying rise in income inequality. If income inequality is a measure of subjective poverty, then the poverty debate becomes more complex and China's progress against poverty may not be as impressive on this measure. Nevertheless, in terms of the numbers of people who have been lifted out of poverty, China's achievement has been remarkable.

5.1 Growth, Poverty and Inequality in China

China's growth experience must be viewed in the context of its status as a developing country which is also in transition. As mentioned already, China is a developing country, where the bulk of its population (81% in 1980 and around 56% in 2008) lives in rural areas and many are still employed in agriculture. However, it is also an economy that is reforming its previously centrally planned economy into one that is increasingly market-oriented and driven by market forces. This set of challenges informs the approach to economic growth undertaken by China and the ensuing impact on poverty reduction.

China essentially adopted a gradual or incremental approach to reform. Importantly, it started in rural areas. The implementation of the Household Responsibility System, which gave a profit incentive to farmers from the late 1970s, greatly boosted agricultural productivity. Chen and Ravallion (2007) conducted a detailed analysis of the causes of the fall in poverty in China and concluded that growth of the agricultural sector accounted for three-quarters of the total decline in poverty in China from 1981–2001. By contrast, they found that globalisation and opening up to international trade were not important. In fact, given that China's 'open door policy' was not implemented until after 1992 and then with restrictions, it is perhaps not surprising that half of the fall in the poverty rate occurred in the first half of the 1980s, when China was still largely a closed economy.

The picture of inequality stands in contrast to China's record on poverty. Recall that in a centrally planned economy, economic activity is directed by the state. China thus industrialised under central direction and became oriented toward heavy industry. This approach resulted in an 'urban bias' policy that extended into the reform period, in which urban residents in the industrialising sector were favoured. Industrialisation in China was achieved through a 'price scissors' policy, whereby agricultural food prices were kept low, while industrial goods prices were kept high, so that the rural sector in a sense permitted the development of the urban sector. This unsurprisingly resulted in a growing rural-urban income gap, where the Gini coefficient measuring absolute income inequality in China rose from around 0.3 to around 0.45. China is today a more unequal economy than the US.

In a sense, where the reforms in China produced a pro-poor outcome, other policies have contributed to worsening inequality. By initially focusing on the bulk of the population in the rural areas which were predominantly agrarian, China unleashed market-oriented forces which gave incentives to farmers to produce and gain returns to their labour. Although it was accompanied by urbanisation and industrialisation, China managed to prevent the expected migration of rural residents to urban areas. In other words, the farmers farmed the land instead of moving to the urban industrial sector with higher wages. In other developing countries, this process often leads to urban overcrowding and unemployment. China, by contrast, maintained strict controls over migration through the *hukou* system, which restricted the movement of both rural and urban residents. In some ways, this worked because rural reforms were undertaken first.

However, as urban incomes began to substantially outpace rural incomes, rural-urban migration occurred in any case, leading to an estimated 70–200 million migrants moving to urban areas in the 1990s and 2000s.

This was exacerbated by the gradual opening of the Chinese economy through creating Special Economic Zones (SEZs), which were located first in the coastal provinces. These SEZs were permitted to engage in trade and attract foreign direct investment. As a result of the market orientation of these areas, the three coastal regions of China account for the bulk (three-quarters) of total GDP (that is, the Bohai river region, Pearl River delta and Yangtze River delta).

Therefore, the adoption of rural reforms first resulted in the decline in overall poverty. However, the policy of reindustrialisation to create a market-driven industrial base for China and the imposition of the house-hold registration system to segregate the rural and urban areas at the same time caused income inequality to rise rapidly. Chen and Ravallion (2007) estimate that the total proportion of the poor in China would be just 1.5% instead of 8% if China's growth had occurred on a more equitable basis. The rise in the so-called 'new' urban poverty in the late 1990s adds a further dimension to the incidence of poverty. Previously, the 'iron rice bowl' protected urban workers, but restructuring state-owned enterprises led to layoffs and a new class of urban poor for the first time (see Li and Sato 2006). Rising levels of income inequality have been associated with scores of people who were plunged into poverty in urban areas after the massive layoffs of the state-owned sector under the Ninth Five Year Plan (1997–2001).

5.2   Policy or Growth?

When China's experience with poverty is assessed, the question that comes to mind must be whether China's economic policies were pro-poor or whether the poverty reduction was a result of rapid economic growth. Some of China's economic policies were explicitly geared at reducing poverty and indeed inequality. For instance, the Western Development Project, launched in 1999, which was designed to stimulate the poor interior provinces and later versions, geared at attracting foreign investment into provinces such as Ningxia, have not been very successful in lifting incomes. China's poorest provinces remain in the western region. However, other policies, such as the Household Responsibility System and cutting agricultural taxes to stimulate rural incomes, have contributed to growth that is associated with massive falls in the number of people living in poverty.

The outcomes of policy, though, are not straightforward. There have been policies such as the urban-biased industrialisation and the selective opening of China's coastal provinces which have not contributed significantly to poverty reduction but have resulted in a growing level of inequality in China.

However, even if the pro-poor policies of China did not seem to work as well, the fiscal redistribution from richer to poorer provinces, from the non-state sector to the lagging state sector, have helped increase incomes. It is these welfare-improving measures which have led some to argue that China's growth is Pareto-improving and 'without losers' (Lau et al. 2001).

This interpretation, though, hinges on the dual characteristic of China's economy being a transition economy as well as a developing country. The centralisation of ownership from the period of the administered economy gave the state the assets to distribute. However, economic growth from decentralisation has resulted in inequality which stands in contrast to the presumed equality during the pre-reform period.

In conclusion, it would seem that China adopted reforms in order to stimulate economic growth which had the consequence of reducing poverty, while its explicit efforts were not as successful. However, China's economic reforms can in general be viewed as a product of a sequence of practical steps to overcome economic barriers rather than a centrally directed, organised plan of reform. The decentralised and regionally driven nature of the reforms give a flavour of why China's growth path is often described as incremental or gradual, since reforms tended to be adopted when successful and not centrally prescribed. In that sense, whether poverty reduction in China is due to policy or growth is not seemingly so important to answer.

However, the consequences of growth in China also include a high level of income inequality. The inequitable nature of growth is itself a source of debate. For China, though, it is argued that poverty would have fallen further if there had been a more balanced growth path, while inequality could itself threaten growth.

Inequality may well rise when marketisation takes hold and factors of production (capital, labour) receive differential returns, because the government did not implement redistributive policies along the way. For instance, policies such as those undertaken by other East Asian countries generated a path of growth with equity. The forms of inequality unsurprisingly follow from the transition and economic development path of China. The experimental, and at times competitive, development of provinces fuelled by export-oriented policies benefiting the coast contributed to a coastal–interior divide. Continuing industrialisation fuels a gap between the still largely agricultural rural community and urban residents. The processes of gradually reforming SOEs and halting privatisation generate a public sector versus private sector gap, reflecting lingering favourable treatment of SOEs vis-à-vis the non-state sector. Regional, rural-urban, state versus non-state – all contribute to a level of income inequality in China that has grown alongside its remarkable growth in the past three decades. Inequality remains a social and economic challenge for China.

Nevertheless, the result of China's growth in the past 30 years is undoubtedly a society with a substantially higher standard of living. For instance, if the US has grown at 3% per annum for the past 30 years while China has grown at 8% per annum, then GDP per capita will double approximately every 23 years in the US and every nine years in China. Within a generation, the average American will be three times as rich as his grandparents, while a Chinese person will be more than 18 times richer. Over a fairly short period of time, small differences in compound growth rates can lead to large differences in per capita incomes. More than this, China's growth has lifted an impressive 400 million people (which is about a quarter larger than the entire population of the US) out of poverty in 30 years. Whether this is a model for poverty reduction, however, is a much more difficult question to answer, along with the challenge of addressing the lingering issue of income inequality.

6.   CONCLUSION

Social coverage in China raises numerous challenges for its continuing growth. Chief among these is the provision of pensions and health care. Both of these benefits had been provided by SOEs until most became loss-making and could not continue to support these services. This created a need for a national system for providing social securities, which the Chinese government has begun to address. The reforms are steps in the right direction, but much more still needs to be done to secure pensions in an aging population and health care provision in a fragmented governmental system.

The legacy of the centrally planned economy has been more positive with respect to education. Gender equality and high rates of educational enrolment exist in both rural and urban China. The main area in need of reform is China's imperfect labour market, which provides the incentives for acquiring education. The dismantling of the administered wage structure and improved mobility has resulted in a labour market that increasingly rewards productive characteristics, such as human capital. The focus on technical education follows from the government's industrial policy, and has successfully generated a significant number of science students who are in a position to contribute to innovation and sustain economic growth.

Poverty has also fallen substantially, marking China's growth as one that has lifted hundreds of millions of people out of abject poverty. However, there are still 100 million living in poverty and new forms have arisen even in the previously privileged urban areas. Moreover, income inequality has resulted from China's particular transition and development path, which could cause growth to stall, if instability derails the gradual marketisation process.

In conclusion, there are numerous difficult challenges for China as it proceeds with some hard areas of reform. Reforms have been halting in the area of social security provision. Continuing progress in these areas will be essential if China is to maintain its impressive rate of economic growth, which has led to such remarkable falls in poverty.

NOTE

* See further my paper 'Parental Investment in Children's Human Capital in Urban China', *Applied Economics*, 38(18), 2006, 2089–111.

10. International trade, foreign investment and the global economy*

1. EXTERNAL SECTOR POLICY

Institutional change is nowhere more apparent than in China's external policy, where policies since 1979 have transformed its exports and investment sectors. For developing countries such as China, one of the key driving forces in economic development operates not only through domestic expenditure but also by attracting foreign direct investment (FDI). For poor countries, in particular, the availability of foreign funds and technologies is crucial. These economies tend to have few domestic resources, either public or private, to invest in developing crucial physical and other technical infrastructure to underpin economic growth. The use of FDI to further economic development is well understood (see, for example, Stern 2002). For instance, the movement of capital from more to less developed countries, where returns are greater, is a key component of the 'catching up' process in the growth literature.

The track record of developing countries in attracting foreign long-term capital rather than short-term capital is mixed. Many developing countries have attracted short-term capital flows, which are useful for improving the liquidity of their usually 'thin' financial markets, but they have also often brought about destabilising financial crises, seen in the second half the 1990s, in particular in the Asian financial crisis. In contrast, long-term capital or foreign investment in manufacturing capacity, research and development (R&D) facilities, and infrastructure is more attractive insofar as this type of investment is geared toward building and developing national capacity. This type of capital is also unlikely to be fickle or as subject to capital flight. However, FDI raises questions about increasing foreign ownership of valuable assets in a developing country and questions of market dominance by large, foreign multinational corporations. However, the potential of foreign investment to bring new technologies and know-how from more developed to emerging economies is an attractive prospect even for successful developing countries.

China has been a particularly successful example of the advantages of utilising industrial policy to attract FDI in order to develop manufacturing and export capacity as well as to meet its infrastructure needs. China has relied on foreign direct investment to a great extent in developing its manufacturing export sector in the coastal regions. Although it has a high savings rate, so that FDI doesn't constitute more than 10% of investment funds, China is still keen to attract foreign investment for the technology and know-how embodied in capital from more advanced economies. As such, its FDI policy is closely intertwined with China's industrial upgrading to move into higher value sectors.

Moreover, the competitive pressures of selling to global markets makes for productivity improvements and allows for learning in exporting firms, such that openness should enhance China's 'catching up' prospects. To ensure this, China's 'open door' policy was geared at attracting foreign investment to gain know-how to help its firms establish a foothold in global markets. With WTO accession in 2001 giving China access to over 90% of world trade through the multilateral trade organisation, exports have become a strong driver of GDP growth and competition has increased in the Chinese economy, while FDI complements rather than displaces domestic capital formation.

This chapter will explore China's successful development of industrial policy to attract FDI during the reform period, including the central role played by the export-processing zones known as SEZs in allowing China to experiment with economic reforms and the Chinese government's objective of using industrial policy to develop these zones to foster technological advancement, whilst promoting export development. Trade liberalisation and WTO accession are key parts of the picture. China's tremendous growth in trade has propelled it to become the world's largest trader, with not unexpected consequences for the global economy. To complete the picture of the external sector, the exchange rate and China's RMB policy will be analysed. Finally, given the importance of China in the global economy, the 'China effect' and its wider implications will conclude the chapter and the book.

2.   'OPEN DOOR' POLICY: TRADE LIBERALISATION AND FDI POLICY

In 1978, the reform period began when market-oriented measures, which included the 'open door' policy designed to encourage foreign trade and investment, were launched. China's approach to economic reforms, though, is and has been gradual, as it tends to adopt policies slowly. China's reform programme progressed in a gradualist way that has also been referred to as 'crossing the stream while feeling the stones'. China's

approach is to wait until a particular policy has been successfully implemented in one region before the 'experiment' is extended nationally. As
a result, China's 'open door' policy did not move forward until reforms
were implemented in urban areas in the mid 1980s and then did not pick
up again until Deng Xiaoping's tour of the southern coastal provinces in
1992. Since then, China has been tremendously successful in attracting
FDI, developing its infrastructure and utilising foreign investment, particularly with respect to its manufacturing capacity and exports.

The first reforms in the area of FDI policy created what are known as
Special Economic Zones (SEZs). SEZs were first introduced in 1979 in the
south-eastern coastal provinces of Fujian and Guangdong and located in
urban areas. The SEZs are similar to special customs areas (Lardy 1991).
Foreign invested enterprises (FIEs) receive preferential treatment, including a reduction of up to 50% in custom duties, lower corporate income
tax, and were granted duty-free imports. This resulted in extremely rapid
growth in these areas due to their attractiveness to foreign investment.
Guangdong has variably been the leading exporting province in China on
account of the successful growth of the SEZ city of Shenzhen on the Hong
Kong border and that of the capital city, Guangzhou. Although the SEZs
were successful even at the start, the Chinese authorities believed that they
tended to attract investment in low-technology and light industry sectors.
These were indeed consistent with China's comparative advantage in abundant, low-cost labour. However, China was keen to attract more advanced
technologies to prompt industrial upgrading and the combination of these
factors paved the way for further reforms.

In 1984, Economic and Trade Development Zones (ETDZ) or 'Open
Port Cities' (OPC) were created. The 'Open Port Cities' were originally
created to address the perceived shortcomings of the SEZs. These OPCs
became ETDZs in 1985. They are located along China's eastern coastline
and were granted preferential investment, as well as import treatment.
There are officially 12 ETDZs sanctioned by the central government,
but there are thought to be many more such areas under local authority
governance (Lin et al. 2003). These were considered to be more successful
then SEZs in attracting higher technological investments, particularly in
consumer electronics and computer-related goods. Guangzhou remains a
strong example of the success of this policy initiative.

In 1992, Free Trade Zones (FTZs) were created following the success
of the earlier initiatives. Free Trade Zones are specially designated urban
areas selected to receive preferential treatment and trading privileges.
The investment incentives in FTZs are extremely attractive since exports
and imports are free of any taxes or tariffs so long as the imports are not
re-sold in China. Items intended for re-sale in China were, by contrast,

subject to high tariff rates. The best-known FTZs are Shanghai's Pudong district, particularly Waigaoqiao, Tianjin Harbour, Futian, an area of Shenzhen, Dalian, and Haikou on Hainan Island.

China continued its push to attract more advanced technologies by developing High-Technology Development Zones (HTDZs) in 1995, just three years after the successful creation of FTZs. The intent of the HTDZs was to increase China's research and development (R&D) capabilities through fostering both domestic and foreign investment. With the exception of the three inner provinces (Xinjiang, Tibet and Ningxia Autonomous Regions), every province has at least one of the 53 HTDZs. Each zone includes a number of 'industrial parks' and 'science and technology parks' open to domestic and foreign high-tech investors. There are also numerous zones that have not been sanctioned by the State Council, as with the ETDZs. HTDZs comprise cities or certain areas of urban China, such as the well-known 'Haidian' district in Beijing. These zones are intended to promote industrial applications of technology and tend to be located in proximity to existing or planned research institutions, or research and development centres. A characteristic of the HTDZs is the '3-in-1' development system, whereby every zone must include a university-based research centre, an innovation centre to utilise applied technology for product development, and a partnership with a commercial enterprise to manufacture and market the products. Foreign investors continue to be offered preferential treatment as an incentive to establish high-tech joint ventures in these zones. The HTDZs are expected to contribute significantly to China's science and technology infrastructure, though it is questionable whether domestic firms have gained in innovative ability as a result of FDI. Although more than 50% of China's exports have been produced by foreign invested enterprises since the mid 1990s, an estimated 80% of China's high-tech goods are currently produced by FIEs (see Yueh 2006).

The policies have contributed to the coastal areas growing more rapidly than the interior and western regions, as over 90% of FDI is located on China's 'gold coast'. Efforts to promote inland areas as potential locations for FDI have faced more obstacles, as poor infrastructure and less dense populations deter investment, though rising wages on the coast and significant investment in roads in the central region have begun to shift economic activity westward, if not all the way to the western regions.

2.1   The Forms of Foreign Direct Investment in China

This section will examine the data on foreign direct investment in China and the forms of foreign investment. Both the successes and shortcomings

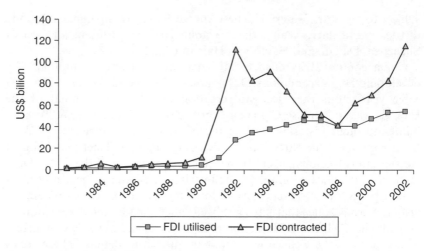

Source: China Statistical Yearbook, various years.

Figure 10.1   Foreign direct investment in China, 1983–2003

of China's industrial policy will be assessed, with a particular focus on the difference between FDI that is contracted for or agreed on and actually utilised investment, the changing composition of the vehicles of investment in China before and after WTO accession, and the sectoral destination of inward FDI in China.

Figure 10.1 shows that China has enjoyed an explosive rate of growth in FDI since the 'open door' policy geared up in the mid 1980s. Figure 10.2 shows the corresponding number of FDI projects in China. These figures are particularly notable in contrast to the early part of the reform period. From 1979 to 1982, China received utilised FDI of only $1.17 billion and contracted FDI of $6.01 billion from just 922 FDI projects. The comparison with the period beginning in 1983 is remarkable. In 1984 alone, the number of FDI projects exceeded the number for the preceding period since 1979. Moreover, between 1991 and 1992 after Deng's southern tour, contracted FDI increased from $11.98 billion to $58.12 billion. The peak in 1992 can also be seen clearly in Figure 10.2. By 2003, China's utilised FDI was $53.50 billion and contracted FDI was an impressive $115.07 billion. By 2007, before the global financial crisis, China received around $60 billion in FDI each year.

The other factor of note in Figure 10.1 is in the early 1990s when FDI began to pour into China primarily through the SEZs. During the early efforts to establish China's export capacity, the divergence between contracted and utilised FDI was significant. As China's technological

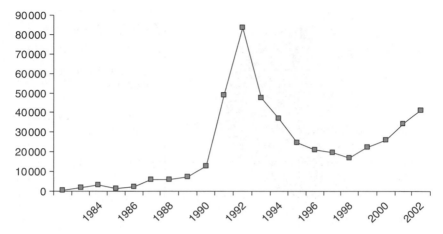

Source: *China Statistical Yearbook*, various years.

Figure 10.2   Number of foreign direct investment projects, 1983–2003

capabilities in those areas of investment, namely, light industry and low technology products, increased, it was thought to be better able to use the agreed FDI and thus the gap between contracted and utilised FDI began to close. A similar pattern may be emerging corresponding to China's initiatives in the mid 1990s geared toward attracting more sophisticated technologies through ETDZs and HTDZs. There is again a trend toward divergence between the amount of contracted-for FDI and the amount that can be used. This interpretation is consistent with evidence of the increasingly complex technological make-up of China's exports, while China's domestic capacity lags somewhat behind.

The types of investment forms and the rules governing FIEs in China warrant further consideration. The vehicle for FDI in China has tradition-ally been Chinese-foreign joint ventures (JVs), particularly equity joint ventures. Until recently, wholly foreign-owned enterprises were permitted only in selected sectors and selectively so. For instance, wholly-owned foreign-owned enterprises (WOFEs) were prohibited from operating in many areas and joint ventures were only permitted if the Chinese partner held a controlling share. Those categories, though, often disguised further nuances. For instance, wholly-owned foreign-owned enterprises were pro-hibited from operating in certain areas of the transportation sector, with respect to some raw materials and aspects of financial services, but encour-aged to operate in others. As one example, the construction and operation of local railways and bridges were prohibited, but investment in highway construction and rural railways was encouraged.

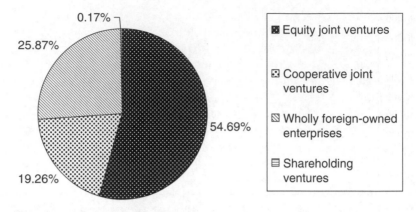

Source: *China Statistical Yearbook.*

Figure 10.3   FDI investment vehicles, 2000

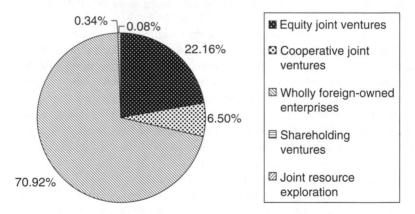

Source: *China Statistical Yearbook.*

Figure 10.4   FDI investment vehicles, 2003

The results of China's strict control of the form of FIEs can be seen in Figure 10.3 for 2000. Figure 10.4, which follows, shows the rapid loosening of the vehicles for investment by 2003. In 2000, prior to China's accession to the World Trade Organisation, wholly-owned foreign-owned enter-prises constituted about 26% of all FDI investment vehicles. Joint ven-tures, equity and cooperative, comprise around three-quarters of all FIEs, around 74%. In Figure 10.4, which shows the same chart of FDI invest-ment vehicles for 2003, wholly foreign-owned enterprises then comprised nearly three-quarters of all FIEs in China. Joint ventures account for just about 29%. This shift has implications for China's industrial policy.

Prior to WTO accession and further opening of its economy, China exerted significant control over the form and destination of inward FDI. For instance, joint ventures were not approved unless they met two criteria. First, the foreign partner had to have superior technology that was of interest to China. In fact, many of the joint venture agreements included annexes designating technology transfers. Second, the manufactured products had to be suitable for export and demanded on global markets. These rules governing joint ventures meant that Chinese enterprises had more potential to benefit from both explicit and implicit (such as through learning and know-how) technology transfers from foreign partners and thus to develop its domestic innovative capacity, in a process known as 'catching up' in economic growth. Moreover, joint ventures were usually nearly 50-50 in ownership (with the Chinese partner holding 51% of shares), reducing the threat of foreign capital taking over or dominating domestic markets. It may also be that the change in the vehicles of FDI means that China will be less able to direct the type of investment that comes into China, shifting the investment potential of FDI away from manufacturing and into the retail sector, where less positive spillover is likely. But it may reflect foreign investors moving into a growing consumer market that has opened substantially since WTO accession.

Inward FDI in China has primarily been invested in manufacturing capacity, which is consistent with the aim of its industrial policy. Figure 10.5 gives the sectoral breakdown of FDI in China between 1999 and 2001. Manufacturing has been the main sector of inward FDI, comprising over 22% of all foreign investment in 1999 and rising to 30% in 2001. Real estate comprises a consistent share of about 5% of sectoral share of FDI, and this consistency characterises most of the sectoral shares. The sector of energy infrastructure, including electricity, power, gas and water, accounts for just over 2% over this period, making it the fourth most popular sector for investment.

It is important to note the growth in sectoral shares over this period. Table 10.1 shows that manufacturing's share of FDI grew 36% over this period, which encompasses WTO accession. Aside from the rather minor sector of geological prospecting, the only sector which achieved faster growth than manufacturing was mining and quarrying, which grew at over 45%, though from a lower starting point. FDI in sales and catering services, interestingly, grew at the fifth fastest rate, of over 21%, during this period. This is consistent with the increased liberalisation of China's domestic consumer market and opening up to foreign invested enterprises in anticipation of WTO accession. In respect of investment

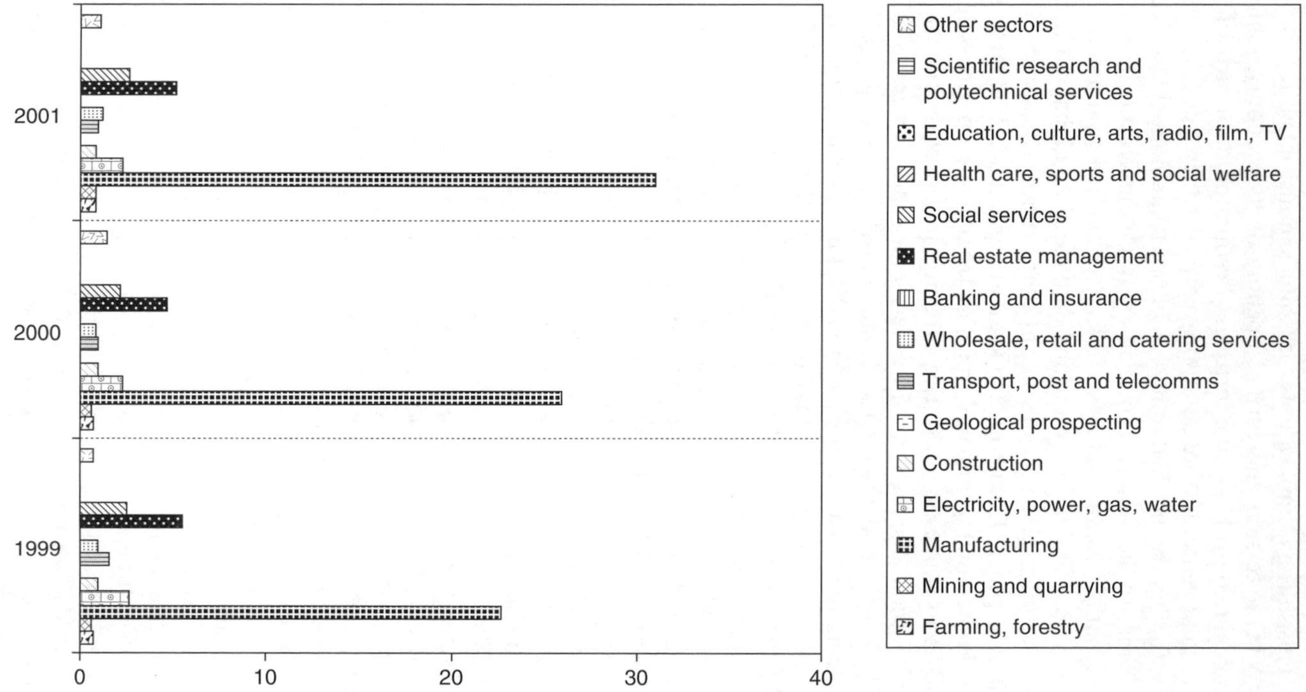
2001
2000
1999
0
10
20
30
40
Other sectors
Scientific research and polytechnical services
Education, culture, arts, radio, film, TV
Health care, sports and social welfare
Social services
Real estate management
Banking and insurance
Wholesale, retail and catering services
Transport, post and telecomms
Geological prospecting
Construction
Electricity, power, gas, water
Manufacturing
Mining and quarrying
Farming, forestry

Source: *China Statistical Yearbook*, various years.

Figure 10.5 FDI by sector, 1999–2001 (US$ billion)

Table 10.1   FDI by sector (in US$ billion)

	1999	2000	2001	Growth rate (1999–2001)
Farming, forestry	0.71	0.68	0.90	26.55%
Mining and quarrying	0.56	0.58	0.81	45.57%
Manufacturing	22.60	25.84	30.91	36.74%
Electricity, power, gas, water	2.70	2.24	2.27	−15.91%
Construction	0.92	0.91	0.81	−11.99%
Geological prospecting	0.00	0.00	0.01	132.08%
Transport, post and telecommunications	1.55	1.01	0.91	−41.40%
Wholesale, retail and catering services	0.97	0.86	1.17	21.10%
Banking and insurance	0.10	0.08	0.04	−63.89%
Real estate management	5.59	4.66	5.14	−8.08%
Social services	2.55	2.19	2.59	1.73%
Health care, sports and social welfare	0.15	0.11	0.12	−19.67%
Education, culture, arts, radio, film, TV	0.06	0.05	0.04	−40.78%
Scientific research and polytechnic services	0.11	0.06	0.12	9.36%
Other sectors	0.75	1.45	1.05	39.62%

Source: China Statistical Yearbook, various years.

in infrastructure, though, FDI in the energy sector declined by a notable 16%. The growth in sales and catering services and fall in infrastructure underscore the challenges that confront China in fashioning an industrial policy in its increasingly open economy, particularly after WTO accession in 2001. However, the growth in FDI in manufacturing and the mounting evidence of increasingly sophisticated technologies that have been invested in China suggest that China's overall policy is effective.

China recognises the need, in particular, to develop its energy infrastructure, as well as the physical and technological infrastructure in the western regions, in order to sustain its remarkable growth rate. In order to attract FDI to its interior, though, China must invest in infrastructure and transport linkages to those areas to make them attractive to FDI. The large-scale infrastructure investment programme to build roads, rail and other infrastructure started in 2006 as part of the Ninth Five Year Plan to develop a national highway and transportation grid, which received a further boost of funds with the fiscal stimulus package of 4 trillion RMB implemented during the 2008 global financial crisis, is a step in the right direction, though it is only the first of many which will have to be taken to bridge the wide coastal–interior gap.

Also, the northward movement of FDI from Guangdong to the Shanghai region, where access to the domestic market is more ready, and the opening of its domestic markets following WTO accession further suggest that China will increasingly need to look to formulate policies that are not simply reliant on foreign investment. There are signs that China is indeed doing this, as it beefs up domestic investment in innovation, as discussed in Chapter 8.

China's industrial policy has focused on developing horizontal partnerships between domestic enterprises and foreign partners, usually well-established multinational corporations. China has been remarkably successful in attracting foreign direct investment, despite a lack of formal private property rights and transparent institutions, and its significant degree of bureaucratic 'red tape'. The creation of export-oriented zones and parks was undoubtedly important in this process.

In terms of infrastructure, China's policy toward FIEs has been successful in directing investment into technologically superior products and this has helped China to carve out a significant share of the global market in manufacturing exports in the space of only a decade. China's technological infrastructure has been bolstered by this process. However, China faces challenges in that the investment forms of FDI are changing, its control is loosening as fewer FIEs now enter China as joint venture partners, and its domestic markets are opening up to foreign firms, attributable largely to WTO accession.

What is also notable is that China's development of its physical infrastructure, for example, roads, transport links, telecommunications, energy, has used largely domestic rather than foreign capital. That China was able to undertake these investments and continues to do so is probably due to a number of factors. China's early successful growth in the 1980s while under a largely planned economy meant that it had resources for investment. During the later period, China has run budget deficits in order to continue investment in the western and interior regions to provide the institutional underpinnings for attracting foreign capital. China has also invested significantly in developing an energy and telecommunications infrastructure to promote industrial upgrading.

Control over FDI, the decision to build infrastructure and to protect certain sectors are all central aspects of China's industrial policy. China is indeed rather unique in that it is a transition economy with a centralised governmental apparatus for economic policy and it has also not relied on foreign aid or borrowing to any large extent. It has been largely unfettered in pursuing its successive Five Year Plans, which since 1979, have aimed at modernising key sectors of its economy. For economies which share some but not all of China's characteristics, designing and implementing a similar industrial policy to enhance their attractiveness to FDI would necessarily be a formidable task.

3.   WTO MEMBERSHIP

After 15 years of negotiation, China gained entry to the World Trade Organisation (WTO), which made it a part of the multilateral trade arrangements with other members that account for a near totality of world trade in manufactured goods. As discussed earlier, agreeing to open up has implications for its FDI policy, as WTO membership entailed opening up more of its domestic market to foreign competitors and removed long-standing barriers such as the geographical restrictions that had previously prevented national expansion of foreign businesses in China.

On the eve of accession, China was already a strong international competitor in a large range of industrial products, led by simple labour-intensive manufactures, but quickly diversifying into complex, capital and technology-intensive goods, as described in the previous section. While accession may not have given China an immediate advantage in markets where it already enjoys Most Favoured Nation (MFN) status, it did give it unprecedented access to other markets. Accession also assured it access in the future and so induce more sustained investment in the development of exports.

Entry into the WTO allowed China to take advantage of other forms of global trade liberalisation, the most important being the removal of restrictions on textiles and garments at the start of 2005, which allowed China to become the largest exporter of clothing and textiles in the world as the labour-intensive sector capitalised on its comparative advantage of abundant labour. China is expected now to move toward a regime based on tariffs so that quotas, licences and designated trading are to be phased out. State trade of commodities is still permitted, subject to WTO rules. China has agreed to bind to all industrial and agricultural tariffs, so that the average tariff on manufactures is reduced to 6.95% and to 17% on agricultural products. The pace of tariff reform has also been rapid, where following significant tariff reform in 1997, rates were less than 20% across the board. The issue of agricultural protection remains, as comparative advantage shifts against China in this area, whilst most of its people live in rural areas, with agriculture as their means of livelihood. As state trading of commodities will still be permitted, significant changes are not expected in agricultural policy after WTO accession. However, trade specialisation in manufacturing will hasten China's shift away from agriculture and China's becoming a net food importer in the mid 2000s is the start of an expected decline in the sector that will have welfare implications for its farmers and rural residents unless new industries and services can arise to absorb rural labour.

Regarding textiles, China has indeed become integrated into the GATT Uruguay Round on textiles and clothing. By 2005, all existing quotas on China's exports of textiles and clothing were phased out and by 2008, any special textile safeguards were also phased out. However, economies such as the US and the EU have instituted quotas against Chinese exports in these areas and developing countries in South Asia like Bangladesh are struggling to cope with China's competitiveness. This is the only instance in which China will benefit from access to foreign markets rather than obtaining the gains from trade that came from reducing its own trade barriers (see also Lall and Albaladejo 2004). As for reciprocal entry into the domestic market, China has reduced the number of products subject to non-tariff barriers (that is, quotas and licences) from an estimated 1200 or so in the early 1990s to approximately 200 on accession.

Foreign investors have been the major drivers of China's export success, and inward FDI has increased from an average of $50 billion per year in the late 1990s to around $80–90 billion in the mid 2000s after WTO accession. WTO principles call for transparency in legal rules and China's business environment has improved as it has confronted the need to develop laws that govern markets, not only to support greater marketisation in its own economy, but also to meet the expectations of foreign firms gaining access to China's domestic market. Although imperfect, the legal system has undergone rapid reform, including passing a law governing mergers and acquisitions (M&A), unifying the various codes that governed foreign and domestic corporations separately, and passing an anti-monopoly law for the first time. Market access remains a key point of contention for foreign firms and is often the subject of disputes at summits between China and its largest trading partners of the EU and US, but the composition of FDI inflows is changing. In the initial stages, most export-oriented FDI came from neighbouring economies, particularly from Hong Kong. Over time, advanced industrial countries have accounted for larger shares of FDI, mostly in the hope of serving the domestic market.

Indeed, some view as the most significant part of WTO accession China's agreement to open its services sector, which has been described as 'breathtaking' in its scope, as it includes not only financial services, but also professional services such as law, accounting, etc. And this is in spite of much evidence of considerable financial weakness. However, in many respects, as discussed in Chapter 6, China's aim is to utilise foreign know-how to reform its lagging banking and capital markets. And, China continues to impose limitations on the operations of foreign firms in this area, so the opening up of the sector is not unfettered.

The opening up includes substantial liberalisation of the Chinese market in banking, insurance, securities, fund management and other financial services. Historically, China has either precluded or severely restricted the ability of foreign firms to compete with domestic firms in these areas (see Lardy 1998). These restrictions are most dramatically demonstrated in the area of banking. Although foreign banks have operated in China for two decades, their role remains extremely limited. In 2005, they accounted for only 2% of China's total banking assets, but 20% of foreign currency business. Under the terms of China's protocol for acceding to the WTO, China will lift all of the existing restrictions on foreign banks. For example, the number of cities in which foreign banks can offer domestic currency services is scheduled to increase until 2005, when all geographic restrictions will be lifted. However, the requirement remains in force that only one foreign branch can be opened per year, which when starting from a small number of locations in China, is a significant impediment. Most importantly, foreign banks will be able to conduct local currency business with Chinese corporations two years after entry and with Chinese households five years after entry, and they will enjoy full national treatment five years after accession. That means that the central bank will no longer be able to restrict the growth of the domestic currency business of foreign banks by limiting their ratio of domestic to foreign currency liabilities or by using any other non-prudential ratios to restrict their operations.

In December 2006 (five years after WTO accession), China's new rules governing foreign banks came into effect. Foreign banks and branches would be permitted to engage in a similar range of financial services as Chinese banks, and they would be treated and regulated in the same way as domestic banks. Geographic restrictions were lifted on conducting domestic currency business, but foreign banks must satisfy certain requirements before they can be granted approval to do so. Foreign banks must establish an incorporated affiliate in China, with minimum capital of RMB 1 billion and each branch must have minimum capital of RMB 100 million. Also, foreign financial institutions must have three years of business operation experience in China and have been profitable for two consecutive years prior to applying. When starting from a low level, it will be some time before foreign banks become a significant presence, particularly as they will be competing against a large state-owned banking system and state-owned commercial banks which are among the largest in the world, particularly in the aftermath of the 2008 global financial crisis.

Foreign financial firms also expect to play a role in China's securities and fund management industries. China's WTO commitments in these areas, however, are less extensive than in either banking or insurance. Foreign financial institutions regard China as a huge, under-served market. The financial sector is in an early stage of development, and the national savings rate has averaged over 40% in recent years, most of which was generated in the household sector. A major household financial asset is outsized holdings of currency. Foreign banks have long believed that most of these funds could be used more effectively with the introduction of a modern payments system, among other things. Regulations passed in 2002 and 2005 ease the way for securities and fund management companies as a result of WTO agreements, but non-tariff restrictions remain, as with the banking sector.

China's leadership has agreed to a significant opening up of its financial sector and believes that competition from foreign banks can accelerate the development of a commercial credit culture in the domestic banking system. This potential is being weighed carefully against the risks associated with premature financial liberalisation in the context of admittedly weak capital markets and a relatively new central bank, with insufficient supervisory and regulatory experience. Added to these concerns is the issue of full currency convertibility. The Chinese authorities are under increasing pressure to speed up currency liberalisation.

4.   THE EXCHANGE RATE

Since 1994, China's currency, the renminbi or RMB, has been effectively pegged to the US dollar, despite its official description as a managed float. The exchange rate at that time was set at RMB 8.7 per US dollar. From 1994 to 1997, the exchange rate appreciated by 5% to RMB 8.29 against the US dollar. Before the onset of the Asian financial crisis in 1998, the peg was at 8.6 to the dollar. After that and before the new peg to a trade-weighted basket in 2005, the RMB was effectively pegged to the US dollar in a narrow band of 8.276 to 8.280.

China implemented a new exchange rate policy in July 2005. On the one hand, China allowed the RMB to appreciate by 2% against the US dollar (from 8.27 to 8.11). China's aim was to gradually adjust its exchange rate within a narrow range, as it did between 1994 and 1997. With the decline of the US dollar by around 35% against a floating currency such as the euro since 2002 and China's ballooning trade surplus with industrial nations, the pressure on the RMB intensified until the 2008 global financial crisis when Chinese current account surpluses exceeded 10% of GDP. Before then, because export processing is estimated to account for half of Chinese exports, imports had grown as quickly as exports, rendering net exports to be nearly in balance in many years during the reform period. But the picture changed in the 2000s after WTO accession, when China began to run significant current account surpluses that added more speculative as well as political pressure on the value of the RMB.

Thus, in 2005, the RMB was pegged to a trade-weighted basket of currencies. China runs a trade deficit with its Asian trading partners and trade surpluses with the Western economies. Thus, the multilateral or effective exchange rate is in many respects more appropriate than a bilateral peg against a depreciating dollar. The move to a currency basket better reflects China's overall trade position, which is much more in balance than its trade with the US alone. The US will remain a significant trading partner, though, so many of the issues noted above will remain.

It is difficult to determine the fundamental value of a currency in the short run. Ultimately, the value of a currency is determined by the balance of payments, in other words, the current (trade balance plus net investment inflows) and capital accounts. Roughly speaking, due to capital controls, China should have minimal portfolio flows so the balance of payments (the sum of the trade balance and net foreign direct investment or FDI flows) would constitute the RMB's underlying pressure. However, portfolio flows have been creeping in nevertheless. In any case, because of China's trade surplus, in particular its significant surpluses with the US and EU, import restrictions and attractiveness to FDI, the RMB was viewed as undervalued.

The timing of reform will certainly be driven by macroeconomic fundamentals in China. But the expense of maintaining a fixed exchange rate in the face of speculative pressures is evident. Given China's massive foreign exchange reserves exceeding $2 trillion, the largest in the world, it is able to defend the currency. However, it is expensive to do so, particularly given relatively low returns on the US bonds that it is holding in its reserves. Moreover, it will not be easy for China to diversify its holdings. An estimated 70–80% of its reserves are US dollar holdings. A move to diversify into euros is not particularly viable due to the erosion of the value of its own foreign exchange reserves. If the dollar falls due to diversification, then the RMB will require more intervention. If the dollar falls in value on account of increased holdings of euros, then again, the PBOC will need to spend more money stabilising the peg.

However, although China does not sterilise all of its intervention, it has not witnessed inflationary pressures in its economy. As inflation is one of the most expensive elements of a fixed exchange rate and it has not appeared in China, the pressures to change its exchange rate policy are not severe, but they do exist, particularly in terms of the accumulation of foreign exchange reserves and excess liquidity in its economy, creating possible asset bubbles in the real estate and stock markets. Also, since the global financial crisis of 2008, China has become concerned about the inflationary aspects of the US programme of deficit spending to ease itself out of recession. Amid the clamour for a new global reserve currency separate from the US dollar, China is sitting uncomfortably on large dollar holdings, though its exchange rate regime leads it to accumulate more dollar-denominated assets in any case.

A variety of scenarios exist. One possible move would be revaluation of the peg. However, in many respects, speculation about a possible revaluation of the current fixed exchange rate has become self-fulfilling. Speculative capital inflows can erode the impact of a revaluation, making future revaluations likely. This reduces the effectiveness of intermediate measures, such as revaluation. There are indications that the Chinese authorities may test a wider trading band. However, if expectations continue to build, then the results are similar to a revaluation.

Alternatively, China could float the RMB. The Chinese authorities have indicated that they would eventually consider moving to a more flexible exchange rate. However, the lack of depth in its financial markets will undermine the effective use of monetary policy and the stability of international investment in a flexible exchange rate regime. Therefore, the Chinese authorities have a number of possible solutions and there are as yet no serious macroeconomic issues within its economy that demand a speeding up of reforms. However, 'hot money' continues to flow into and out of China irrespective of capital controls. With the extent of global integration of China, this was inevitable.

Thus, in 2009, China began to liberalise its capital account and allow for greater convertibility of the RMB with select trading partners. Specifically, its 'going out' policy, formed in the mid 1990s (discussed in Chapter 3), was pursued in the aftermath of the global financial crisis. China declared that its foreign exchange reserves will be used to help finance the global expansion of its firms and thus allow capital outflows and reduce its balance of payments surplus, which has the effect of lessening reserve accumulation. At the same time, cheap equity investments in the US and Europe suffering a 'credit crunch' from the near collapse of the Western banking system can help Chinese firms become global players, which have yet to establish global brands and multinational operations.

In 2008, outward FDI totalled $55.6 billion, a 194% increase over a year earlier; of which, $40.7 billion was in the financial sector and $11.9 billion in the non-financial sector. As China receives around $60–80 billion per annum in inward FDI, it may become a capital exporter in the next few years, especially as investments in energy, minerals, raw materials accelerated in the late 2000s and its commercial firms begin to expand overseas. In addition to easing the pressures on its external account, global ambitions could herald an era of Chinese multinationals.

Taken together, the concerns over the accumulation of US dollar holdings and a push for the RMB to be included in a new supranational reserve currency all point in one direction. RMB liberalisation and relaxation of the fixed exchange rate are on the cards, somewhere down the road.

5.   CHINA'S IMPACT ON THE GLOBAL ECONOMY

The book will conclude with an assessment of China's re-emergence in the global economy to place in context the growth impact of such a sizeable nation. Even though China is a developing country in the midst of making the transition to a market economy, it is already emerging as a major force in the world economy – one that accounts for 20% of the world's population, more than four times the size of the United States and nearly three times that of the European Union.

China's size and integration with the world economy have contributed to uncertainty about the global inflationary environment; its currency has been the subject of contention, as discussed in the last section; its trade has raised concerns for workers and firms in both developed and developing countries; its demand for energy has led to competition and conflict; it has rivalled the United States, the UK and developing countries as a destination for foreign direct investment; and the effects of its own overseas investments have begun to be felt across the world. As a result, China has generated incremental growth in the global economy that has made its success significant for the welfare of other countries.

In this section, the 'China effect' is presented and it will be argued that the rise of China will benefit the process of globalisation, but also raise significant challenges for national economic structures and competitiveness in the rest of the world.

5.1   Chinese Growth and Trade

Since the process of economic liberalisation began in 1979, Chinese trade with the rest of the world has risen by a factor of 30. In terms of GDP, China has overtaken Canada, Italy and the UK in the last decade, and Germany in 2008. It is the world's third largest economy, after the United States and Japan.

A startling aspect of China's economic performance is its degree of openness to international trade. Total Chinese trade (exports plus imports) amounts to 70% of its GDP, which compares with 37% for the UK and just 20% for the United States. China's trade-to-GDP ratio is all the more remarkable given that one of the main determinants of this number is country size – large countries typically have low shares of trade in GDP (for example, the United States compared with the UK).

One reason why China's trade-to-GDP ratio is so large is the valuation of the denominator, which, at market exchange rates, understates the true size of the economy. But even allowing for this, the Chinese economy is extremely open, reflecting its export-oriented growth strategy. China now accounts for 7% of world merchandise exports, a proportion that is a historic high for major trading nations.

5.2 Mechanisms of the China Effect

How does the growth of such a big economy affect other parts of the world? The primary mechanism is via China's effects on the global supply of, and demand for, goods, services and assets. The resulting shifts in supply and demand cause changes in prices and hence lead to adjustment in other countries.

The changes that other countries experience can be broken down into 'quantity effects' and 'income effects'. Quantity effects involve some sectors of a national economy contracting and other sectors expanding, requiring workers to be reallocated. In these circumstances, there may be adjustment costs, but if an economy is operating at full employment, they are likely to be temporary as workers are re-employed elsewhere.

Income effects involve changes in a country's 'terms of trade' – the relationship between the prices of its exports and imports. A country will be better off if the prices of its exports increase relative to the prices of its imports – and worse off the other way round. So if the 'China effect' is to increase the prices of oil and other commodities while reducing the prices of some manufactured goods, commodity-exporting countries will have their incomes raised while commodity importers will have their incomes reduced.

Something similar will happen with manufactures, depending on the composition of the manufacturing trade of the countries concerned. Countries that tend to export goods similar to Chinese exports will lose out, while countries that import the goods that China is exporting will gain.

In addition to these national level effects, there will be gainers and losers within countries as the relative wages of different types of workers change.

The simple prediction is that unskilled workers will lose and skilled workers will gain, since what China brings to the world economy is a large increase in the supply of unskilled labour.

The mechanisms are changes in the prices of goods, with the expectation that the largest price falls will be for goods where production relies on unskilled labour, such as textiles and garments. As Chinese exports of such goods expand, so their prices will fall, contracting production and employment of unskilled labour in other countries.

So the overall predictions for the China effect are that other countries will gain or lose depending on their trade patterns. Similarly for workers: expect to lose out if a worker's skill mix is similar to that embodied in Chinese exports – and to gain otherwise.

5.3   The Changing Structure of Chinese Trade

Since the income and quantity effects of China are transmitted through trade, the next step is to analyse the composition of China's trade. The first point to note is increasing Chinese imports of primary commodities. The reform of the state sector in the 1990s and the rise of the non-state sector have heralded a second industrialisation in China, which requires energy and raw materials. While these commodities constitute a relatively small share of total Chinese imports, they are large enough to have a major impact on world markets.

Since the mid 1990s, China has become a net oil importer even though it is also one of the top ten world producers of oil. China is the world's second largest consumer of oil after the United States. And, in 2004, with 4.4% of total world GDP, China consumed 30% of the world's iron ore, 31% of its coal, 27% of its steel and 25% of its aluminium. Between 2000 and 2003, China's share of the increase in global demand for aluminium, steel, nickel and copper was, respectively, 76%, 95%, 99% and 100% (Kaplinsky 2006).

Highly speculative estimates suggest that demand from China is responsible for about 50% of the 2000s boom in world commodity prices. One effect of this is to redistribute income between other countries in the world. Thus, primary commodity exporters have experienced dramatic improvements in their export earnings and terms of trade, which have been paid for by importers of these commodities, some of them developed countries.

At the same time, Chinese exports of a range of manufactures have resulted in some substantial price falls. China's terms of trade for manufactured goods fell by 14% between 1993 and 2000 (Zheng and Zhao 2002). Its overall terms of trade worsened by 17% between 1980 and 2003

(UNCTAD 2004). Moreover, in one-third of 151 industrial sectors, the prices of Chinese imports into the European Union have fallen (Kaplinsky 2006).

Which countries gain and which lose from these changes? The answer depends on whether a country is an importer of these goods (hence benefiting from the lower prices) or an exporter. Lower prices of many basic manufactures have been beneficial for high-income countries that have already moved out of production in these sectors, and also for low-income countries without such manufacturing capacity.

Lower import prices have also contributed to a more benign inflationary environment. Up until the real commodity boom peaking in 2008, China's rapid global integration and remarkable growth generated a favourable terms of trade shock that produced lower than expected levels of inflation in the global economy (Rogoff 2006).

But China nevertheless poses a competitive threat. In some countries in Latin America (Chile, Costa Rica and El Salvador), 60–70% of exports are directly threatened by China's rise because of a similar export product mix (Lall et al. 2005). There remain concerns for other developing countries. For example, the phasing out of the WTO Multi-fibre Agreement in 2005, which had previously limited China's exports of clothing and textiles through a global quota system, raised concerns for Bangladesh and Sri Lanka, whose export sectors are dominated by these goods. And while China's rise has induced more imports from its Asian neighbours, this has not been enough to offset displacement of their exports in third-country markets (Greenaway et al. 2008).

But exports of labour-intensive products like clothing, apparel, textiles and footwear, though large, are a rapidly declining share of China's trade. These have gone from 40% of exports in the early 1990s to less than 20% in 2006, as much of the fastest export growth has been in more advanced manufactured products, particularly electrical equipment.

A key aspect of this technological upgrading is the growth of high levels of two-way trade in similar items, particularly electronics. This 'intra-industry trade' reflects cross-border production networks. For example, electrical and electronic equipment comprises 39% of all China's exports to Malaysia and 44% of China's imports from Malaysia. Electrical and electronic equipment is 33% of China's exports to, and 28% of imports from, Singapore (Wang 2003). And the phenomenon is not limited to developing countries: vertical intra-industry trade between China and OECD countries is rising and accounted for around 20% of trade in the early 1990s (Hellvin 1996). Since around half of China's exports have been produced by foreign-owned enterprises since the mid 1990s, the rise of intra-industry trade should not be surprising (Yueh 2006). Multinational corporations seek low-cost manufacturing bases and often diversify their production and supply chains.

5.4 Wages, Costs and Comparative Advantage

What is the China effect on wages? The simple prediction for the rest of the world is that skilled workers gain, while unskilled workers lose. The doubling of the global labour force that has occurred since the early 1990s, as Asian and former communist countries have opened up to trade, points to the likely impact of this on wages (Freeman 2004). But neither the theory nor the evidence is quite this clear cut.

On the theory side, offshoring and global production chains increase the efficiency of firms, enabling them to continue to maintain a presence in high-income countries (Grossman and Rossi-Hansberg 2006). On the empirical side, there has been stagnation of the wages of unskilled workers, particularly in the United States. But the evidence suggests that skill-biased technical change has as least as much to do with this as does the rise of trade with developing countries like China (Feenstra and Hanson 2003).

It is also interesting to record the changing patterns of wages in China. Figure 10.6 shows that economic growth has driven up wages in coastal areas, including Beijing and Guangdong, to levels double that of interior provinces like Sichuan and Guizhou. There has also been an increasing skill premium, on the rise since the beginning of market-oriented reforms. This may be because China's administered labour system meant that

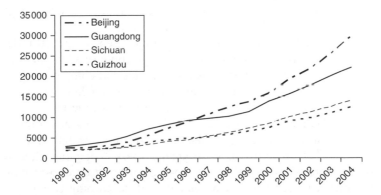

Source: *China Statistical Yearbook*, various years.

Figure 10.6   Average annual real wages, in selected provinces (in RMB), 1990–2004

wages used to be centrally determined and not linked to productivity or skills, as discussed in Chapter 4.

China's comparative advantage is seemingly no longer being driven simply by low-cost, abundant labour. Some interior provinces may still compete on that basis, but for areas on the coast this advantage has been substantially eroded and competitive advantage is increasingly based on skills. China's industrial policies are aimed at technological upgrading, and China is now graduating well over a million scientists and engineers each year and a fast-growing number of Ph.D's.

This upgrading will alter the set of industries that experience competitive pressure from China, but not all sectors will suffer. Relative prices and exchange rates will change, and aggregate effects will turn on terms of trade effects, as described above.

6. CONCLUSION

China's remarkable economic growth in the past 30 years has propelled it to become the third largest economy in the world, recently surpassing the UK and Germany. Within the next couple of years, it is likely that the G2 will consist of the United States and China, as China nears the size of a stagnating Japan and grows eight times faster. China's WTO accession and its high degree of openness hold several implications for the global economy.

First, there will be sectoral and employment shifts in other economies, as some industries grow and others shrink. The development of outsourcing, offshoring and vertical production networks, together with the rapid skill upgrading of the Chinese economy, means that these effects will not just be felt in unskilled labour-intensive industries.

Second, countries that import from China (such as the OECD) will gain from lower priced manufactures that contribute to a low inflationary environment, while putting pressure on countries that compete in the same products (including those in Latin America). But vast Chinese demand for raw materials and commodities will redistribute income from countries that also demand these resources (developed countries plus other fast-growing industrialising countries like India) to countries that export these products (such as in Africa). With greater market opening after WTO accession, there will be the further prospect of horizontal intra-industry trade, which will benefit both developed and developing countries with competitive products and services to sell to China.

Third, China's comparative advantage is, increasingly, not determined by low-cost labour. A sophisticated technical mix of export products and a policy focus on science and technology have resulted in a diverse set of determinants of international trade, with a great deal of provincial variability. The evidence suggests that China's growing competitiveness will put pressure on the productivity of firms and workers around the world.

Fourth, there is some evidence of increasing wage inequality in developed countries arising from the growth of developing countries, including China. But China's skills upgrading suggests that it will not only compete in terms of cost, but also in more technically advanced goods, which would affect the returns to skilled labour.

Fifth, as covered in Chapter 6, but not repeated here, China was part of the global imbalances which characterised the 2008 global financial crisis, highlighting yet another facet of its integration, along with other emerging countries, into the world economy.

China's continuing economic growth is not assured, the road to development is rocky and the transition to a market economy is rife with instability. Institutional change has been a recurring feature of China's marketisation and growth process. Yet the country's remarkable success so far has already fundamentally transformed its own society and made its economic impact felt worldwide. The continued growth and global integration of China will undoubtedly be of importance for the world economy, and countries will need to focus on their own competitiveness to benefit.

NOTE

* See further my 'Perspectives on China's Growth: Prospects and Wider Impact, in N. Dinello and S. Wang (eds), *China, India and Beyond: Drivers and Limitations of Development*, Cheltenham, UK and Northampton, MA, USA: Edward Elgar, Global Development Network Series Volume 4, 2009.

Bibliography

Acemoglu, D. and S. Johnson (2005), 'Unbundling institutions', *Journal of Political Economy,* 113, 949–95.

Acemoglu, D., Johnson, S. and J. Robinson (2005), 'Institutions as the fundamental cause of long-run economic growth', in P. Aghion and S. Durlauf (eds), *Handbook of Economic Growth*, Amsterdam: Elsevier, pp. 385–472.

Akin, J.S., Dow, W.H. and P.M. Lance (2004), 'Did the distribution of health insurance in China continue to grow less equitable in the nineties? Results from a longitudinal survey', *Social Science & Medicine,* 58, 293–304.

Allen, F., Qian, J. and M. Qian (2005), 'Law, finance and economic growth in China', *Journal of Financial Economics,* 77, 57–116.

Bai, C., Li, D.D., Tao, Z. and Y. Wang (2000), 'A multitask theory of state enterprise reform', *Journal of Comparative Economics*, 28, 716–38.

Banerjee, A. and A. Newman (1993), 'Occupational choice and the process of development', *Journal of Political Economy*, 101, 274–98.

Bian, Y. (1994), *Work and Inequality in Urban China*, Albany, NY: State University of New York.

Blanchflower, D.G. and A.J. Oswald (1998), 'What makes an entrepreneur?', *Journal of Labor Economics*, 16, 26–60.

Blomström, M. and A. Kokko (1998), 'Multinational corporations and spillovers', *Journal of Economic Surveys*, 12, 1–31.

Bloom, N., Griffith, R. and J. Van Reenen (2002), 'Do R&D tax credits work?', *Journal of Public Economics*, 85, 1–31.

Borensztein, E. and J.D. Ostry (1996), 'Accounting for China's growth performance', *American Economic Review*, 86, 225–8.

Bosworth, D. and D. Yang (2000), 'Intellectual property law, technology flow and licensing opportunities in the People's Republic of China', *International Business Review*, 9, 453–77.

Brandt, L., Giles, J. and A. Park (2003), 'Competition under credit rationing: theory and evidence from rural China', *Journal of Development Economics*, 71, 463–95.

Brandt, L. and H. Li (2003), 'Bank discrimination in transition economies: ideology, information, or incentives?', *Journal of Comparative Economics,* 31, 387–413.

Brandt, L. and Z. Zhu (2000), 'Redistribution in a decentralized economy: growth and inflation in China under reform', *Journal of Political Economy*, 108, 422–51.

Brock, G.J. (1998), 'Foreign direct investment in Russia's regions 1993–95: why so little and where has it gone?', *Economics of Transition*, 6, 349–60.

Chang, D.W. (1988), *China under Deng Xiaoping,* London: Macmillan Press.

Che, J. and Y. Qian (1998), 'Institutional environment, community government, and corporate governance: understanding China's township-village enterprises', *Journal of Law, Economics, and Organization*, 14, 1–23.

Chen, S. and M. Ravallion (2007), 'China's (uneven) progress against poverty', *Journal of Development Economics*, 82, 1–42.

Chen, Z. (2003), 'Capital markets and legal development: the China case', *China Economic Review*, 14, 451–72.

Cheung, K. and P. Lin (2004), 'Spillover effects of FDI on innovation in China: evidence from provincial data', *China Economic Review*, 15, 25–44.

Choo, C. and X. Yin (2000), 'Contract management responsibility system and profit incentives in China's state-owned enterprises', *China Economic Review,* 11, 98–112.

Chow, G.C. (1994), *Understanding China's Economy,* London: World Scientific Publishing Co. Pte. Ltd.

Clarke, D.C. (2003), 'Economic development and the rights hypothesis: the China problem', *American Journal of Comparative Law*, 51, 89–111.

Clarke, D.C., Murrell, P. and S. Whiting (2006), 'The role of law in China's economic development', George Washington University Law School Public Law and Legal Theory Working Paper No. 187.

Coase, R. (1937), 'The nature of the firm', *Economica*, 4, 386–405.

Coffee, Jr., J.C. (2001), 'The rise of dispersed ownership: the roles of law and the states in the separation of ownership and control', *Yale Law Journal*, 111, 1–82.

Cordell, D.D., Gregory, J.W. and V. Piche (1998), *Hoe and Wage: A Social History of a Circular Migration System in West Africa,* Boulder, CO: Westview Press.

Cull, R. and L.C. Xu (2005), 'Institutions, ownership, and finance: The determinants of profit reinvestment among Chinese firms', *Journal of Financial Economics,* 77, 117–46.

de Brauw, A., Huang, J. and S. Rozelle (2000), 'Responsiveness, flexibility and market liberalization in China's agriculture', *American Journal of Agricultural Economics,* 82, 1133–9.

Djankov, S., Miguel, E., Qian, Y., Roland, G. and E. Zhuravskaya (2005), 'Who are Russia's Entrepreneurs?', *Journal of the European Economic Association*, 3, 587–97.

Djankov, S., Qian, Y., Roland, G. and E. Zhuravskaya (2006), 'Who are China's entrepreneurs?', *American Economic Review Paper and Proceedings*, 96, 348–52.

Dong, X. and L.C. Xu (2008), 'The impact of China's millennium labor restructuring program on firm performance and employee earnings', *Economics of Transition*, 16, 223–45.

Du, J. and C. Xu (2006), 'Regional competition and regulatory decentralization: case of China', Working paper, Chinese University of Hong Kong, London School of Economics and Hong Kong University of Science and Technology.

Du, J. and C. Xu (2009), 'Which firms went public in China? A study of financial market regulation', *World Development*, 37, 812–24.

Fan, G. (1994), 'Incremental change and dual-tack transition: understanding the case of China', *Economic Policy*, 19, 100–122.

Fan, J.P.H., Morck, R., Xu, L.C. and B. Yeung (2009), 'Institutions and foreign direct investment: China versus the rest of the world', *World Development*, 37, 852–65.

Farber, H.S. (1999), 'Alternative and part-time employment arrangements as a response to job loss', *Journal of Labor Economics*, 17, S142–69.

Farber, H.S. (1999), 'Mobility and stability: the dynamics of job change in labor markets', in O. Ashenfelter and D. Card (eds), *Handbook of Labor Economics*, Vol 3B, Amsterdam: North-Holland, Ch 37.

Feenstra, R. and G. Hanson (2003), 'Global production sharing and rising inequality: a survey of trade and wages', in K. Choi and J. Harrigan (eds), *Handbook of International Trade*, Oxford: Basil Blackwell, pp. 146–87.

Franks, J.R., Mayer, C. and S. Rossi (2009), 'Ownership: evolution and control', *Review of Financial Studies*, 22, 4009–56.

Freeman, R. (2004), 'Doubling the global work force: the challenge of integrating China, India and the former Soviet bloc into the world economy', Institute for International Economics presentation, Washington, DC.

Frye, T. and E. Zhuravskaya (2000), 'Rackets, regulation and the rule of law', *Journal of Law, Economics and Organization*, 16, 478–502.

Fujita, M., Krugman, P., and A.J. Venables (1999), *The Spatial Economy: Cities, Regions, and International Trade*, Cambridge, MA: MIT Press.

Garnaut, R., Song, L.G., Tenev, S. and Y. Yao (2005), *China's Ownership Transformation: Process, Outcomes, Prospects*, Washington, DC: The World Bank.

Glaeser, E., La Porta, R., Lopez-de-Silanes, F. and A. Shleifer (2004), 'Do institutions cause growth?', *Journal of Economic Growth,* 9, 271–303.

Greif, A. (1993), 'Contract enforceability and economic institutions in early trade: the Maghribi traders' coalition', *American Economic Review*, 83, 525–48.

Greenaway, D., Mahabir, P. and C.R. Milner (2008), 'Has China displaced other Asian countries' exports?', *China Economic Review,* 19, 152–69.

Grossman, G. and E. Rossi-Hansberg (2006), 'The rise of offshoring: it's not wine for cloth anymore', paper presented at the symposium on 'The New Economic Geography: Effects and Policy Implications', sponsored by the Federal Reserve Bank of Kansas City, Jackson Hole, Wyoming, 24–6 August 2006.

Groves, T., Hong, Y., McMillan, J. and B. Naughton (1995), 'China's evolving managerial market', *Journal of Political Economy,* 103, 873–92.

Hausman, J., Hall, B.H. and Z. Griliches (1984), 'Econometric models for count data with an application to the patents-R&D relationship', *Econometrica*, 52, 909–38.

Hay, D.A., Morris, D., Liu, G. and D. Lo (1994), *Economic Reform and State-owned Enterprises in China, 1979–1987*, Oxford: Clarendon Press.

Heckman, J.J. (1979), 'Sample selection bias as a specification error', *Econometrica*, 47, 153–61.

Hellvin, L. (1996), 'Vertical intra-industry trade between China and OECD countries', OECD Development Centre Working Chapter No. 114.

Ho, P. (2006), *Institutions in Transition: Land Ownership, Property Rights and Social Conflict in China,* Oxford: Oxford University Press.

Hu, A.G.Z. and G.H. Jefferson (2009), 'A great wall of patents: what is behind China's recent patent explosion?', *Journal of Development Economics,* 90, 57–68.

Huang, J. and S. Rozelle (1996), 'Technological change: the re-discovery of the engine of productivity growth in China's rural economy', *Journal of Development Economics*, 49, 337–69.

Huang, Y. (2006), *Selling China*, Cambridge: Cambridge University Press.

Hugo, G. (1982), 'Circular migration in Indonesia', *Population and Development Review*, 8, 59–84.

Javorcik, B.S. (2004), 'Does foreign direct investment increase the productivity of domestic firms? In search of spillovers through backward linkages', *American Economic Review,* 94, 605–27.

Jefferson, G. and T. Rawski (1994), 'Enterprise reform in Chinese industry', *Journal of Economic Perspectives*, 8, 47–70.

Jefferson, G.H. and T. Rawski (2002), 'China's emerging market for property rights', *Economics of Transition*, 10, 585–617.

Jefferson, G.H., Rawski, T.G., Li, W. and Y. Zheng (2000), 'Ownership, productivity change, and financial performance in Chinese industry', *Journal of Comparative Economics*, 28, 786–813.

Jefferson, G.H. and Rawski, T. and Y. Zheng (1992), 'Growth, efficiency, and convergence in China's state and collective industry', *Economic Development and Cultural Change*, 40, 239–66.

Jefferson, G.H. and J. Su (2006), 'Privatization and restructuring in China: evidence from shareholding ownership, 1995–2001', *Journal of Comparative Economics*, 24, 146–66.

Jones, C.I. (1995), 'R&D-Based models of economic growth', *Journal of Political Economy*, 103, 759–84.

Jones, W.C. (2003), 'Trying to understand the current Chinese legal system', in C. S. Hsu (ed.), *Understanding China's Legal System: Essays in Honor of Jerome A. Cohen*, New York and London: New York University Press.

Kaplinsky, R. (2006), 'Revisiting the revisited terms of trade: will China make a difference?', *World Development*, 34, 981–95.

Kaufmann, D., Kraay, A. and M. Mastruzzi (2007), 'Governance matters VI: governance indicators for 1996–2006', World Bank Policy Research Working Paper No. 4280.

Kipnis, A.B. (1997), *Producing Guanxi*, Durham, NC: Duke University Press.

Knight, J. (1995), 'Price scissors and intersectoral resource transfers: who paid for industrialization in China?', *Oxford Economic Papers*, 47, 117–35.

Knight, J. and L. Song (1999), *The Rural-urban Divide: Economic Disparities and Interactions in China*, Oxford: Oxford University Press.

Knight, J. and L. Song (2005), *Towards a Labour Market in China*, Oxford: Oxford University Press.

Knight, J., Song, L. and H. Jia (1999), 'Chinese migrants in urban China: three perspectives', *Journal of Development Studies*, 35, 73–104.

Knight, J. and L. Yueh (2004), 'Job mobility of residents and migrants in urban China', *Journal of Comparative Economics*, 32, 637–60.

Knight, J. and L. Yueh (2008), 'The role of social capital in China's urban labour market', *Economics of Transition*, 16, 389–414.

Komter, A. (2005), *Social Solidarity and the Gift*, Cambridge: Cambridge University Press.

Koo, A.Y.C. (1990), 'The contract responsibility system: transition from a planned to a market economy', *Economic Development and Cultural Change*, 38, 797–820.

Kornai, J. (1992), *The Socialist System*, Oxford: Clarendon Press.

Kraay, A. (2006), 'Exports and economic performance: evidence from a panel of Chinese enterprises', in B.M. Hoekman and B. Javorcik (eds), *Global Integration and Technology Transfer,* Washington, DC: The World Bank, pp. 139–60.

Lall, S. and M. Albaladejo (2004), 'China's competitive performance: a threat to East Asian manufactured exports?', *World Development*, 32, 1441–66.

Lall, S., Weiss, J. and H. Oikawa (2005), 'China's competitive threat to Latin America: an analysis for 1990–2002', *Oxford Development Studies,* 33, 163–94.

La Porta, R., Lopez-de-Silanes, F., Shleifer, A. and R. Vishny (1997), 'Legal determinants of external finance', *Journal of Finance*, 54, 1131–50.

La Porta, R., Lopez-de-Silanes, F., Shleifer, A. and R. Vishny (1998), 'Law and finance', *Journal of Political Economy*, 106, 1113–55.

Lardy, N. (1991), *Foreign Trade and Economic Reform in China, 1978–1990,* Cambridge: Cambridge University Press.

Lardy, N.R. (1998), *China's Unfinished Economic Revolution*, Washington, DC: Brookings Institution Press.

Lau, L.J., Qian, Y. and G. Roland (2001), 'Reform without losers: an interpretation of China's dual-track approach to transition', *Journal of Political Economy*, 108, 120–43.

Li, S., and H. Sato (eds) (2006), *Unemployment, Inequality and Poverty in Urban China*, London and New York: Routledge.

Lin, J.Y. (1992), 'Rural reforms and agricultural growth in China', *American Economic Review*, 82, 34–51.

Lin, J.Y. (2007), 'Developing small and medium banks to improve the financial structure', China Center for Economic Research, Peking University, working chapter (in Chinese).

Lin, J.Y., Cai, F. and L. Zhou (2003), *The China Miracle: Development Strategy and Economic Reform*, Hong Kong: The Chinese University Press.

Liu, X. and W.C.L. Hsiao (1995), 'The cost escalation of social health insurance plans in China: its implications for public policy', *Social Science & Medicine,* 41, 1095–101.

Liu, Y. (2004), 'Development of the rural health insurance system in China', *Health Policy and Planning,* 19, 159–65.

Lu, F.S. and Y. Yao (2009), 'The effectiveness of the law, financial development, and economic growth in an economy of financial repression: evidence from China', *World Development,* 37, 763–77.

Lubman, G. (2002), *Bird in a Cage: Legal Reform in China after Mao*, Stanford, CA: Stanford University Press.

Maddison, A. (2001), *The World Economy: A Millennial Perspective*, Paris: OECD.

Mohapatra, S., Rozelle, S. and R. Goodhue (2007), 'The rise of self-employment in rural China: development or distress?', *World Development*, 35, 163–81.

Murphy, K.M., Schleifer, A. and R.W. Vishny (1992), 'The transition to a market economy: pitfalls of partial reform', *Quarterly Journal of Economics,* 107, 889–906.

National Bureau of Statistics (NBS) (1999), *Comprehensive Statistical Data and Materials on 50 Years of New China,* Beijing: China Statistics Press (in Chinese).

National Bureau of Statistics (NBS) (various years), *China Statistical Yearbook*, Beijing: China Statistics Press.

Naughton, B. (1996), *Growing Out of the Plan: Chinese Economic Reform, 1978–1993,* Cambridge: Cambridge University Press.

Naughton, B. (2007), *The Chinese Economy*, Cambridge, MA: MIT Press.

Nee, V. (1996), 'The emergence of a market society: changing mechanisms of stratification in China', *American Journal of Sociology*, 101, 908–49.

Oi, J.C. (1999), *Rural China Takes Off: Institutional Foundations of Economic Reform*, Berkeley, CA: University of California Press.

Pistor, K., Martin, R. and S. Gelfer (2000), 'Law and finance in transition economies', *Economics of Transition*, 8, 325–68.

Pistor, K., Keinan, Y., Kleinheisterkamp, J. and M.D. West (2003), 'The evolution of corporate law: a cross-country comparison', *University of Pennsylvania Journal of International Economic Law*, 23, 791–871.

Pistor, K. and C. Xu (2005), 'Governing stock markets in transition economies: lessons from China', *American Law and Economics Review,* 7, 1–27.

Portes, A. (1998), 'Social capital: its origins and applications in modern sociology', *Annual Review of Sociology*, 24, 1–24.

Qian, Y. and Xu, C. (1993), 'The M-form hierarchy and China's economic reform', *European Economic Review*, 37, 541–8.

Rees, H. and A. Shah (1986), 'An empirical analysis of self-employment in the UK', *Journal of Applied Econometrics*, 1, 95–108.

Riedel, J., Jin, J. and J. Gao (2007), *How China Grows: Investment, Finance, and Reform*, Princeton, NJ and Oxford: Princeton University Press.

Riskin, C. (1987), *China's Political Economy: The Quest for Development since 1949,* Oxford: Oxford University Press.

Rodríguez-Clare, A. (1996), 'Multinationals, linkages, and economic development', *American Economic Review*, 86, 852–73.

Rodrik, D. (1999), 'The new global economy and developing countries: making openness work', Overseas Development Council Policy Essay No. 24, Baltimore, Maryland, USA.

Rodrik, D., Subramanian, A. and R. Trebbi (2004), 'Institutions rule: the primacy of institutions over geography and integration in economic development', *Journal of Economic Growth,* 9, 139–65.

Rogoff, K. (2006), 'Impact of globalization on monetary policy', paper presented at the symposium on 'The New Economic Geography: Effects and Policy Implications', sponsored by the Federal Reserve Bank of Kansas City, Jackson Hole, Wyoming, USA, 24–6 August 2006.

Romer, P.M. (1986), 'Increasing returns and long-run growth', *Journal of Political Economy*, 94, 1002–37.

Sicular, T. (1988), 'Plan and market in China's agricultural commerce', *Journal of Political Economy*, 96, 283–307.

Solinger, D. (2004), 'Policy consistency in the midst of crisis: managing the furloughed and the farmers in three cities', in B. Naughton and D. Yang (eds), *Holding China Together: Diversity and National Integration in the Post-Deng Era*, Cambridge: Cambridge University Press.

Solow, R. (1956), 'A contribution to the theory of economic growth', *Quarterly Journal of Economics,* 70, 65–94.

Stern, N. (2002), *A Strategy for Development*, Washington, DC: World Bank Publications.

Sun, L. and D. Tobin (2009), 'International listing as a means to mobilize the benefits of financial globalization: micro-level evidence from China', *World Development,* 37, 825–38.

Sun, Q. and W.H.S. Tong (2003), 'China's share issue privatization: the extent of its success', *Journal of Financial Economics,* 70, 183–222.

United Nations Conference on Trade and Development (UNCTAD) (2004), *UNCTAD Handbook of Statistics*, Geneva: UNCTAD.

Wan, G. (ed.), (2008), *Inequality and Growth in Modern China*, Oxford and New York: Oxford University Press for the World Institute for Development Economics Research of the United Nations University.

Wang, K. (2003), 'China's WTO accession and its trade with the Southeast-Asian nations', University of Washington mimeo.

Wang, Y. and Y. Yao (2003), 'Sources of China's economic growth: 1952–99: incorporating human capital accumulation', *China Economic Review,* 14, 32–52.

Wedeman, A. (2009), *From Mao to Market,* Cambridge: Cambridge University Press.

Weitzman, M. and C. Xu (1994), 'Chinese township village enterprises as vaguely defined cooperatives', *Journal of Comparative Economics*, 18, 121–45.

West, L.A. (1999), 'Pension reform in China: preparing for the future', *Journal of Development Studies,* 35, 153–83.

Woo, W.T. (2007), 'What are the high-probability challenges to continued high growth in China?', Paper prepared for the conference 'Assessing the Power of China: Political, Economic, and Social Dimensions', co-sponsored by the Institute for China Studies at Seoul National University, and the POSCO Research Institute (POSRI) in Seoul, South Korea, 30–31 May 2007.

World Bank (1983), *China: Socialist Economic Development*, Vol. 1, Washington, DC: The World Bank.

World Bank (1997), *World Development Report*, Washington, DC: The World Bank.

Wu, H.X. (2001), 'China's comparative labour productivity performance in manufacturing, 1952–1997: catching up or falling behind?', *China Economic Review,* 12, 172–89.

Xu, D. (1982), *China's Search for Economic Growth: The Chinese Economy since 1949*, Beijing: New World Press.

Yan, Y. (1996), *The Flow of Gifts: Reciprocity and Social Networks in a Chinese Village*, Palo Alto, CA: Stanford University Press.

Yang, M.M. (1994), *Gifts, Favors and Banquets: The Art of Social Relationships in China*, Ithaca, NY: Cornell University Press.

Yao, Y. and L. Yueh (2009), 'Law, finance and economic growth in China: an introduction', *World Development,* 37, 753–62.

Yueh, L. (2004), 'Wage reforms in China during the 1990s', *Asian Economic Journal*, 18, 149–64.

Yueh, L. (2006), 'China's competitiveness, intra-industry and intra-regional trade in Asia', in Y. Yao and L. Yueh (eds), *Globalisation and Economic Growth in China*, London: World Scientific Publishing Co. Pte. Ltd.

Yueh, L. (2007), 'Global intellectual property rights and economic growth', *Northwestern Journal of Technology and Intellectual Property*, 5, 436–48.

Yueh, L. (2009), 'Patent laws and innovation in China', *International Review of Law and Economics*, 29(4), 304–13.

Zhang, J., Zhang, L., Rozelle, S., and S. Boucher (2006), 'Self-employment with Chinese characteristics: the forgotten engine of rural China's growth', *Contemporary Economic Policy*, 24, 446–58.

Zheng, Z. and Y. Zhao (2002), 'China's terms of trade in manufactures', UNCTAD Discussion Chapter No. 161.

Zhu, T. (1998), 'A theory of contract and ownership choice in public enterprises under reformed socialism: the case of China's TVEs', *China Economic Review*, 9, 59–71.

Index